D1110551

COUNTERSTRAP

SELECTED AND EDITED BY
Nancy Carr, Louise Galpine, and Donald H. Whitfield

CONTRIBUTORS
Kelsey Crick
Mary Klein
Dylan Nelson
Tom Pilcher
Devin Ross
Audrey Schlofner
Josh Sniegowski
Jamie Spagnola
Samantha Stankowicz
Mary Williams

Cover graphic design: Audrey Schlofner
Interior design: THINK Book Works

COUNTER PARTS
COUNTER PARTS

THE GREAT BOOKS FOUNDATION

A nonprofit educational organization

Published and distributed by

THE GREAT BOOKS FOUNDATION
A nonprofit educational organization

35 E. Wacker Drive, Suite 400
Chicago, IL 60601
www.greatbooks.org

Shared Inquiry™ is a trademark of the Great Books Foundation. The contents of this
publication include proprietary trademarks and original materials and may be used or
quoted only with permission and appropriate credit to the Foundation.

First printing
9 8 7 6 5 4 3 2 1

Library of Congress Cataloging-in-Publications Data

Counterparts / selected and edited by Nancy Carr, Louise Galpine, and Donald H.
    Whitfield.
        pages cm
    ISBN 978-1-939014-25-2 (pbk.) -- ISBN 978-1-939014-26-9 (ebook)
    1. Literature—Collections. I. Carr, Nancy, editor. II. Galpine, Louise, editor.
    III. Whitfield, Donald H., editor.
    PN6014.C647 2015
    808.8--dc23
                                                                    2015023590

About the Great Books Foundation

The Great Books Foundation is an independent, nonprofit educational organization that creates reading and discussion programs for students and adults with the conviction that literacy and critical thinking help form reflective and well-informed citizens. We believe that civil and open discussion of the world's enduring literature promotes empathy, understanding, and community, and by working to develop reading and thinking skills, we advance the ultimate promise of democracy—participation for all.

The Great Books Foundation was established in 1947 to promote liberal education for the general public. In 1962, the Foundation extended its mission to children with the introduction of Junior Great Books.® Since its inception, the Foundation has helped thousands of people throughout the United States and in other countries begin their own discussion groups in schools, libraries, and community centers. Today, Foundation instructors conduct hundreds of workshops each year, in which educators and parents learn to lead Shared Inquiry™ discussion.

Notes by the author are not bracketed; notes by the Great Books Foundation, an editor, or a translator are [bracketed].

Contents

Introduction

The definition of a counterpart is something that completes another thing, is equivalent to it, has many of the same characteristics, and is a perfect fit. This definition implies that the counterparts exist on a level playing field; though not identical, they are nevertheless capable of closely engaging with each other on common ground.

Counterparts offers ten pairs of readings that engage with each other in a variety of ways, but are always closely related to some idea or concern they have in common. In this sense, they are counterparts: the selections in each pair fit into the same forum of discussion and speak to each other with a common vocabulary of ideas that not only allows, but strongly encourages rewarding exchanges of opinions between each of them and their readers. They often conflict with each other but they do so in such a way that promotes, rather than prevents, productive debate.

The selections in *Counterparts* represent many genres including fiction, nonfiction, poetry, and essay. Among the issues explored by the writers are the ethics of biological experimentation (Hawthorne and Bernard); romantic love and self-interest (Andersen and Gardam); patriotism and the realities of armed combat (Horace and Owen); the politics and sociology of education for women (Ruskin and Friedan); and the nature of liberal and conservative political positions (Dworkin and Hayek). We hope that as you read and discuss the selections in *Counterparts*, you will find many other interesting interconnections among them that will greatly enrich your experience.

In Great Books anthologies, individual works are not only powerful statements of an author's ideas but also dynamic components of an enduring inquiry with other writers concerning important universal questions. Just as the world's greatest writers are engaged in a dialogue with other writers near and far in time and space, we too can participate in this ongoing conversation. By examining their ideas and adding our own voices, *Counterparts* provides readers with access to this ongoing inquiry in a manner that we hope you will find stimulating, provocative, and enjoyable.

To help prompt lively discussion, each pair of selections is preceded by an introduction giving brief background about the authors and introducing the topics explored. Following each pair is a brief set of discussion questions to encourage exploration of the authors' ideas. Some of the questions ask about something very specific in a selection, such as the meaning of a statement or the motivation of a character in a story. Others ask about more general issues related to the themes; these questions are broader and invite discussion of personal insights and opinions. Addressing both kinds of questions during a discussion, without tipping the balance heavily toward one or the other, will make for a more satisfying experience that not only engages with each author's distinctive voice, but also allows for participants in the group to contribute their insights in their own individual way.

About Shared Inquiry

The Great Books Foundation's Shared Inquiry™ method of discussion builds habits of civil and open discussion, while promoting empathy, critical thinking, understanding, and the kind of intellectual community in which democracy can flourish. A Shared Inquiry discussion begins when the leader of the discussion group poses an interpretive question about the meaning of a reading selection. The question is substantial enough that no single answer can resolve it. Instead, several answers—even answers that are in conflict—may be valid. In effect, the leader is telling the group: "Here is a problem of meaning that seems important. Let's try to resolve it."

From that moment on, participants are free to offer answers and opinions to the group, to request clarification of points, and to raise objections to the remarks of other participants. They also discuss specific passages in the selection that bear on the interpretive question and compare their differing ideas about what these passages mean. The leader, meanwhile, asks additional questions, clarifying and expanding the interpretive question and helping group members arrive at more cogent answers. All participants don't have to agree with all of the answers—each person can decide which answer seems most convincing. This process is called Shared Inquiry.

In Shared Inquiry discussion, three kinds of questions can be raised about a reading selection: factual questions, interpretative questions, and evaluative questions.

Interpretation is central to a Shared Inquiry discussion but factual questions can bring to light evidence in support of interpretations and can clear up misunderstandings. On the other hand, evaluative questions invite participants to compare the experiences and opinions of an author with their own and can introduce a personal dimension into the discussion.

In order for your discussions to be most rewarding, we strongly recommend that a significant amount of time be spent coming to an understanding of what the authors are saying by continually returning to the text during the discussion. Doing so will provide a strong central focus for whatever personal accounts participants introduce into the conversation, as they evaluate the authors' ideas in light of their own experiences.

The following guidelines will help keep the conversation focused on the text and assure all the participants a voice:

1. **Read the selection carefully before participating in the discussion.** This ensures that all participants are equally prepared to talk about the ideas in the reading.

2. **Discuss the ideas in the selection, and try to understand them fully.** Reflecting as individuals and as a group on what the author says makes the exploration of both the selection and related issues that will come up in the discussion more rewarding.

3. **Support interpretations of what the author says with evidence from the reading, along with insights from personal experience.** This provides focus for the group on the selection that everyone has read and builds a strong foundation for discussing related issues.

4. **Listen to other participants and respond to them directly.** Shared Inquiry is about the give and take of ideas, the willingness to listen to others and talk with them respectfully. Directing your comments and questions to other group members, not always to the leader, will make the discussion livelier and more dynamic.

5. **Expect the leader to mainly ask questions.** Effective leaders help participants develop their own ideas, with everyone gaining a new understanding in the process. When participants hang back and wait for the leader to suggest answers, discussion tends to falter.

LOVE
LOVE

British novelist Angela Carter once joked that asking about the origin of fairy tales is like asking who invented the meatball. Centuries of oral tradition have shaped the fairy tales we know today, and innumerable retellings have imbued these stories with universal themes, such as love and family. As fairy tales have evolved, new storytellers have embellished and adapted the narratives, contributing to an ongoing reimagining of these stories for new generations of listeners and readers. Yet the themes remain constant in each retelling. The search for love and family and the perilous path to a happy ending are consistent elements of many fairy tales, however differently they are approached.

Hans Christian Andersen (1805–1875) was a Danish author celebrated for his literary fairy tales. "The Little Mermaid" (1837), like many of his works, has been adapted over the years into numerous popular forms, including film, opera, and other works of art. However, Andersen's little mermaid differs from many later portrayals of the character in that her self-sacrificing love for the prince remains unrequited. In Andersen's tale she is unable to break the spell of the sea witch and is denied the fairy-tale ending we might expect. Instead of true love fulfilled, we are left with unanswered questions about loyalty, sublimation, and effacement.

One hundred and fifty years after Andersen, British author **Jane Gardam** (1928–) penned "The Pangs of Love" (1983). In this sequel to "The Little Mermaid," she challenges Andersen's theme of self-sacrificing love. After the tragic death of the little mermaid, the only sister unimpressed by the little mermaid's romantic legacy is Gardam's creation, the seventh mermaid. The seventh mermaid is openly critical of her selfless sister and the selfish prince. Yet when the seventh mermaid visits the surface, she too is drawn to the prince. Her different expectations and demands upon his commitment exemplify the interaction that can occur between authors—counterparts centuries apart—who are drawn to the same themes and universal questions of love and romance.

The Little Mermaid

Hans Christian Andersen

Far out at sea the water's as blue as the petals of the loveliest cornflower, and as clear as the purest glass; but it's very deep, deeper than any anchor can reach. Many church steeples would have to be piled up one above the other to reach from the bottom of the sea to the surface. Right down there live the sea people.

Now you mustn't for a moment suppose that it's a bare white sandy bottom. Oh, no. The most wonderful trees and plants are growing down there, with stalks and leaves that bend so easily that they stir at the very slightest movement of the water, just as though they were alive. All the fishes, big ones and little ones, slip in and out of the branches just like birds in the air up here. Down in the deepest part of all is the sea King's palace. Its walls are made of coral, and the long pointed windows of the clearest amber; but the roof is made of cockleshells that open and shut with the current. It's a pretty sight, for in each shell is a dazzling pearl; any single one of them would be a splendid ornament in a Queen's crown.

The sea King down there had been a widower for some years, but his old mother kept house for him. She was a clever woman, but proud of her noble birth; that's why she went about with twelve oysters on her tail, while the rest of the nobility had to put up with only six. But apart from that, she was deserving of special praise, because she was so fond of the little sea Princesses, her grandchildren. They were six pretty children, but the youngest was the loveliest of them all. Her skin was as clear and delicate as a rose leaf, her eyes were as blue as the deepest lake, but like the others she had no feet; her body ended in a fish's tail.

All the long day they could play down there in the palace, in the great halls where living flowers grew out of the walls. The fishes would swim in to them, just as with us the swallows fly in when we open the windows; but the fishes swam right up to the little Princesses, fed out of their hands, and let themselves be patted.

Outside the palace was a large garden with trees of deep blue and fiery red; the fruit all shone like gold, and the flowers like a blazing fire with stalks and leaves that were never still. The soil itself was the finest sand, but blue like a sulphur flame. Over everything down there lay a strange blue gleam; you really might have thought you were standing high up in the air with nothing to see but sky above and below you, rather than that you were at the bottom of the sea. When there was a dead calm you caught a glimpse of the sun, which looked like a purple flower pouring out all light from its cup.

Each of the small Princesses had her own little plot in the garden, where she could dig and plant at will. One of them gave her flower bed the shape of a whale, another thought it nicer for hers to look like a little mermaid; but the youngest made hers quite round like the sun, and would only have flowers that shone red like it. She was a curious child, silent and thoughtful; and when the other sisters decorated their gardens with the most wonderful things they had got from sunken ships, she would have nothing but the rose-red flowers that were like the sun high above, and a beautiful marble statue. It was the statue of a handsome boy, hewn from the clear white stone and come down to the bottom of the sea from a wreck. Beside the statue she planted a rose-red weeping willow, which grew splendidly and let its fresh foliage droop over the statue right down to the blue sandy bottom. Here the shadow took on a violet tinge and, like the branches, was never still; roots and treetop looked as though they were playing at kissing each other.

Nothing pleased her more than to hear about the world of humans up above the sea. The old grandmother had to tell her all she knew about ships and towns, people and animals. One thing especially surprised her with its beauty, and this was that the flowers had a smell—at the bottom of the sea they hadn't any—and also that the woods were green and the fishes you saw in among the branches could sing as clearly and prettily as possible. It was the little birds that the grandmother called fishes; otherwise, never having seen a bird, the small sea Princesses would never have understood her.

"As soon as you are fifteen," the grandmother told them, "you shall be allowed to rise to the surface, and to sit in the moonlight on the rocks and watch the great ships sailing past; you shall see woods and towns." That coming year one of the sisters was to have her fifteenth birthday, but the rest of them—well, they were each one year younger than the other; so the youngest of them had a whole five years to wait before she could rise up from the bottom and see how things are with us. But each promised to tell the others what she had seen and found most interesting on the first day; for their grandmother didn't really tell them enough—there were so many things they were longing to hear about.

None of them was so full of longing as the youngest: the very one who had most time to wait and was so silent and thoughtful. Many a night she stood at the open window and gazed up through the dark blue water, where the fishes frisked their tails and fins. She could see the moon and the stars, though it's true their light was rather pale; and yet through the water they looked much larger than they do to us, and if ever a kind of black cloud went gliding along below them, she knew it was either a whale swimming above her or else a vessel with many passengers; these certainly never imagined that a lovely little mermaid was standing beneath and stretching up her white hands toward the keel of their ship.

By now the eldest Princess was fifteen and allowed to go up to the surface.

When she came back, she had a hundred things to tell; but the loveliest, she said, was to lie in the moonlight on a sandbank in a calm sea and there, close in to the shore, to look at the big town where the lights were twinkling like a hundred stars; to listen to the sound of music and the noise and clatter of carts and people; to see all the towers and spires on the churches and hear the bells ringing. And just because she couldn't get there, it was this above everything that she longed for.

Oh, how the youngest sister drank it all in! And, when later in the evening she stood at the open window and gazed up through the dark blue water, she thought of the big town with all its noise and clatter, and then she seemed to catch the sound of the church bells ringing down to her.

The following year, the second sister was allowed to go up through the water and swim wherever she liked. She came to the surface just as the sun was setting, and that was the sight she found most beautiful. The whole sky had looked like gold, she said, and the clouds—well, she just couldn't describe how beautiful they were as they sailed, all crimson and violet, over her head. And yet, much faster than they, a flock of wild swans flew like a long white veil across the water where the sun was setting. She swam off in that direction, but the sun sank, and its rosy light was swallowed up by sea and cloud.

The year after that, the third sister went up. She was the boldest of them all, and she swam up a wide river that flowed into the sea. She saw delightful green slopes with grape vines; manors and farms peeped out among magnificent woods; she heard all the birds singing; and the sun was so hot that she often had to dive under the water to cool her burning face. In a small cove she came upon a swarm of little human children splashing about quite naked in the water. She wanted to play with them, but they ran away terrified, and a little black animal came up; it was a dog. She had never seen a dog before. It barked at her so dreadfully that she got frightened and made for the open sea. But never could she forget the magnificent woods, the green slopes and the darling children, who could swim on the water although they had no fishes' tails.

The fourth sister was not so bold. She kept far out in the wild waste of ocean, and told them that was just what was so wonderful: you could see for miles and miles around you, and the sky hung above like a big glass bell. She had seen ships, but a long way off, looking like sea gulls. The jolly dolphins had been turning somersaults, and enormous whales had spirted up water from their nostrils, so that they seemed to be surrounded by a hundred fountains.

And now it was the turn of the fifth sister. Her birthday happened to come in winter, and so she saw things that the others hadn't seen the first time. The sea appeared quite green, and great icebergs were floating about; they looked like pearls, she said, and yet were much larger than the church towers put up by human beings. They were to be seen in the most fantastic shapes, and they glittered like diamonds. She had sat down on one of the biggest, and all the ships gave it a wide berth as they sailed in terror past where she sat with her long hair streaming in the wind. But late in the evening the sky became overcast with clouds; it lightened and thundered, as the dark waves lifted the great blocks of ice right up, so that they flashed in the fierce red lightning. All the ships took in sail, and amidst the general horror and alarm, she sat calmly on her floating iceberg and watched the blue lightning zigzag into the glittering sea.

The first time one of the sisters went up to the surface, she would always be delighted to see so much that was new and beautiful; but afterwards, when they were older and could go up as often as they liked, it no longer interested them; they longed to be back again, and when a month had passed they said that, after all, it was nicest down below—it was such a comfort to be home.

Often of an evening the five sisters used to link arms and float up together out of the water. They had lovely voices, more beautiful than any human voice; and when a gale sprang up threatening ship-wreck, they would swim in front of the ships and sing tempting songs of how delightful it was at the bottom of the sea. And they told the sailors not to be afraid of coming down there, but the sailors couldn't make out the words of their song; they thought it was the noise of the gale, nor did they ever see any of the delights the mermaids prom-ised, because when the ship sank the crew were drowned, and only as dead men did they come to the palace of the sea King.

When of an evening the sisters floated up through the sea like this, arm in arm, their little sister stayed back all alone gazing after them. She would have cried, only a mermaid hasn't any tears, and so she suffers all the more.

"Oh, if only I were fifteen!" she said. "I'm sure I shall love that world up there and the people who live in it."

And then at last she was fifteen.

"There, now you'll soon be off our hands," said her grandmother, the old Dowager Queen. "Come now, let me dress you up like your sisters;" and she put a wreath of white lilies on her hair, but every petal of the flowers was half a pearl. And the old lady made eight big oysters nip tight on to the Princess's tail to show her high rank.

"Oo! that hurts," said the little mermaid.

"Yes," said the grandmother, "one can't have beauty for nothing."

How she would have liked to shake off all this finery and put away the heavy wreath! The red flowers in her garden suited her much better, but she didn't dare make any change. "Goodbye," she said, and went up through the water as light and clear as a bubble.

The sun had just set, as she put her head up out of the sea, but the clouds had still a gleam of rose and gold; and up in the pale pink sky the evening star shone clear and beautiful. The air was soft and fresh, and the sea dead calm. A large three-masted ship was lying there, with only one sail hoisted because not a breath of wind was stirring, and sailors were lolling about in the rigging and on the yards. There was music and singing, and as it grew dark hundreds of lanterns were lit that, with their many different colors, looked as if the flags of all nations were flying in the breeze.

The little mermaid swam right up to the porthole of the cabin and, every time she rose with the swell of the wave, she could see through the clear glass a crowd of splendidly dressed people; but the handsomest of them all was a young Prince with large dark eyes. He couldn't have been much more than sixteen; it was his birthday and that's why there was all this set out. As the young Prince came out on to the deck where sailors were dancing, over a hundred rockets swished up into the sky—and broke into a glitter like broad daylight. That frightened the little mermaid, and she dived down under the water; but she quickly popped up her head again, and look! it was just as if all the stars in heaven were falling down on her. Never had she seen such fireworks. Great suns went spinning around, gorgeous firefishes swerving into the blue air, and all this glitter was mirrored in the clear still water. On board the ship herself it was so light that you could make out every little rope, let alone the passengers. Oh, how handsome the young Prince was; he shook hands with the sailors, he laughed and smiled, while the music went floating out into the loveliness of the night.

It grew late, but the little mermaid couldn't take her eyes off the ship and the beautiful Prince. The colored lanterns were put out, the rockets no longer climbed into the sky, and the cannon were heard no more; but deep down in the sea there was a mumbling and a rumbling. Meanwhile the mermaid stayed on the water, rocking up and down so that she could look into the cabin. But the ship now gathered speed; one after another her sails were spread. The waves increased, heavy clouds blew up, and lightning flashed in the distance. Yes, they were in for a terrible storm; so the sailors took in their sails, as the great ship rocked and scudded through the raging sea. The waves rose higher and higher like huge black mountains, threatening to bring down the mast, but the ship dived like a swan into the trough of the waves and then rode up again on their towering crests. The little mermaid thought, why, it must be fun for a ship to sail like that—but the crew didn't. The vessel creaked and cracked, the stout planks crumpled up under the heavy pounding of the sea against the ship, the mast snapped in the middle like a stick, and then the ship gave a lurch to one side as the water came rushing into the hold. At last the little mermaid realized that they were in danger; she herself had to look out for the beams and bits of wreckage that were drifting on the water. One moment it was so pitch dark that she couldn't see a thing, but then when the lightning came it was so bright that she could make out everyone on board. It was now a case of each man for himself. The young Prince was the one she was looking for and, as the ship broke up, she saw him disappear into the depths of the sea. Just for one moment she felt quite pleased, for now he would come down to her; but then she remembered that humans can't live under the water and that only as a dead man could he come down to her father's palace. No, no, he mustn't die. So she swam in among the drifting beams and planks, with no thought for the danger of being crushed by them; she dived deep down and came right up again among the waves, and at last she found the young Prince. He could hardly swim any longer in the heavy sea; his arms and legs were beginning to tire, the fine eyes were closed, he would certainly have drowned if the little mermaid had not come. She held his head above water and then let the waves carry her along with him.

By morning the gale had quite gone; not the smallest trace of the ship was to be seen. The sun rose red and glowing out of the water and seemed to bring life to the Prince's cheeks, but his eyes were still shut. The mermaid kissed his fine high forehead and smoothed back his dripping hair. He was like the marble statue down in her little garden; she kissed him again and wished that he might live.

Presently she saw the mainland in front of her, high blue mountains with the white snow glittering on their peaks like nestling swans. Down by the shore were lovely green woods and, in front of them, a church or a convent—she wasn't sure which, but anyhow a building. Lemon and orange trees were growing in the garden, and tall palm trees in front of the gate. At this point the sea formed a little inlet, where the water was quite smooth but very deep close in to the rock where the fine white sand had silted up. She swam here with the handsome Prince and laid him on the sand with his head carefully pillowed in the warm sunshine.

Now there was a sound of bells from the large white building, and a number of young girls came through the garden. So the little mermaid swam further out behind some large boulders that were sticking out of the water and covered her hair and breast with seafoam, so that her face wouldn't show; and then she watched to see who would come to the help of the unfortunate Prince.

It wasn't long before a young girl came along. She seemed quite frightened, but only for a moment; then she fetched several others, and the mermaid saw the Prince come round and smile at those about him; but no smile came out to her, for of course he didn't know she had rescued him. She felt so sad that, when he was taken away into the large building, she dived down sorrowfully into the sea and went back to her father's palace.

Silent and thoughtful as she had always been, she now became much more so. Her sisters asked her what she had seen on her first visit to the surface, but she wouldn't say.

Many a morning and many an evening she rose up to where she had left the Prince. She saw the fruit in the garden ripen and be gathered, she saw the snow melt on the peaks, but she never saw the Prince, and so she always turned back more despondent than ever. Her one comfort was to sit in the little garden with her arms round the beautiful marble statue which was so like the Prince. She never looked after her flowers, and they grew into a sort of wilderness, out over the paths, and braided their long stalks and leaves on to the branches of the trees, until the light was quite shut out.

At last she could keep it to herself no longer, but told one of her sisters; and immediately all the rest got to know, but nobody else— except a few other mermaids who didn't breathe a word to any but their nearest friends. One of these was able to say who the Prince was; she, too, had seen the party that was held on board the ship, and knew where he came from and whereabouts his kingdom was.

"Come on, little sister!" said the other Princesses. And with arms round each other's shoulders they rose in one line out of the sea, just in front of where the Prince's castle stood. It was built in a glistening stone of pale yellow with great flights of marble steps; one of these led straight into the sea. Splendid gilt domes curved above the roof, and between the pillars that went right round the building were life-like sculptures in marble. Through the clear glass in the tall windows you could see into the most magnificent rooms; these were hung with sumptuous silk curtains and tapestries and their walls were covered with large paintings that were a delight to the eye. In the middle of the biggest room was a huge splashing fountain; its spray was flung high up to the glass dome in the ceiling, through which the sun shone down on to the water and the beautiful plants growing in the great pool.

Now she knew where he lived, and many an evening and many a night she would come to the surface at that spot. She swam much closer to the shore than any of the others had ever dared. She even went up the narrow creek under the fine marble balcony that threw its long shadow across the water. Here she would sit and gaze at the young Prince, who imagined he was quite alone in the clear moonlight.

Often in the evening she saw him go out to the strains of music in his splendid vessel that was dressed with flags. She peeped out from among the green rushes and, when the wind caught her long silvery veil and someone saw it, they fancied it was a swan spreading its wings.

On many nights, when the fishermen were at sea with their torches, she heard them speaking so well of the young Prince, and that made her glad she had saved his life when he drifted about half-dead on the waves; and she thought of how closely his head had rested on her bosom and how lovingly she had kissed him. But he knew nothing whatsoever about that, never even dreamed she existed.

Fonder and fonder she became of human beings, more and more she longed for their company. Their world seemed to her to be so much larger than her own. You see, they could fly across the ocean in ships, climb the tall mountains high above the clouds; and the lands they owned stretched with woods and meadows further than her eyes could see. There was so much she would have liked to know, but her sisters couldn't answer all her questions, and so she asked the old grandmother, for she knew all about the upper world—as she so aptly called the countries above the sea.

"If people don't drown," asked the little mermaid, "can they go on living forever? Don't they die, as we do down here in the sea?"

"Yes, yes," said the old lady. "They, too, have to die; their life-time is even shorter than ours. We can live for three hundred years, but when our life here comes to an end we merely turn into foam on the water; we haven't even a grave down here among those we love. We've no immortal soul; we shall never have another life. We're like the green rush—once it's been cut it can't grow green again. But human beings have a soul which lives forever; still lives after the body is turned to dust. The soul goes climbing up through the clear air, up till it reaches the shining stars. Just as we rise up out of the sea and look at the countries of human beings, so they rise up to beautiful unknown regions—ones we shall never see."

"Why haven't we got an immortal soul?" the little mermaid asked sadly. "I would give the whole three hundred years I have to live, to become for one day a human being and then share in that heavenly world."

"You mustn't go worrying about that," said the grandmother. "We're much happier and better off here than the people who live up there."

"So then I'm doomed to die and float like foam on the sea, never to hear the music of the waves or see the lovely flowers and the red sun. Isn't there anything at all I can do to win an immortal soul?"

"No," said the old lady. "Only if a human being loved you so much that you were more to him than father and mother—if he clung to you with all his heart and soul, and let the priest put his right hand in yours as a promise to be faithful and true here and in all eternity—then his soul would flow over into your body and you, too, would get a share in human happiness. He would give you a soul and yet keep his own. But that can never happen. The very thing that's so beautiful here in the sea, your fish's tail, seems ugly to people on the earth; they know so little about it that they have to have two clumsy supports called legs, in order to look nice."

That made the little mermaid sigh and look sadly at her fish's tail.

"We must be content," said the old lady. "Let's dance and be gay for the three hundred years we have to live—that's a good time, isn't it?—then one can have one's fill of sleep in the grave all the more pleasantly afterward. Tonight we're having a Court ball."

That was something more magnificent than we ever see on the earth. In the great ballroom walls and ceiling were made of thick but quite clear glass. Several hundred enormous shells, rose-red and grass-green, were ranged on either side, each with a blue-burning flame which lit up the whole room and, shining out through the walls, lit up the sea outside as well. Countless fishes, big and small, could be seen swimming toward the glass walls; the scales on some of them shone purple-red, and on others like silver and gold . . . Through the middle of the ballroom flowed a wide running stream, on which mermen and mermaids danced to their own beautiful singing. No human beings have voices so lovely. The little mermaid sang the most sweetly of them all, and they clapped their hands for her, and for a moment there was joy in her heart, for she knew that she had the most beautiful voice on earth or sea. But then her thoughts soon returned to the world above her; she couldn't forget the handsome Prince and her sorrow at not possessing, like him, an immortal soul. So she crept out of her father's palace and, while all in there was song and merriment, she sat grieving in her little garden. Suddenly she caught the sound of a horn echoing down through the water, and she thought, "Ah, there he is, sailing up above—he whom I love more than father or mother, he who is always in my thoughts and in whose hands I would gladly place the happiness of my life. I will dare anything to win him and an immortal soul. While my sisters are dancing there in my father's palace, I will go to the sea witch; I've always been dreadfully afraid of her, but perhaps she can help me and tell me what to do."

So the little mermaid left her garden and set off for the place where the witch lived, on the far side of the roaring whirlpools. She had never been that way before. There were no flowers growing, no sea grass, nothing but the bare grey sandy bottom stretching right up to the whirlpools, where the water went swirling round like roaring mill wheels and pulled everything it could clutch down with it to the depths. She had to pass through the middle of these battering eddies in order to get to the sea witch's domain; and here for a long stretch there was no other way than over hot bubbling mud—the witch called it her swamp. Her house lay behind it in the middle of an extraordinary wood. All the trees and bushes were polyps, half animals and half plants. They looked like hundred-headed snakes growing out of the earth; all the branches were long slimy arms with supple worm-like fingers, and joint by joint from the root up to the very tip they were continuously on the move. They wound themselves tight round everything they could clutch hold of in the sea, and they never let go. The little mermaid was terribly scared as she paused at the edge of the wood. Her heart was throbbing with fear; she nearly turned back. But then she remembered the Prince and the human soul, and that gave her courage. She wound her long flowing hair tightly round her head, so that the polyps shouldn't have that to clutch her by, she folded both her hands across her breast and darted off just as a fish darts through the water, in among the hideous polyps which reached out for her with their supple arms and fingers. She noticed how each of them had something they had caught, held fast by a hundred little arms like hoops of iron. White skeletons of folk who had been lost at sea and had sunk to the bottom looked out from the arms of the polyps. Ship's rudders and chests were gripped tight, skeletons of land animals, and—most horrible of all—a small mermaid whom they had caught and throttled.

Now she came to a large slimy open space in the wood where big fat water snakes were frisking about and showing their hideous whitish-yellow bellies. In the middle was a house built of the bones of human folk who had been wrecked. There sat the sea witch letting a toad feed out of her mouth, just as we might let a little canary come and peck sugar. She called the horrible fat water snakes her little chicks and allowed them to sprawl about her great spongy bosom.

"I know well enough what you're after," said the sea witch. "How stupid of you! Still, you shall have your way, and it'll bring you into misfortune, my lovely Princess. You want to get rid of your fish's tail and in its place have a couple of stumps to walk on like a human being, so that the young Prince can fall in love with you and you can win him and an immortal soul"—and with that the witch gave such a loud repulsive laugh that the toad and the snakes fell to the ground and remained sprawling there. "You've just come at the right time," said the witch. "Tomorrow, once the sun's up, I couldn't help you for another year. I shall make you a drink, and before sunrise you must swim to land, sit down on the shore and drink it up. Then your tail will divide in two and shrink into what humans call 'pretty legs'. But it'll hurt; it'll be like a sharp sword going through you. Everyone who sees you will say you are the loveliest human child they have ever seen. You will keep your graceful movements—no dancer can glide so lightly—but every step you take will feel as if you were treading on a sharp knife, enough to make your feet bleed. Are you ready to bear all that? If you are, I'll help you."

"Yes," said the little mermaid, and her voice trembled; but she thought of her Prince and the prize of an immortal soul.

"Still, don't forget this," said the witch. "Once you've got human shape, you can never become a mermaid again. You can never go down through the water to your sisters and to your father's palace; and if you don't win the Prince's love, so that he forgets father and mother for you and always has you in his thoughts and lets the priest join your hands together to be man and wife, then you won't get an immortal soul. The first morning after the Prince marries someone else, your heart must break and you become foam on the water."

"I'm ready," said the little mermaid, pale as death.

"Then there's me to be paid," said the witch, "and you're not getting my help for nothing. You have the loveliest voice of all down here at the bottom of the sea. With that voice, no doubt, you think to enchant him; but that voice you shall hand over to me. I demand the best that you have for me to make a rich drink. You see, I have to give you my own blood, in order that the drink may be as sharp as a two-edged sword."

"But if you take my voice," said the little mermaid, "what shall I have left?"

"Your lovely form," said the witch, "your graceful movements, and your speaking eyes. With those you can so easily enchant a human heart. . . . Well, where's your spunk? Put out your little tongue and let me cut it off in payment; then you shall be given the potent mixture."

"Go on, then," said the little mermaid, and the witch put the kettle on for brewing the magic drink. "Cleanliness before everything," she said, as she scoured out the kettle with a bundle of snakes she had knotted together. Next, she scratched her breast and let her black blood drip down into the kettle; the steam took on the weirdest shapes, terrifying to look at. The witch kept popping fresh things into the kettle, and when it boiled up properly it sounded like a crocodile in tears. At last the brew was ready; it looked like the clearest water.

"There you are!" said the witch and cut off the little mermaid's tongue; she was now dumb and could neither sing nor speak.

"If the polyps should catch hold of you, as you go back through the wood," said the witch, "throw but a single drop of this drink on them, and their arms and fingers will burst into a thousand pieces." But the little mermaid had no need to do that. The polyps shrank from her in terror when they saw the dazzling drink that shone in her hand like a glittering star. So she quickly came through the wood, the swamp, and the roaring whirlpools.

She could see her father's palace; the lights were out in the great ballroom. They were all certain to be asleep in there by this time; but she didn't anyhow dare to look for them, now that she was dumb and was going to leave them forever. She felt as if her heart must break for grief. She stole into the garden, picked one flower from each of her sisters' flower beds, blew a thousand finger kisses toward the palace, and rose then through the dark blue sea.

The sun was not yet up, as she sighted the Prince's castle and climbed the magnificent marble steps. The moon was shining wonderfully clear. The little mermaid drank the sharp burning potion, and it was as if a two-edged sword pierced through her delicate body—she fainted and lay as though dead. Then the sun, streaming over the sea, woke her up, and she felt a sharp pain. But there in front of her stood the handsome young Prince. He stared at her with his coal-black eyes, so that she cast down her own—and saw that her fish's tail had gone and she had the sweetest little white legs that any young girl could wish for; but she was quite naked and so she wrapped herself in her long flowing hair. The Prince asked who she was and how she had come there, and she could only look back at him so gently and yet so sadly out of her deep blue eyes; for of course she couldn't speak. Then he took her by the hand and led her into the castle. Every step she took, as the witch had foretold, was as though she were treading on sharp knives and pricking gimlets; but she gladly put up with that. By the side of the Prince she went along as lightly as a bubble; and he and all of them marvelled at the charm of her graceful movements.

Costly dresses were given her of silk and muslin; she was the most beautiful in all the castle. But she was dumb; she could neither sing nor speak. Lovely slave girls in gold and silk came out and danced before the Prince and his royal parents; one of them sang more beautifully than all the rest, and the Prince clapped his hands and smiled at her. This saddened the little mermaid, for she knew that she herself had sung far more beautifully. And she thought, "Oh, if only he knew that I gave my voice away forever, in order to be with him!"

Next, the slave girls danced a graceful gliding dance to the most delightful music; and then the little mermaid raised her pretty white arms, lingered on the tips of her toes and then glided across the floor, dancing as no one had danced before. She looked more and more lovely with every movement, and her eyes spoke more deeply to the heart than the slave girls' singing.

Everyone was enchanted, and especially the Prince, who called her his little foundling. Still she went on dancing, although every time her foot touched the ground it felt as though she was treading on sharp knives. The Prince said that she must never leave him, and she was allowed to sleep on a velvet cushion outside his door.

He had boys' clothes made for her, so that she could go riding with him on horseback. They rode through the sweet-smelling woods, where the green boughs grazed her shoulders and the little birds sang among the cool foliage. She went climbing with the Prince up high mountains and, although her delicate feet bled so that others could see it, she only laughed and went on and on with him, until they could see the clouds sailing below them like a flock of birds migrating to other lands.

Back at the Prince's castle, when at night the others were asleep, she would go out on to the broad marble steps and cool her tingling feet in the cold sea water; and then she would think of those down there in the depths of the sea.

One night her sisters rose up arm in arm singing so mournfully as they swam on the water. She made signs to them, and they recognized her and told her how unhappy she had made them all. After that, they used to visit her every night; and once, in the far distance, she saw her old grandmother who hadn't been above the water for many years, and also the sea King wearing his crown. They both stretched out their hands toward her, but they didn't venture in so near to the shore as the five sisters.

Day by day she became dearer to the Prince. He loved her as one loves a dear good child, but he didn't dream of making her his Queen; and yet she had to become his wife, or else she would never win an immortal soul, but on his wedding morning would be turned to foam on the sea.

"Do you like me best of all?" the little mermaid's eyes seemed to say, when he took her in his arms and kissed her lovely brow.

"Yes," said the Prince. "You're the dearest of all, because you have the kindest heart. You are the most devoted to me, and you remind me of a young girl I once saw but shall probably never see again. I was sailing in a ship that was wrecked; the waves drove me ashore near a sacred temple where a number of young girls were serving. The youngest, who found me on the beach and saved my life—I only saw her twice. She was the only one I could ever love in this world, but you are so like her that you almost take the place of her image in my heart. She belongs to the holy temple, so that fortune has been kind in sending you to me. We will never part."

"Ah, little does he know that it was I who saved his life," thought the mermaid; "that I carried him across the sea to the temple in the wood; that I waited in the foam and watched if anyone would come.

I saw the pretty girl he loves better than me"—and the mermaid sighed deeply, for she didn't know how to cry. "The girl belongs to the sacred temple, he says; she'll never come out into the world, and they'll never meet again. I am with him. I see him every day. I will take care of him, love him, give up my life to him."

But now the Prince was getting married they said—married to the pretty daughter of the neighboring King, and that was why he was fitting out such a splendid ship. The Prince was going off to take a look at his neighbor's kingdom—that was how they put it, meaning that it was really to take a look at his neighbor's daughter. A large suite was to go with him, but the little mermaid shook her head and laughed. She knew the Prince's thoughts far better than all the others. "I shall have to go," he said to her. "I shall have to visit the pretty Princess, as my parents are so insistent. But force me to bring her back here as my wife, that they will never do. I can't love her. She's not like the beautiful girl in the temple, as you are. If I ever had to find a bride, I would rather have you, my dear mute foundling with the speaking eyes," and he kissed her red mouth, played with her long hair and laid his head against her heart, so that it dreamed of human happiness and an immortal soul.

"You've no fear of the sea, have you, my dumb child?" he asked, as they stood on board the splendid ship that was to take him to the neighboring kingdom. And he told her of stormy gales and dead calms, of strange fishes at the bottom of the ocean, and all that the diver had seen there; and she smiled at his tales, for she knew better than anyone else about the bottom of the sea.

At night, when there was an unclouded moon and all were asleep but the helmsman at his wheel, she sat by the ship's rail and stared down through the clear water; and she seemed to see her father's palace, with her old grandmother standing on the top of it in her silver crown and gazing up through the swift current at the keel of the vessel. Then her sisters came up on to the water and looked at her with eyes full of sorrow, wringing their white hands. She beckoned to them and smiled and would have liked to tell them that all was going well and happily with her; but the cabin boy came up at that moment, and the sisters dived down, so that the boy felt satisfied that the white something he had seen was foam on the water.

Next morning the ship sailed into the harbor of the neighboring King's magnificent capital. The church bells all rang out; and trumpets were blown from the tall battlements, while the soldiers saluted with gleaming bayonets and flying colors. Every day there was a fête. Balls and parties were given one after another, but nothing had yet been seen of the Princess; it was said that she was being educated abroad in a sacred temple, where she had lessons in all the royal virtues. At last she arrived.

The little mermaid was eager for a glimpse of her beauty, and she had to admit that she had never seen anyone more charming to look at. Her complexion was so clear and delicate, and behind the long dark lashes smiled a pair of trusting deep blue eyes.

"It's you!" cried the Prince. "You who rescued me, when I was lying half-dead on the shore." And he clasped his blushing bride in his arms. "Oh, I'm too, too happy," he said to the little mermaid. "My dearest wish—more than I ever dared to hope for—has been granted me. My happiness will give you pleasure, because you're fonder of me than any of the others." Then the little mermaid kissed his hand, and already she felt as if her heart was breaking. The morrow of his wedding would mean death to her and change her to foam on the sea.

All the church bells were ringing, as the heralds rode round the streets to proclaim the betrothal. On every altar sweet oil was burning in rich lamps of silver. The priests swung their censers, and bride and bridegroom joined hands and received the blessing of the bishop. Dressed in silk and gold, the little mermaid stood holding the bride's train; but her ears never heard the festive music, her eyes never saw the holy rites; she was thinking of her last night on earth, of all she had lost in this world.

That same evening, bride and bridegroom went on board the ship; the cannon thundered, the flags were all flying, and amidships they had put up a royal tent of gold and purple, strewn with luxurious cushions; here the wedded couple were to sleep that calm cool night.

The sails filled with the breeze and the ship glided lightly and smoothly over the clear water.

As darkness fell, colored lanterns were lit, and the crew danced merrily on the deck. The little mermaid could not help thinking of the first time she came up out of the sea and gazed on just such a scene of joy and splendor. And now she joined in the dance, swerving and swooping as lightly as a swallow that avoids pursuit; and shouts of admiration greeted her on every side. Never had she danced so brilliantly. It was as if sharp knives were wounding her delicate feet, but she never felt it; more painful was the wound in her heart. She knew that this was the last evening she would see the Prince for whom she had turned her back on kindred and home, given up her beautiful voice, and every day suffered hours of agony without his suspecting a thing. This was the last night she would breathe the same air as he, gaze on the deep sea and star-blue sky. An endless night, without thoughts, without dreams, awaited her who had no soul and could never win one. . . . All was joy and merriment on board until long past midnight. She laughed and danced with the thought of death in her heart. The Prince kissed his lovely bride, and she toyed with his dark hair, and arm in arm they went to rest in the magnificent tent.

The ship was now hushed and still; only the helmsman was there at his wheel. And the little mermaid leaned with her white arms on the rail and looked eastward for a sign of the pink dawn. The first ray of the sun, she knew, would kill her. Suddenly she saw her sisters rising out of the sea. They were pale, like her; no more was their beautiful long hair fluttering in the wind—it had been cut off.

"We have given it to the witch, so that she might help us to save you from dying when tonight is over. She has given us a knife—look, here it is—do you see how sharp it is? Before sunrise you must stab it into the Prince's heart. Then, when his warm blood splashes over your feet, they will grow together into a fish's tail, and you will become a mermaid once more; you will be able to come down to us in the water and live out your three hundred years before being changed into the dead salt foam of the sea. Make haste! Either he or you must die before the sun rises. Our old grandmother has been sorrowing till her white hair has fallen away, as ours fell before the witch's scissors. Kill the Prince and come back to us! But make haste—look at that red gleam in the sky. In a few minutes the sun will rise, and then you must die." And with a strange deep sigh they sank beneath the waves.

The little mermaid drew aside the purple curtain of the tent, and she saw the lovely bride sleeping with her head on the Prince's breast. She stopped and kissed his handsome brow, looked at the sky where the pink dawn glowed brighter and brighter, looked at the sharp knife in her hand, and again fixed her eyes on the Prince, who murmured in his dreams the name of his bride—she alone was in his thoughts. The knife quivered in the mermaid's hand—but then she flung it far out into the waves; they glimmered red where it fell, and what looked like drops of blood came oozing out of the water. With a last glance at the Prince from eyes half-dimmed in death she hurled herself from the ship into the sea and felt her body dissolving into foam.

And now the sun came rising from the sea. Its rays fell gentle and warm on the death chilled foam, and the little mermaid had no feeling of death. She saw the bright sun and, hovering above her, hundreds of lovely creatures—she could see right through them, see the white sails of the ship and the pink clouds in the sky. And their voice was the voice of melody, yet so spiritual that no human ear could hear it, just as no earthly eye could see them. They had no wings, but their own lightness bore them up as they floated through the air. The little mermaid saw that she had a body like theirs, raising itself freer and freer from the foam.

"To whom am I coming?" she asked, and her voice sounded like that of the other beings, more spiritual than any earthly music can record.

"To the daughters of the air," answered the others. "A mermaid has no immortal soul and can never have one unless she wins the love of a mortal. Eternity, for her, depends on a power outside her. Neither have the daughters of the air an everlasting soul, but by good deeds they can shape one for themselves. We shall fly to the hot countries, where the stifling air of pestilence means death to mankind; we shall bring them cool breezes. We shall scatter the fragrance of flowers through the air and send them comfort and healing. When for three hundred years we have striven to do the good we can, then we shall win an immortal soul and have a share in mankind's eternal happiness. You, poor little mermaid, have striven for that with all your heart; you have suffered and endured, and have raised yourself into the world of the spirits of the air. Now, by three hundred years of good deeds, you too can shape for yourself an immortal soul."

And the little mermaid raised her crystal arms toward God's sun, and for the first time she knew the feeling of tears.

On board the ship there was bustle and life once more. She saw the Prince with his pretty bride looking about for her; sorrowfully they stared at the heaving foam, as if they knew she had thrown herself into the waves. Unseen, she kissed the forehead of the bride, gave a smile to the Prince, and then with the other children of the air she climbed to a rose-red cloud that was sailing to the sky.

"So we shall float for three hundred years, till at last we come into the heavenly kingdom."

"And we may reach it even sooner," whispered one. "Unseen we float into human homes where there are children and, for every day we find a good child who makes father and mother happy and earns their love, God shortens our time of trial. The child never knows when we fly through the room and, if that makes us smile with joy, then a year is taken away from the three hundred. But if we see a child who is naughty or spiteful, then we have to weep tears of sorrow, and every tear adds one more day to our time of trial."

The Pangs of Love

Jane Gardam

t is not generally known that the good little mermaid of Hans Christian Andersen, who died for love of the handsome prince and allowed herself to dissolve in the foam of the ocean, had a younger sister, a difficult child of very different temper.

She was very young when the tragedy occurred, and was only told it later by her five elder sisters and her grandmother, the Sea King's mother with the twelve important oyster shells in her tail. They spent much of their time, all these women, mourning the tragic life of the little mermaid in the Sea King's palace below the waves, and a very dreary place it had become in consequence.

"I don't see what she did it for," the seventh little mermaid used to say. "Love for a man—ridiculous," and all the others would sway on the tide and moan, "Hush, hush—you don't know how she suffered for love."

"I don't understand this 'suffered for love'," said the seventh mermaid. "She sounds very silly and obviously spoiled her life."

"She may have spoiled her life," said the Sea King's mother, "but think how good she was. She was given the chance of saving her life, but because it would have harmed the prince and his earthly bride she let herself die."

"What had he done so special to deserve that?" asked the seventh mermaid.

"He had *done* nothing. He was just her beloved prince to whom she would sacrifice all."

"What did he sacrifice for her?" asked Signorina Settima.

"Not a lot," said the Sea King's mother, "I believe they don't on the whole. But it doesn't stop us loving them."

"It would me," said the seventh mermaid. "I must get a look at some of this mankind, and perhaps I will then understand more."

"You must wait until your fifteenth birthday," said the Sea King's mother. "That has always been the rule with all your sisters."

"Oh, shit," said the seventh mermaid (she was rather coarse). "Times change. I'm as mature now as they were at fifteen. Howsabout tomorrow?"

"I'm sure I don't know what's to be done with you," said the Sea King's mother, whose character had weakened in later years. "You are totally different from the others and yet I'm sure I brought you all up the same."

"Oh no you didn't," said the five elder sisters in chorus, "she's always been spoiled. We'd never have dared talk to you like that. Think if our beloved sister who died for love had talked to you like that."

"Maybe she should have done," said the dreadful seventh damsel officiously, and this time in spite of her grandmother's failing powers she was put in a cave for a while in the dark and made to miss her supper.

Nevertheless, she was the sort of girl who didn't let other people's views interfere with her too much, and she could argue like nobody else in the sea, so that in the end her grandmother said, "Oh for goodness' sake then—go. Go now and don't even wait for your *fourteenth* birthday. Go and look at some men and don't come back unless they can turn you into a mermaid one hundredth part as good as your beloved foamy sister."

"Whoops," said Mademoiselle Sept, and she flicked her tail and was away up out of the Sea King's palace, rising through the coral and the fishes that wove about the red and blue seaweed trees like birds, up and up until her head shot out into the air and she took a deep breath of it and said, "Wow!"

The sky, as her admirable sister had noticed stood above the sea like a large glass bell, and the waves rolled and lifted and tossed towards a green shore where there were fields and palaces and flowers and forests where fishes with wings and legs wove about the branches of green and so forth trees, singing at the tops of their voices. On a balcony sticking out from the best palace stood, as he had stood before his marriage when the immaculate sister had first seen him, the wonderful prince with his chin resting on his hand as it often did of an evening—and indeed in the mornings and afternoons, too.

"Oh help!" said the seventh mermaid, feeling a queer twisting around her heart. Then she thought, "Watch it." She dived under water for a time and came up on a rock on the shore, where she sat and examined her sea-green fingernails and smoothed down the silver scales of her tail.

She was sitting where the prince could see her and after a while he gave a cry and she looked up. "Oh," he said, "how you remind me of someone. I thought for a moment you were my lost love."

"Lost love," said the seventh mermaid. "And whose fault was that? She was my sister. She died for love of you and you never gave her one serious thought. You even took her along on your honeymoon like a pet toy. I don't know what she saw in you."

"I always loved her," said the prince. "But I didn't realise it until too late."

"That's what they all say," said Numera Septima. "Are you a poet? They're the worst. Hardy, Tennyson, Shakespeare, Homer. Homer was the worst of all. And he hadn't a good word to say for mermaids."

"Forgive me," said the prince, who had removed his chin from his hand and was passionately clenching the parapet. "Every word you speak reminds me more and more—"

"I don't see how it can," said the s.m., "since for love of you and because she was told it was the only way she could come to you, she let them cut out her tongue, the silly ass."

"And your face," he cried, "your whole aspect, except of course for the tail."

"She had that removed, too. They told her it would be agony and it was, so my sisters tell me. It shrivelled up and she got two ugly stumps called legs—I daresay you've got them under that parapet. When she danced, every step she took was like knives."

"Alas, alas!"

"Catch me getting rid of my tail," said syedmaya krasavitsa, twitching it seductively about, and the prince gave a great spring from the balcony and embraced her on the rocks. It was all right until half way down but the scales were cold and prickly. Slimy, too, and he shuddered.

"How dare you shudder," cried La Septieme. "Go back to your earthly bride."

"She's not here at present," said the p., "she's gone to her mother for the weekend. Won't you come in? We can have dinner in the bath."

The seventh little mermaid spent the whole weekend with the prince in the bath, and he became quite frantic with desire by Monday morning because of the insurmountable problem below the mermaid's waist. "Your eyes, your hair," he cried, "but that's about all."

"My sister did away with her beautiful tail for love of you," said the s.m., reading a volume of Descartes over the prince's shoulder as he lay on her sea-green bosom. "They tell me she even wore a disgusting harness on the top half of her for you, and make-up and dresses. She was the saint of mermaids."

"Ah, a saint," said the prince. "But without your wit, your spark. I would do anything in the world for you."

"So whats about getting rid of your legs?"

"Getting rid of my *legs*?"

"Then you can come and live with me below the waves. No one has legs down there and there's nothing wrong with any of us. As a matter of fact, aesthetically we're a very good species."

"Get rid of my *legs*?"

"Yes—my grandmother, the Sea King's mother, and the Sea Witch behind the last whirlpool who fixed up my poor sister, silly cow, could see to it for you."

"Oh, how I love your racy talk," said the prince. "It's like nothing I ever heard before. I should love you even with my eyes shut. Even at a distance. Even on the telephone."

"No fear," said the seventh m., "I know all about this waiting by the telephone. All my sisters do it. It never rings when they want it to. It has days and days of terrible silence and they all roll about weeping and chewing their handkerchieves. You don't catch me getting in that condition."

"Gosh, you're marvellous," said the prince, who had been to an old-fashioned school, "I'll do anything—"

"The legs?"

"Hum. Ha. Well—the legs."

"Carry me back to the rocks," said the seventh little mermaid, "I'll leave you to think about it. What's more I hear a disturbance in the hall which heralds the return of your wife. By the way, it wasn't your wife, you know, who saved you from drowning when you got shipwrecked on your sixteenth birthday. It was my dear old sister once again. 'She swam among the spars and planks which drifted on the sea, quite forgetting they might crush her. Then she ducked beneath the water, and rising again on the billows managed at last to reach you who by now' (being fairly feeble in the muscles I'd guess, with all the stately living) 'was scarcely able to swim any longer in the raging sea. Your arms, your legs' (ha!) 'began to fail you and your beautiful eyes were closed and you must surely have died if my sister had not come to your assistance. She held your head above the water and let the billows drive her and you together wherever they pleased.' "

"What antique phraseology."

"It's a translation from the Danish. Anyway, 'when the sun rose red and beaming from the water, your cheeks regained the hue of life but your eyes remained closed. My sister kissed—'

("No!")

" '—your lofty handsome brow and stroked back your wet locks . . . She kissed you again and longed that you might live.' What's more if you'd only woken up then she could have spoken to you. It was when she got obsessed by you back down under the waves again that she went in for all this tongue and tail stuff with the Sea Witch."

"She was an awfully nice girl," said the prince, and tears came into his eyes—which was more than they ever could do for a mermaid however sad, because as we know from H. C. Andersen, mermaids can never cry which makes it harder for them.

"The woman I saw when I came to on the beach," said the prince, "was she who is now my wife. A good sort of woman but she drinks."

"I'm not surprised," said the seventh mermaid. "I'd drink if I was married to someone who just stood gazing out to sea thinking of a girl he had allowed to turn into foam," and she flicked her tail and disappeared.

"Now then," she thought, "what's to do next?" She was not to go back, her grandmother had said, until she was one hundredth part as good as the little m. her dead sister, now a spirit of air, and although she was a tearaway and, as I say, rather coarse, she was not altogether untouched by the discipline of the Sea King's mother and her upbringing. Yet she could not say that she exactly yearned for her father's palace with all her melancholy sisters singing dreary stuff about the past. Nor was she too thrilled to return to the heaviness of water with all the featherless fishes swimming through the amber windows and butting in to her, and the living flowers growing out of the palace walls like dry rot. However, after flicking about for a bit, once coming up to do an inspection of a fishing boat in difficulties with the tide and enjoying the usual drop-jawed faces, she took a header home into the front room and sat down quietly in a corner.

"You're back," said the Sea King's mother. "How was it? I take it you now feel you are a hundredth part as good as your sainted sister?"

"I've always tried to be good," said the s.m., "I've just tried to be rationally good and not romantically good, that's all."

"Now don't start again. I take it you have seen some men?"

"I saw the prince."

At this the five elder sisters set up a wavering lament.

"Did you feel for him—"

"Oh, feelings, feelings," said the seventh and rational mermaid, "I'm sick to death of feelings. He's good looking, I'll give you that, and rather sweet-natured and he's having a rough time at home, but he's totally self-centred. I agree that my sister must have been a true sea-saint to listen to him dripping on about himself all day. He's warm-hearted though, and not at all bad in the bath."

The Sea King's mother fainted away at this outspoken and uninhibited statement, and the five senior mermaids fled in shock. The seventh mermaid tidied her hair and set off to find the terrible cave of the Sea Witch behind the last whirlpool, briskly pushing aside the disgusting polypi, half plant, half animal, and the fingery seaweeds that had so terrified her dead sister on a similar journey.

"Aha," said the Sea Witch, stirring a pot of filthy black bouillabaisse, "you, like your sister, cannot do without me. I suppose you also want to risk body and soul for the human prince up there on the dry earth?"

"Good afternoon, no," said the seventh mermaid. "Might I sit down?" (For even the seventh mermaid was polite to the Sea Witch.) "I want to ask you if, when the prince follows me down here below the waves, you could arrange for him to live with me until the end of time?"

"He'd have to lose his legs. What would he think of that?"

"I think he might consider it. In due course."

"He would have to learn to sing and not care about clothes or money or possessions or power—what would he think of that?"

"Difficult, but not impossible."

"He'd have to face the fact that if you fell in love with one of your own kind and married him he would die and also lose his soul as your sister did when he wouldn't make an honest woman of her."

"It was not," said the seventh mermaid, "that he wouldn't make an honest woman of her. It just never occurred to him. After all—she couldn't speak to him about it. You had cut out her tongue."

"Aha," said the s.w., "it's different for a man, is it? Falling in love, are you?"

"Certainly not," said Fräulein Sieben. "Certainly not."

"Cruel then, eh? Revengeful? Or do you hate men? It's very fashionable."

"I'm not cruel. Or revengeful. I'm just rational. And I don't hate men. I think I'd probably like them very much, especially if they are all as kind and as beautiful as the prince. I just don't believe in falling in love with them. It is a burden and it spoils life. It is a mental illness. It killed my sister and it puts women in a weak position and makes us to be considered second class."

"They fall in love with us," said the Sea Witch. "That's to say, with women. So I've been told. Sometimes. Haven't you read the sonnets of Shakespeare and the poems of Petrarch?"

"The sonnets of Shakespeare are hardly all about one woman," said the bright young mermaid. "In fact some of them are written to a man. As for Petrarch, (there was scarcely a thing this girl hadn't read) he only saw his girl once, walking over a bridge. They never exactly brushed their teeth together."

"Well, there are the Brownings."

"Yes. The Brownings were all right," said the mermaid. "Very funny looking though. I don't suppose anyone else ever wanted them."

"You are a determined young mermaid," said the Sea Witch. "Yes, I'll agree to treat the prince if he comes this way. But you must wait and see if he does."

"Thank you, yes I will," said the seventh mermaid. "He'll come," and she did wait, quite confidently, being the kind of girl well-heeled men do run after because she never ran after them, very like Elizabeth Bennet.

So, one day, who should come swimming down through the wonderful blue water and into the golden palaces of the Sea King and floating through the windows like the fishes and touching with wonder the dry-rot flowers upon the walls, but the prince, his golden hair floating behind him and his golden hose and tunic stuck tight to him all over like a wet suit, and he looked terrific.

"Oh, princess, sweet seventh mermaid," he said, finding her at once (because she was the sort of girl who is always in the right place at the right time). "I have found you again. Ever since I threw you back in the sea I have dreamed of you. I cannot live without you. I have left my boozy wife and have come to live with you forever."

"There are terrible conditions," said the seventh mermaid. "Remember. The same conditions which my poor sister accepted in reverse. You must lose your legs and wear a tail."

"This I will do."

"You must learn to sing for hours and hours in unison with the other mermen, in wondrous notes that hypnotise simple sailors up above and make them think they hear faint sounds from Glyndebourne or Milan."

"As to that," said the prince, "I always wished I had a voice."

"And you must know that if I decide that I want someone more than you, someone of my own sort, and marry him, you will lose everything, as my sister did—your body, your immortal soul, and your self-respect."

"Oh well, that's quite all right," said the prince. He knew that no girl could ever prefer anyone else to him.

"*Right*," said the mermaid. "Well, before we go off to the Sea Witch, let's give a party. And let me introduce you to my mother and sisters."

Then there followed a time of most glorious celebration, similar only to the celebration some years back for the prince's wedding night when the poor little mermaid now dead had had to sit on the deck of the nuptial barque and watch the bride and groom until she had quite melted away. Then the cannons had roared and the flags had waved and a royal bridal tent of cloth of gold and purple and precious furs had been set upon the deck and when it grew dark, coloured lamps had been lit and sailors danced merrily and the bride and groom had gone into the tent without the prince giving the little mermaid a backward glance.

Now, beneath the waves the sea was similarly alight with glowing corals and brilliant sea-flowers and a bower was set up for the seventh mermaid and the prince and she danced with all the mermen who had silver crowns on their heads and St. Christophers round their necks, very trendy like the South of France, and they all had a lovely time.

And the party went on and on. It was beautiful. Day after day and night after night and anyone who was anyone was there, and the weather was gorgeous—no storms below or above and it was exactly as Hans Christian Andersen said: "a wondrous blue tint lay over everything; one would be more inclined to fancy one was high up in the air and saw nothing but sky above and below than that one was at the bottom of the sea. During a calm, too, one could catch a glimpse of the sun. It looked like a crimson flower from the cup of which, light streamed forth." The seventh mermaid danced and danced, particularly with a handsome young merman with whom she seemed much at her ease.

"Who is that merman?" asked the prince. "You seem to know him well."

"Oh—just an old friend," said the seventh m., "he's always been about. We were in our prams together." (This was not true. The seventh m. was just testing the prince. She had never bothered with mermen even in her pram.)

"I'm sorry," said the prince, "I can't have you having mermen friends. Even if there's nothing in it."

"We must discuss this with the Sea Witch," said the seventh mermaid, and taking his hand she swam with him out of the palace and away and away through the dreadful polypi again. She took him past the last whirlpool to the cave where the Sea Witch was sitting eating a most unpleasant-looking type of caviar from a giant snail shell and stroking her necklace of sea snakes.

"Ha," said the Sea Witch, "the prince. You have come to be rid of your legs?"

"Er—well—"

"You have come to be rid of your earthly speech, your clothes and possessions, and power?"

"Well, it's something that we might discuss."

"And you agree to lose soul and body and self-respect if this interesting mermaid goes off and marries someone?"

There was a very long silence and the seventh mermaid closely examined some shells round her neck, tiny pale pink oyster shells each containing a pearl which would be the glory of a Queen's crown. The prince held his beautiful chin in his lovely, sensitive hand. His gentle eyes filled with tears. At last he took the mermaid's small hand and kissed its palm and folded the sea-green nails over the kiss (he had sweet ways) and said, "I must not look at you. I must go at once," and he pushed off. That is to say, he pushed himself upwards off the floor of the sea and shot up and away and away through the foam, arriving home in time for tea and early sherry with his wife, who was much relieved.

It was a very long time indeed before the seventh little mermaid returned to the party. In fact the party was all but over. There was only the odd slithery merman twanging a harp of dead fisherman's bones and the greediest and grubbiest of the deep water fishes eating up the last of the sandwiches. The Sea King's old mother was asleep, her heavy tail studded with important oyster shells coiled round the legs of her throne.

The five elder sisters had gone on somewhere amusing.

The seventh mermaid sat down at the feet of her grandmother and at length the old lady woke up and surveyed the chaos left over from the fun. "Hello, my child," she said. "Are you alone?"

"Yes. The prince has gone. The engagement's off."

"My dear—what did I tell you? Remember how your poor sister suffered. I warned you."

"Pooh—I'm not suffering. I've just proved my point. Men aren't worth it."

"Maybe you and she were unfortunate," said the Sea King's mother. "Which men you meet is very much a matter of luck, I'm told."

"No—they're all the same," said the mermaid who by now was nearly fifteen years old. "I've proved what I suspected. I'm free now—free of the terrible pangs of love which put women in bondage, and I shall dedicate my life to freeing and instructing other women and saving them from humiliation."

"Well, I hope you don't become one of those frowsty little women who don't laugh and have only one subject of conversation," said the Sea King's mother. "It is a mistake to base a whole philosophy upon one disappointment."

"Disappointment—pah!" said the seventh mermaid. "When was I ever negative?"

"And I hope you don't become aggressive."

"When was I ever aggressive?" said Senorita Septima ferociously.

"That's a good girl then," said the Sea King's mother. "So now—unclench that fist."

QUESTIONS FOR DISCUSSION

In Andersen's story, why is the little mermaid's reward a chance to earn an immortal soul through three hundred years of good deeds?

1. Why does the little mermaid long for the human world so much more than her sisters?

2. Why is the little mermaid willing to give up her voice in order to get human legs and try to win the Prince?

3. Why does the little mermaid continue to laugh and dance "with the thought of death in her heart"? (23)

4. Why won't the little mermaid kill the Prince, even though it is the only way to save her life?

At the end of Gardam's story, why does the seventh mermaid believe she is "free of the terrible pangs of love which put women in bondage"? (37)

1. What does the seventh mermaid mean when she says her sister was "the saint of mermaids"? (30)

2. What does the seventh mermaid mean when she says, "I've just tried to be rationally good and not romantically good"? (32)

3. Why does the prince ultimately refuse to give up his legs and meet the seventh mermaid's other conditions?

4. At the end of the story, why does the Sea King's mother tell the seventh mermaid, "So now—unclench that fist"? (37)

FOR FURTHER REFLECTION

1. What is it that gives fairy tales their lasting power and appeal? Why do authors rewrite or reimagine fairy tales?

2. What similarities and differences do you see in the ways that Andersen and Gardam define love?

3. Do you think love requires self-sacrifice?

4. Why do some people define themselves by their romantic relationships?

ASPIRATION

In aspiring to fulfill our dreams and ambitions, we often yearn to live elsewhere, in a place that holds out the promise—real or illusory—of wealth, health, and contentment. Throughout human history, people have pulled up stakes and sought new homelands, hoping for a better life. In nineteenth-century America, as the frontier settlements pushed farther west, the region known as California became for many the goal of their aspirations. With the advent of the Hollywood entertainment industry in the twentieth century, the mystique of California assumed worldwide stature. For many, California represented the pinnacle of fame and fortune, but these enticements could also lead to bitter disappointment and broken dreams. Using California as the emblem of the human aspiration to find a better place, the following selections invite us to consider both the uplifting and degrading consequences of our need to maintain such a vision and to act on it.

The poet **Walt Whitman** (1819–1892), considered by some to be the first quintessentially American poet, wrote during the period of westward expansion in the United States. His poem "Facing West from California's Shores" comes from *Leaves of Grass*, and this version matches the 1867 edition. In it, Whitman reflects on the entire course of human migration: he completes the age-old circling of the globe, and, in reaching the West Coast of America, simultaneously looks forward and backward to the origins of all aspiration.

American novelist and screenwriter **Daniel Fuchs** (1909–1993) lived in California and often wrote about the dreams of fictionalized characters working in the film industry. In his short story "The Golden West," Fuchs chronicles several friends at a party of Hollywood insiders, sharply depicting the intersections of their personal and professional lives.

Facing West from California's Shores

Walt Whitman

Facing west from California's shores,
Inquiring, tireless, seeking what is yet unfound,
I, a child, very old, over waves, towards the house of maternity, the
    land of migrations, look afar,
Look off the shores of my Western sea, the circle almost circled;
For starting westward from Hindustan, from the vales of
    Kashmere,
From Asia, from the north, from the God, the sage, and the hero,
From the south, from the flowery peninsulas and the spice islands,
Long having wander'd since, round the earth having wander'd,
Now I face home again, very pleas'd and joyous,
(But where is what I started for so long ago?
And why is it yet unfound?)

The Golden West

Daniel Fuchs

As everyone knows, the movie business isn't what it used to be. For many of us who used to work at the studios, the pleasant, oversized checks that came every Thursday have stopped. The blow fell softly, mainly because when the crisis developed we couldn't believe or didn't want to believe that it was upon us. Some of us went back to the kind of work we had done before we were brought out to Hollywood. Others, like a certain group of people I had come to know, and saw almost every week, simply stayed on, hanging.

The California sunshine continued to pour down. The streets, the stucco mansions, the lawns and shrubbery sparkled with light. These friends of mine went on visiting one another's homes, and giving outdoor dinner parties, the ladies in their lovely frocks scattered over the terrace at the tables, chattering and affectionate, while their husbands stood off by themselves in small clusters, nodding and smiling and smoking; my friends kept on their housekeepers and gardeners and children's nurses; they still sent their children to dancing school, to supervised play groups. "And every month," as a man named Curtis Spogel once remarked sadly to me, "another few Defense Bonds cashed in at the bank and dissipated."

Spogel was a certified public accountant by profession, and he was also in the movie business. He was in the exhibition end, the non-creative side, but he was mixed in with the creative people through his brother-in-law Julie Vencie, a top producer in the industry, now no longer attached to any major studio. "If they would only awaken to the realities. If they would only face the facts and do something,"

Spogel said. "But what?" he added immediately. His movie houses, eight-hundred-seaters, were upstate in Kern County—in rural communities, far from the cities, from the television stations. His income was relatively unaffected by the debacle, and he didn't want to seem unfeeling.

One Sunday afternoon, I drove over to his home in Beverly Hills, high up on Angelo Drive. As I left my car in the parking space near the garage, I could tell at once I was the first to arrive. The garden lay fresh and still, the water was quiet in the swimming pool, and Mrs. Vencie, Mrs. Spogel's mother, was sitting on the terrace, in the shade, reading a foreign-language newspaper. Mrs. Vencie lived with the Spogels.

I wanted to avoid the old lady. I knew she would fasten on to me and talk, about the bad times, about her son Julie—her golden boy, she used to call him.

A row of large, old oleander bushes separated the garage area from the grounds and the house. I went up the row of oleanders and made my way around the terrace, reached the house, and slipped inside by the front way. Passing through the entrance hall, I saw Edith Spogel standing alone in the living room, leaning against the back of the couch in the dimness there, her eyes shut. She was listening to the New York Philharmonic concert on the radio and was lost in the music. I started to speak to her, but just then I became aware of Spogel creeping up on her. He was wearing a pair of tennis trunks and carrying a box of chocolates. "Boo!" he said.

"Oh, Curtis!" she said startled.

"Have a sweet!" Spogel said, playful and eager.

"No, thanks," Edith said, and then, as he kept pressing the chocolates on her, she said, "Oh, Curtis, really! How can you, in the middle of the day—Oh, hello, David," she said, seeing me. She smoothed her eyebrows with her fingertips and sighed. "How are you?" she said to me. "How's the family? Come—let's go out on the terrace. Let's listen to the music there." She touched the switches on the little box that controlled the various radio speakers, and went outside.

"Everything these days is like walking on eggshells," Spogel said to me, disappointed, the candy box still in his hands. "We seem to exist in perpetual tension."

Auditing other people's books, working on the inside, Spogel was able to spot good business opportunities. That was how he had wandered into the movie field, buying that chain of theaters upstate; that was how he had met Julie Vencie, and then Julie's sister. Edith was a year or two older than her brother, and getting on. The marriage was one of those arranged, matchmaker's affairs. At the time, Julie was a big producer, under contract, bustling and sprightly, four thousand a week at the majors, and there was a certain atmosphere, a kind of glamour. But now the glamour was gone, and Spogel saddled with the support of his wife's mother, too. He was awed by this whole circle of movie people among whom he had, so to speak, blundered. He admired them. He thought they possessed some quality, some mystery, that he lacked. He always felt inferior and apologetic with them. He was apologetic and self-conscious over everything he did—because he showed Gene Autrys and Randolph Scotts at his movie houses, or sex-and-sands with Yvonne de Carlo, because he ate candy in the daytime and had no personality, because he neglected his reducing exercises. He wanted to reduce, he sincerely meant to do the exercises every day, but they made his stomach muscles hurt, and so he would forget and then, later, feel guilty. "I am a sybarite!" he said one day, daringly, when we came upon him with one of those thirty-cent chocolate bars in his hands. And then, when no one smiled, he said, "I don't smoke, I don't drink—so this is my vice, sweets. Everybody has a vice or two . . ." That was the way he was.

When we went out on the terrace, Mrs. Vencie was chattering at full speed, every word getting on Edith's nerves.

"Rich, rich—famous!" the old lady was saying, meaning her son Julie, of course. "He always wanted to be a big shot. I used to argue patiently with him by the hour. 'Julie,' I would say to him, 'you'll give yourself a breakdown. You'll bust a spring in your head! Julie, what do you want it for, who needs it—the ulcers, the hypertension, the Cadillacs? A trolley car won't get you there just the same?' "

"Ma," Edith said.

"When he was a boy," Mrs. Vencie went on, ignoring the interruption, "when we lived on the East Side, you know what he did? He walked! He couldn't stand the tenements—the babies crying, the dumbwaiters, the garbage. He would walk for miles and miles, making up dreams in his head, having ambitions. He would go and find a dime and ride on the Fifth Avenue bus—he couldn't live if he didn't look at the fancy stores, at the rich people!"

"Ma," Edith said again.

"Dear," Spogel said to his wife. "Why must you aggravate yourself and take everything to heart so? What difference does it make if Mother harmlessly—"

"Curtis, please," Edith said, and he stopped at once, turning aside.

"I know nothing," he murmured to me. "I am a businessman, bourgeois—sex-and-sands."

"Reaching for the stars!" Mrs. Vencie said. "They say if you don't give them affection when they're little, it will have bad aftereffects on them and give them scars. So it was my fault? I didn't give him enough affection? Who had time for affection? I had seven small little children. I had to scrub floors, cook supper, wash the clothes—not like the modern women nowadays, believe me. Everything the children wore, I sewed by myself on the machine—the jumpers, the knee pants, the dresses for the girls. When I gave birth to Edith and had to lay in bed for three whole days, naturally, of course, I couldn't watch out, and so that's how we had the tragedy—that's how we lost Freddie."

"Ma!" Edith cried.

"Ma!" Mrs. Vencie burst out, nettled. "What are you hollering on me 'Ma' for? It ain't the truth? Poor little Freddie didn't go up on the roof to play, and they didn't push him off?"

"Nobody's interested," Edith said. "You told us the whole story a dozen times. It happened a hundred years ago. I'm trying to listen to the Symphony!"

"Symphony!" Mrs. Vencie said. "Fancy lady! What's the matter—I embarrass you? I didn't do enough for you? When the doctor took out your tonsils and I gave you the wrong medicine by mistake; didn't I hurry up quick and drink the whole bottle?"

"Oh, it's hopeless, it's hopeless," Edith said. "Again the story with the tonsils and the medicine, again the whole repertoire!" She turned away and went back into the house.

Mrs. Vencie's shoulders started to shake, and I saw she was laughing. "David, you could make a book!" she said, chortling, and wiping her nose with the back of her hand. "It was a regular Charlie Chaplin! See, innocently, I thought I poisoned her—that's why I hurried up and drank the whole bottle. But in the excitement, in the hoorah I made, Edith vomited it up—excuse me, David—but me, I kept my share down and I still got it in me to this day! I was furious! Poor Papa," she said, her mood suddenly shifting. She was thinking now, it turned out, of Freddie, of the tragedy. Mr. Vencie had worked in fur, but he had caught the furrier's lung disease and had been totally incapacitated. At the time of the accident, he had just been getting on his feet again—he had a small candy stand. "It took ten years off his life, that's why he died so soon," Mrs. Vencie said. "When the police officers came and they informed him, he went running home from the candy store, hitting his head with his hands and hollering in the street, 'Gevalt, gevalt!' . . . Oh, look, look, look," she said, her face lighting up. Another pair of visitors had emerged from the parking space. "Now we have the newlyweds," Mrs. Vencie said with satisfaction, settling herself.

The newcomers were the Kittershoys, Boris and Daisy. Boris was Julie's partner, the "kay" in Veeankay Pictures, an independent producing company they were trying to get started.

"Curtis! Curtis!" Daisy cried as she came scampering across the garden. "You should feel my thighs—like iron bands!" She was taking ballet and tennis lessons—that was all she meant by the reference to her thighs. She and Boris had recently been married, and although she was by no means in her first youth, she acted like a bride. "Doom, doom," she said as she joined us on the terrace, chiding her husband as well as Spogel. They both had long faces. "Smile!" she said. "Show optimism! The world is not coming to an end."

Boris Kittershoy came to the Spogels's hoping to see Julie, who was unpredictable, with a violent temper, and hard to approach. These meetings at the Spogels's parties were about the only chance Boris had to talk to his partner. I knew all this, so I knew what it meant to Boris when Julie failed to appear and, instead, his wife, Imogene, came, not long after the Kittershoys. She had an overnight bag. She and Julie were fighting again, it developed. She had left him or he had left her or had driven her away.

"He is an *enfant terrible*," Boris said. The Spogels and I were huddled around Imogene in the living room—away from Mrs. Vencie, on the terrace. "We are going under, perishing," Boris said, "and he must pick this time to fight with his wife! He is clinical."

"How irresponsible they are," Spogel whispered to me. "How temperamental and undisciplined." His eyes kept wavering and he glanced constantly at Edith, to see how she was managing under the new strain.

Boris and Julie had gone ahead with their independent picture largely on assurances given to them by an executive at a major studio. He had promised, orally, to furnish them with a release, with the principle financing, with a director, with name stars. The deal had fallen through, as Hollywood deals do. The executive hadn't reneged or double-crossed them; his studio had simply decided at the last moment to withdraw. It was a change of policy, but it left Veeankay with two hundred thousand dollars hard cash, or more, sunk in the venture, and no place to go. "He is a mass of contradictions, and he poses, and nobody can get along with him," Boris said, half rocking there in the dim light, on his upholstered chair.

"It never fails!" Daisy said. "When a man is in the dumps and business is bad, he immediately gets infatuated with his wife all over again. They put you on a pedestal, and think you are the most beautiful woman in the world, and they give you no peace!"

"I suppose," Imogene said, listless. "He's crazy."

Whenever they had their fights, she drove straight up the hill to the Spogels's, because she was safe there; she knew Julie couldn't suspect her of wrongdoing while she was with Spogel and her in-laws. She was very pretty. She had been in show business, had gone to work in her teens, and you always had the feeling that she was helpless and vulnerable. Julie had been giving her a bad time the last year or so. She had been crying all morning, and her face was blurry and she still had a Frownie—those things women wear when they sleep, to avoid wrinkles—stuck on her forehead, between the eyebrows. "I don't know what he wants from me," she said. "Who am I? I'm just a person. I'm not even intelligent, like he always says when he throws it up at me, I'm common and have no background. Well, actually, you know, he's not wrong. I mean, what was I before I met him, what sort of a life did I have? I always had the blues. I was ordinary. You know, he can be awfully nice when he wants to. He's disadjusted."

The quarrel had been going on since early the previous morning. She had made a face at him—that was how it had all started. She and Julie used separate bedrooms. She had gone into his room yesterday morning, looked, and seen he was still asleep, and then—on an impulse, thoughtlessly—she had made a face at him. Only he hadn't been asleep. He had been peeking at her, through his eyelashes.

She went on talking, hopeless, tearful. Time was passing, she said, and what did she do, where did she go? All she ever did was look at the television set, switching the dial all evening from channel to channel, watching the news and the wrestling and "This Is Your Life," and it was depressing. She had a lump under her arm, she said, and everybody talked about hysterectomies and she ought to go and see the doctor, and every time she combed her hair she saw more gray. "I used to sing with a band in Atlantic City," she said. "I got a hundred a week. Only two shows a night and the rest of the time to myself. I used to sunbathe on the beach all day. I ought to have my head examined for giving that all up."

She rose. Julie always came after her at the Spogels's—to fight some more or to make up—and she had to change her clothes and be ready for him. She looked around now for her overnight bag.

"You're too good to him," Daisy said. "You're too loyal. You should have an affair!"

"That's all we need now," Boris said. "That's a fine piece of advice you're giving her. Thank you very much."

"No, I'm right!" Daisy insisted gaily. "She must make herself precious to him. She must teach him a lesson. Have an affair!"

"You think it's so easy?" Imogene said. "Try it sometime yourself and you'll see. What do you think—you can just go up to a man and confront him? Everybody can always tell you exactly what to do. It's not so simple." She saw the little suitcase on the floor and stooped to pick it up. "Once I called up Eversall and I said to him—What could I say? I didn't know what to say. So I asked him did he want to take me out to dinner. And you know Eversall, how tight he is. He refused. You'd be surprised," she said, dabbing at her eyes with her handkerchief. "They know your husband or you know their wives, or you can't stand them in the first place—there are all kinds of things that crop up."

She went off to one of the bedrooms in the back of the house. Everyone remained silent for several moments. Even Daisy.

"What is there to mourn?" she said suddenly.

"There she goes again," Boris said, hitting the arm of his chair.

"No, seriously," she said. "I mean, after all, what is there for us to get so all worked up about? In the last analysis, what do we really possess? We have our naked bodies, just ourselves. That's all that really matters. I mean—" In addition to the ballet and tennis lessons, Daisy took courses at U.C.L.A., and she was also having her teeth straightened, and at parties she would scream out how the Kittershoy wives were spirited, like race horses—but nothing helped. It was her money Boris had put into the independent company. She had owned a children's-wear factory before their marriage. Boris hadn't had a dime. He had married her; he had taken the earnings of a lifetime in the children's-wear trade and had put every penny of it into the Veeankay disaster, and at night it was an agony for her to fall asleep.

"Yes, yes, we understand—we know what you mean," Spogel said, trying to head her off, but she wouldn't stop. She couldn't stop.

"No, truth," she said. "Ultimately there is only truth. Truth and goodness and beauty—those are the only basic values!"

"Sweetheart, say nothing!" Boris roared at his wife. "When I am without you, I am without an arm. But when I am *with* you, I am without a head—shut up! You don't understand conditions. You don't know what's going on. For God's sakes, do not try to be cheerful and alleviate the situation!"

"Oh, look at her, look at her!" Daisy cried, turning, for no reason, to Edith, who had been sitting by quietly all this time. "Isn't she dainty? Isn't she darling?"

"Truth! Truth! Beauty!" Boris shouted. "Life is worth living! She don't want to hear bad news; it don't exist for her. There are lines standing all around the corner—the box office is booming!"

"Oh, I love her, I love her, I love her!" Daisy said. "Curtis, you must always be kind to her. You must never hurt her. She is my very best friend!"

She subsided abruptly. The living room became still again.

The Spogels had a pocket-billiards table in a game room that stood off by itself at the foot of the garden, not far from the garage. We were on the terrace—the Kittershoys, the Spogels, and I—when suddenly we heard the rolling of the balls, the clicks they made as they hit, and we knew it was Julie down there, shooting pool. Edith went to tell Imogene, and in a few minutes Imogene wearily crossed the garden to join her husband. We settled down to wait.

More guests were arriving. They played at the swimming pool or sat in the sun or were waylaid on the terrace by old Mrs. Vencie. Daisy Kittershoy was talking to one of the guests, a doctor, describing her symptoms to him. She had called his office, I heard her say, but then had cancelled the appointment because there was really nothing the matter with her. It was just that she couldn't seem to think clearly or energetically. It was just that she couldn't seem to enjoy anything. She was tired and not tired. If she could only do manual labor or something and get herself really exhausted, she said. She kept waiting for that morning when you wake up and feel bright and everything is sharp and fine again. She had a ringing in her ears—No, not a ringing, not a buzzing—more like telephone wires singing in the wind, a humming.

The doctor kept nodding. "It's very clear. Yes, I know," he said. "Those are the typical symptoms of mental fatigue. Do you perspire?"

"Oh, Doctor, you're so wonderful!" Daisy cried. "That's all I wanted to know—that there was nothing physically wrong with me. That's why you're so popular, Doctor—you always tell your patients exactly what they want to hear!"

"Ridiculous situation." Spogel murmured to me unhappily. "The whole thing just on account of a face she made, over a dirty look she gave him."

He took me along for company as he went walking around the grounds. He pretended to be seeing after his guests, but his real purpose was to get near the game room, to find out how Imogene and

Julie were doing. "Girls are so peculiar," he mused. "To make a face at a sleeping man! Who knows what goes on in their heads? Once—naturally, long before I knew Edith—I had a lady friend. She cooked for me, we went out together, she came to my place—you know, everything. But she wouldn't marry me. Once I asked her, 'Reba, would you marry me if I asked you serious?' And she said 'No.'"

We had reached the game-room window, and he stepped up to it cautiously. We eavesdropped. "Julie, I'll get a cold," we heard Imogene saying. "Julie, it's damp here. It's chilly." She was barefoot, wearing her shorts and sun top, and she was obviously trying to get him away from the game room, into the house, where she apparently felt she could do more with him. "Julie, you know I'm allergic and always catch colds. Julie, I'm shivering," she said.

"Take an allergy pill, dear," Julie said, cheerful and matter-of-fact, going on with his game. We could hear the balls rolling and mixing.

"Anything transpire?" Boris Kittershoy whispered, coming up to us.

Spogel shook his head. "Patience," he said.

Boris started to moan, under his breath. There were industry people here, contacts, items of trade gossip to be picked up. "We could talk, we could inquire—we could try!" he said. A man named Irving Lissak had telephoned Edith, inviting himself over, and the visit might mean something, Boris said; the visit might be an approach, a feeler. There were two Lissaks, brothers. They were an independent company, actively in production, and it might very well be that they could be interested into taking over the Veeankay white elephant. "Who knows—it's a possibility!" Boris exclaimed softly. "But he is incommunicado, fighting with Imogene! Why does he always do this? It seems he was put into the world only to twist and scheme up ways to make life miserable!"

"He is an enigma," Spogel whispered nodding.

"He is a pain in the neck!" Boris said.

Boris took himself off—to inquire, to try—and Spogel and I turned back to the game-room window. "Julie, I'm sick," Imogene was saying now. "Julie, my teeth are chattering. I'll have to go back into the house and leave you all alone. Julie, I'm leaving. Julie, I'm going back to the house."

"Yes, dear. Why don't you do that?" Julie said.

He was probably just waking up. Julie followed a peculiar twenty-four-hour cycle. During the early part of the day, he was dead to the world, groggy and glazed. As the afternoon wore on, the color would start filtering into his face. By nighttime, he was rosy and glowing again, the picture of health, full of energy. He downed a bottle of whiskey every night. He smoked thick, expensive cigars. He made people play cards with him and kept them up till all hours of the night. He worked up gags against his partner. Then, suddenly, unaccountably, he would turn cold sober, troubled and groping. "Why do I like you?" he once said to me, in a bewildering rush of affection. He gripped me by the shoulders. "I mean it David. That's the best thing that's happened to me all year—my meeting you. I mean it. Listen—tell me about yourself," he said, catching himself up abruptly, joking again. "Come on, pappy, you always lay low and play possum. Tell me about your wife. What sort of a girl is she? What do you think of her? What does she think of you?" And in another moment he was throwing himself around the room, drinking and laughing and getting some friend of his at the county morgue to call up Boris, to say that he, Julie, had been killed in an auto accident.

"Tell me you told me," he was saying to Imogene now in the game room. "Tell me you didn't tell me. Tell me *you* lied, *I* lied. Deny everything. Admit everything. Dress, undress, take off your clothes—you think I don't know what you're doing?"

"Oh, my goodness, he is on the warpath," Spogel said. Spogel had begun to shuffle on his feet, out of worry. "Here it's half past four already, getting on five, and I'm still in my tennis trunks. I have to shave and take a shower!"

"You poor, pathetic broad," Julie said to Imogene, "you had me— you won out. Only you were too dumb to realize it."

"When? When did I win out?" Imogene asked.

"Yesterday—when I kicked you, when you started out for your hairdresser's appointment," Julie said. It seemed she had been taking her dress off all day, and all day he had successfully managed to resist the maneuver—up to the hairdresser's appointment, up to the moment when she had started to leave and had turned and he had seen that sweet, little, round whatsis of hers, he said. Then he had caved in. He simply had been unable to hold out any longer—that was why he had kicked her, he said. "You had me in the palm of your hand right then and there," he went on. "Only, you had to go ahead and ruin everything."

"How? Why? What did I do so terrible to spoil everything?" Imogene cried.

"You don't remember?" Julie said. "After I kicked you, you turned around and what did you say? You said, 'Oh, darling, if I could only undo the hurt that I have caused you.' Where do you pick up language like that? Is that the way they talk in the dance-band business? What kind of books do you read?"

"I'm always at fault," Imogene said, sobbing. "No matter what I do, I'm always wrong. I'm responsible for everything."

"Oh, when will be the end?" Spogel said, sighing and jiggling his feet.

Up on the terrace, the extra help had arrived and were setting the tables. The people at the swimming pool had changed back into their clothes, and here and there we could see a guest in a dinner jacket.

Spogel nudged my elbow. "Listen, listen," he said. The game room had turned oddly quiet. Julie had stopped playing pool. We couldn't hear him laughing or talking any longer—just Imogene sobbing—and Spogel thought perhaps this meant they were making up in there at last. "What do you think? David, how does it sound to you?" he said, and then "Now what?" Daisy Kittershoy and Edith were hurrying down to us from the terrace. They appeared to be having some kind of altercation.

"Sh-h-h! He'll hear!" Spogel begged when the two women came up. "Please! Don't make a commotion—he'll think we're peeking!"

It turned out Daisy had heard of the impending visit of Irving Lissak, the active independent producer, and had come hurrying down to ask Spogel what he knew about the visit. Did Spogel think it was business or pleasure? Was Lissak a frequent guest here? Did Spogel know him so very well socially, or was there really something doing? "Daisy, I told you!" Edith cried. "I met him at a party weeks ago, and I told him to drop in any Sunday! You're making a whole hullabaloo over nothing!"

But Daisy wouldn't listen. "No, no!" she said, shaking her head. "I was speaking to Curtis—let Curtis answer!"

"Sh-h-h!" Spogel whispered, gesturing. "He'll hear! You came intruding at the worst possible moment. They're just starting to reconcile!"

"We're not reconciling, don't worry," Imogene said bitterly. She had come out of the game room, her eyes and cheeks smudged with tears. "You can talk all you want—he's not inside to hear."

Daisy and Edith rushed over to her. "He got hungry," Imogene said. "I hate him. He went up to the house to get a snack. He eats and has the time of his life while all the time I'm dying. He enjoys it!"

So that was why the game room had suddenly turned quiet. Spogel was dazed with disappointment. "What will be the outcome?" he said. He meant when would they ever reconcile now, Imogene here, Julie in the house somewhere, everything up in the air? On the terrace, the tables were all set—the tablecloths gleaming, the candles lit and shining quietly. "Oh, why did you do it?" Spogel said to Imogene.

"Leave her alone!" Edith said to her husband. "Can't you see she's miserable enough?"

"Why did I do what?" Imogene said.

"Go into his bedroom yesterday," Spogel said. "Make the face. Why did you needlessly have to provoke him?"

"What should I do? Love him to death because he's so irresistible and tortures me to pieces?"

"But what good did it do?" Spogel said. "What purpose could it have accomplished? What was the *sense*?"

"I thought he was *asleep*!" Imogene wailed. "Oh, Curtis, do you think people know what they do?"

She ran off into the oleander bushes. Spogel wanted to go after her, but Edith checked him. They stood together, squabbling wretchedly. Spogel wanted to bring Imogene back. They had guests to entertain, a dinner party to live through, and it was ridiculous—all this upset, everybody going around in circles, all over a dirty look, a face. "Let her go!" Edith cried. "Didn't you bother her enough? Don't interfere! Don't make difficulties!"

"I'm making difficulties?" Spogel said.

At this moment, old Mrs. Vencie came up. She was taking a little walk. "Isn't it remarkable?" she said, looking up at the ladies in the garden, the guests. She was marvelling at their appearance, at the way they kept themselves, their figures. "Imagine!" the old woman went on, full of wonder. "They get pregnant only when they want to!"

"Ma!" Edith said.

"I give them all the credit in the world," Mrs. Vencie said. "They're smarter than my generation. What, then—they should let themselves go and become sloppy and fat like a horse? Let them make the beauty, let them diet. They're absolutely right!"

"Oh, for heaven's sake, Ma, couldn't you take a day off just once and spare us all your observations and comments?" Edith said, through her teeth.

"Look at her!" Mrs. Vencie said, wiping her nose with the back of her hand. "Somebody would think she's having a miscarriage. What's the matter—I'm killing people?"

"Oh, she comes right out with everything, no inhibitions at all," Edith said.

Just then, Boris Kittershoy came stamping down on us, panting with his news, holding up two fingers in the air. *Both* Lissaks had arrived, not just Irving. The visit definitely had to be a feeler, or else why *both*? Boris couldn't stop talking and pumping. The Lissaks had access to oil money, he said, the Lissaks had a release with U-L, they were in a position where they needed a product, and a deal was perfectly feasible!

"Good, good," Mrs. Vencie said, happy for them. "What a fool I was," she said, going on with her own thoughts. "How ignorant we all were in my time. When I had the twins, I would wash out a whole clothesline of diapers every day, and then I would stand by the window and look out and I would feel *good*—I was so simple—because the diapers came out nice and white. I even used to put in bluing!" She went off, resuming her walk, mingling with the guests.

Spogel was in agonies. He wanted to go looking for Julie immediately. He wanted to tell him about the two Lissaks. But Edith was dead set against it. "Curtis, please!" she cried. "Believe me, you don't know what it is. You just don't understand, so do me a favor and stay out of it!"

Boris, in the meanwhile, had just found out from Daisy that Julie was still incommunicado, that the reconciliation had broken down, and he was putting on a big show of despair. "I have done my best," he said. "I have eaten gall and wormwood, and now I am finished with him. This is the end!"

"But I do, I do—I do understand why he always fights with Imogene!" Spogel was saying hoarsely to Edith. "She is the symbol to him of his youth, of his hopes and dreams and aspirations, and naturally, in his downfall, he takes everything out on her. She is his Mona Lisa! You think I don't know. Don't judge a product by its container. I am not necessarily an ignoramus without sensitivity!"

Daisy urged Boris to start negotiations with the Lissaks by himself; after all, he was vice president, a partner. But he refused. "I should initiate everything so that he can renege on me and make me out a fool again?" he said. "I had my experience once—no, thank you!" Boris was referring to something that happened with Ronnie Fitts—another independent, a man whose wife had made a fortune during the war buying Beverly Hills real estate on margin. Boris had arranged matters with Fitts, had paved the way for a possible deal, and all that had been left was a final meeting. Julie had agreed to the meeting; for once, he had appeared on time; he had promised to behave himself. But when they entered Fitts's home for the conference and Julie saw the original Impressionist paintings hanging on the walls there, he turned wild with fury. He walked straight up to Fitts and insulted him right and left; he was a slob, Julie said, and what right did he have to be owning Cézannes? "He is a madman!" Boris said now, pulling away from Daisy. "He is tactless and antagonizes people. He malingers. He makes practical jokes. Suddenly, he goes flying away on trips and runs up expenses, and let somebody else have the pleasure—I suffered with him long enough!" Boris kept trying to escape from his wife, she kept arguing and clinging to him, and now the two went off together, into the garden.

"Oh, why must you have such a sensitive nature and tremble over every least little thing?" Spogel cried out at Edith. "What harm would there be if I went and talked to him?"

"But it is not my nature!" Edith cried back at him. "You don't know what happened! Believe me, you have no understanding of the situation!"

"But I do! I do!" Spogel said, his eyes shut tight. "I just told you. I do understand—" He stopped. He listened. Edith was complaining about her mother again, saying how the old woman always had to open up her big mouth and talk, talk, talk. "Oh, why do you fix on Mother all the time?" Spogel said, exasperated. "Why must you pick on her now? Don't we have more serious problems?"

"But she made the whole trouble!" Edith said. "Julie was here yesterday. He saw her, and that's when it really started! Oh, really, it's too impossible—it's humiliating!" she said. "I'd rather not talk about it."

But, little by little, the story came out. Julie snored. It was an affliction; he had a deviated septum. That was the reason he and Imogene used separate bedrooms. But yesterday, after Imogene made the face at him, he came to see his mother and asked the old woman if it was really true that he snored. And Mrs. Vencie had told a white lie. She had said he didn't snore at all.

Spogel didn't stay to hear any more. He could see the whole picture in a flash. It was the worst possible thing Mrs. Vencie could have said. Julie, of course, had immediately gone off convinced that Imogene had been avoiding him, that the talk about his snoring had been nothing but a pretext all along.

"Wait! Don't go to him!" Edith cried, clutching at her husband, but Spogel wouldn't be held back this time. He fought free and went rushing away—to find Julie, to tell him, to clear up the whole foolish misunderstanding once for all and restore peace.

"Oh, stop him!" Edith said to me, her eyes big with alarm. "David, do something! He'll go blundering in where he doesn't belong, and it will be awful!" And now she blurted out the rest of the story. She hadn't finished. It wasn't the face, the dirty look; it wasn't Mrs. Vencie's white lie. Imogene had been unfaithful to Julie. She had had an affair, and he had found out all about it. The mischief hadn't ended with Mrs. Vencie. One thing had led to another. After Julie talked to his mother, he had gone straight back to his own home. Simmering with suspicions, furious, he had searched Imogene's room, and there had been some letters. Imogene had been at a hotel at Lake Tahoe not long ago, and she had met a man there, one of the players in the band.

"Oh, run!" Edith cried to me now as we saw Spogel weaving in and out among the guests in the garden, hurrying up to the house. "Run, David—run, or it will be too late!"

By the time I came up to the terrace, I had lost Spogel in the press of people. I looked everywhere for him, but there was too much coming and going—new arrivals crossing over to greet their friends, the extra help passing through with trays of drinks and appetizers, the guests constantly shifting as they formed into groups. I saw the Kittershoys. Off to one side, on the flagstones under the lights, Boris was playing ping-pong, and Daisy hovered nearby. She was with some people, but she kept anxiously watching the ping-pong game. Boris was playing with a Mrs. Ashton, a lady who had an extremely full bosom and wore a low-cut dress. Mrs. Ashton was an intensely serious person, and as she lunged and flung herself about, she clearly had no idea of the violent effect the game was having on her bosom.

"Boris! Boris!" I heard Daisy call out. "Boris, take care—you will overexert!"

A few moments later, making my way through the guests, I stumbled on the Kittershoys again. Daisy had contrived somehow to get her husband away from the ping-pong table, and now, standing in a corner in the shadows, she was warning him against Mrs. Ashton. "She is literal-minded. She is intellectual. She will have a heart-to-heart talk with her husband and ask him for a divorce and then come running back to you, and then what? She has been analyzed!"

"But I am only amusing myself!" Boris said. "What do you want from me? I am only doing what you always preach—smile! Enjoy life! The world isn't coming to an end!" He left her and went off into the crowd.

It occurred to me that Spogel might be in the house. I went inside, and found him right away. He was in the library, but I had spent too much time wandering around outside and listening to the Kittershoys. Julie was already in there with him. Spogel had talked, had told him all about the white lie, and the damage was done.

Julie wouldn't talk about Imogene. He passed over the whole business of the snoring and the unfortunate misunderstanding. His color was high, his eyes shone, and he looked bursting with vigor and good health. "You don't say!" he said when Spogel told him that Imogene was only thoughtless and feminine, that he, Julie, was perhaps being unduly harsh with her. Spogel sensed trouble. He knew something had gone terribly awry, but for the life of him he couldn't imagine what was wrong, and he could only go ahead. "Is that so?" Julie said, in his hearty, friendly manner when Spogel told him about the Lissaks, both brothers appearing at the party, all the signs pointing to the clear-cut possibility of a transaction in the offing. "They do, do they?" Julie said when he heard the Lissaks had connections with oil people. Then he went to work on Spogel and took him apart.

Up in Kern County, Julie said, where Spogel had his theaters, the authorities let you pop the popcorn on the premises, and Spogel worked the contraptions in his houses so that the popcorn smell was piped directly out into the auditoriums, overpowering the audiences. "Not only that," Julie said, "you purposely put too much salt into the popcorn, so all during the show the poor farmers have to keep running out into the lobby to buy drinks. You chop the credits off the Westerns and run the same godforsaken pictures all over again with new titles, and nobody knows the difference. You import burlesque dancers for live shows, raise the prices sky-high, and then you shortchange the yokels on the bumps and grinds because you're scared to death the P.-T.A.'ll kick. And every year you add to your capital. Every month you set aside a nice, tidy sum for another few shares of American Tel. & Tel. What are you yammering to me about the Lissaks for? Who asked you?"

"But they are *here!*" Spogel gasped. "They have financing—they have a release!"

"What do you expect out of the Lissaks? What do you think they're going to do?" Julie said. He wouldn't go near the Lissaks with a ten-foot pole. They were greedy. They were ragpickers, junkmen. They came around shopping for bargains, looking to take advantage of desperation cases. They'd move in and immediately start taking over the whole show. Overnight they'd become experts on scripts, on casting, on cutting. They'd want to hog it all—a Lissak

Brothers Production Produced by Julian Vencie. What are the Lissaks—beginners, children, public benefactors? Didn't they know the score? Didn't they know he had tried the banks everywhere—downtown in Los Angeles, in New York, in Boston? Didn't the Lissaks know he was two hundred thousand dollars in the hole? "Would *you* give me money, just like that?" Julie pounded. The notion struck his fancy. "Come on, Spogel!" he cried. "You're a sport. You're a rich man. You got capital. Why don't *you* give me the money?"

"Gladly!" Spogel said. "I would do it like a shot, only what would be the sense?" The fact of the matter was that he himself was getting out of the business, selling his houses, liquidating, and how would it be to liquidate everything and then jump right back in again, investing in a movie? "Julie, darling, the handwriting is on the wall!" Spogel pleaded.

Julie roared with laughter. He roared because Spogel looked so comical, with his arms extended, his face honest and confounded, and because Spogel was so beautifully right. Spogel had put it perfectly: The handwriting was on the wall. The industry was dead. It was all over—the years of picturemaking, the work, the rush, the all-night sessions at the studio, the whole wonderful excitement and rapture.

The library had two doors, one leading to the hall, the other to the back of the house. Now, as Julie stood shaking with his innocent glee, Edith came running in from the hall. "They're gone! They're gone!" she said to her husband, meaning the Lissaks. "Curtis, they only came in for a cocktail on their way to Malibu. It was purely social!"

Julie was perversely triumphant, enormously delighted to learn that he was so far gone that the Lissaks didn't even want to take advantage of him. Just then, the other door opened. Imogene walked in. She had borrowed one of Edith's dresses, had carefully made up her face, had carefully done her hair, and she came in smiling, and lovely, and hopeful.

"That Bartók baloney!" Julie said to her by the way of greeting. "All you have to do is mention Braque and the art of Arnold Schoenberg, and they drop like flies!" Her face fell, under the fresh makeup.

It turned out that Julie was referring to the letters, to things he had read in the correspondence with the hotel-band player.

"Julie, don't—not here, not in front of everybody!" she said, but he wouldn't spare her. He kept quoting from the letters, mentioning the most delicate intimacies, merrily relishing every tender tidbit.

"Oh, Julie, how can you!" Edith said. She went up to Imogene and put her arm around her, and they moved toward the door.

"I didn't know!" Spogel protested fervently, apologizing to Imogene and Edith both. "I didn't know. Believe me, I meant only for the best!"

"You ought to read that fancy stuff!" Julie said. "They weren't going to live to make money; they would make money to live! They had it all figured out—he would play the fiddle only three days a week, and have the rest of the time for life and love. What were they going to do for four days every week—talk about Bartók?"

Imogene and the Spogels had reached the hall. The door closed behind them, and the room grew quiet. Julie paused. He was still wound up, but he had no one now to rail at. He went to the desk. He picked up the phone and dialed a number. Suddenly, he had become altogether transformed. In another moment, I heard him arguing fiercely over the phone. He was talking business now, blustering and wangling, desperately trying to make a deal. He was talking to Ronnie Fitts—the other independent producer, the one he had insulted, the man whose wife's earnings in real estate had bought him the original French paintings. "I'll let you have control!" Julie was saying. "Now wait a minute, pappy, listen. I'll let you cast the picture. You'll do it all! You'll hire and fire, you'll handle the rushes in the projection room. It'll be your name on the card, not mine!" He cajoled. He begged.

I hadn't intended to stay for the party; I was expected home for dinner. As I began walking down the hall, I heard Spogel calling to me in a stage whisper. He was standing at the door of one of the bedrooms. "David! David, quick, please, come here, help . . ." Imogene had gone in there, and Spogel didn't know what she might be doing to herself. He feared the worst. "There are pills on the dressing table—sleeping pills! Oh, I never would forgive myself! Imogene!"

he whispered frantically, turning back to the door. "Imogene!" He tried the knob.

The door wasn't locked. It opened easily. Imogene was sitting at the dressing table, facing herself in the mirror. She was softly singing "Some Enchanted Evening" and trying on a sequined hair net of Edith's. She stared at Spogel. "I'm not committing suicide on his account, don't worry," she said slowly. "What did you think—" She broke off. It happened that our eyes met, Imogene's and mine, and we looked at each other for a second, suspended in silence. I noticed the curve of her cheek, and in that instant I saw her as a little girl, chubby and fresh and clear-eyed, everything yet to come. She looked at me with defiance, and then she turned away.

"Sorry," Spogel said sadly. He gently closed the door and, without a word, walked off to shave and take his shower.

In the entrance hall, I found Daisy Kittershoy—all alone there, oddly hunched over the wraps and topcoats on the table, searching away through the pile. "All the years, all the years, all the years," she was saying to herself, like a chant. "You can't know, David," she said, speaking straight at me but not really seeing me, "you don't know how much I looked forward to retiring from the business world. I thought, you see—I anticipated—What you must understand, you see, is that all my life I have been a businesswoman, my mind always taken up, every morning in the shop—I expected a paradise on earth!"

She turned back to the pile of clothing on the table. She was looking for Boris's topcoat, she told me—for the car keys in his pocket. He had left the party. She didn't know where he'd gone, and now she wanted to go home. She had a headache. Her ears throbbed. She wanted to take a bath. She wanted to lie down and rest and sleep. "Seventy-eight thousand dollars!" she said, anguish welling up in her. "Seventy-eight thousand dollars. Do you know what that means, David? All the years, all the years—fighting in the shop, fighting with the contractors, with the buyers, the returns, the rejections!" She wept. She held her face in her hands. "No," she said, making an effort, taking a grip on herself. She dropped her hands and straightened her shoulders. "I mustn't. I mustn't. That was always my trouble—I was always overpreoccupied with material values. It teaches me a lesson. It serves me right. I never had time for literature, or lectures—gardening!" she said. She found Boris's topcoat and reached into the pocket for the keys.

Out on the terrace, old Mrs. Vencie was sitting in her usual place, still going strong. She caught my arm as I passed. "Look, look!" she said, pointing to the city below us, to the thousands and thousands of lights spreading for miles all the way out to the ocean. "Isn't it remarkable, David? All the lights, all the people, each and every one a living human being, the blood in their veins just as red as you or me." On the road winding above us there were headlights moving— young people, undergraduates at the university, driving to the top of the hill on a weekend night. Edith and Spogel were always careful to tell Mrs. Vencie the youngsters went up there to see the view, to hold romantic conversations, but the old woman wasn't fooled. She knew what they did in the parked cars—they necked. "And why not?" Mrs. Vencie said.

The Spogels's dinner party was well under way. The servants bustled. The ladies in their lovely frocks chattered over the candlelight, their faces animated and affectionate, while their husbands stood by themselves, quietly smoking, quietly discussing the situation of the industry.

Mrs. Vencie was telling me how she met her husband. "So," she said, "they told me, 'Go to the shop, make believe you don't know anything, look on him, see if you like him—what will it hurt?' So I went there, to the fur shop where he worked. But, unbeknownst to me, they told him the same story. They told him to look and see, too, maybe he would be interested—so there we stood, like two big dumbbells, spying on each other, bashful and ashamed!"

"Outdoor living," I heard someone say. On the hillside below, bulldozers had scooped out level sites. Homes now lay before us in descending tiers. Most people on Angelo Drive had buffet dinners on Sunday evenings, and it made a picture—the splashes of light down there, the guests grouped on the lawns, the blue-tiled swimming pools.

"Poor Papa," Mrs. Vencie said, nodding, remembering. "You should have seen him when he was alive, David. He was elegant. He had a Kaiser Wilhelm mustache, with the points—a prince! On Sunday morning, he bought the breakfast, and if you asked him what did the whitefish cost, the carp, he never knew. He was too aristocratic to ask the storekeeper the price—he just paid the whole bill. Once, when I was in the mountains with the children, he sent me a letter—he was giving me a big surprise. I wondered to myself, what could it be? Was it a new gas range, maybe? A new icebox, even? It was a picture of himself! He went to a photographer and took a picture—with the mustache, with his Palm Beach summer suit, blowing me a kiss. Poor Papa!"

She took time out to marvel at the view. "Look! It shimmers before the eyes!" she said, pointing again, meaning the multitude of lights. She was old. She knew that nothing was out of the ordinary, that hopes were betrayed, that you always started out with illusion, and yet everything was a wonder to her. "Isn't it gorgeous?" she said to me. "It's like a fairyland, David. It's like magic!"

QUESTIONS FOR DISCUSSION

At the end of Whitman's poem, does the speaker still expect to find what he "started for so long ago"?

1. As he looks over the ocean, why does the speaker see "the circle almost circled"?

2. Why does the speaker call himself "a child, very old"?

3. What does the speaker mean when he describes looking west across the Pacific Ocean as facing "the house of maternity, the land of migrations"?

4. Why is the speaker "very pleas'd and joyous" to be facing home again?

Does Fuchs intend us to admire Julie Vencie or to disapprove of him?

1. Why does Curtis Spogel feel that the "whole circle of movie people" have "some quality, some mystery, that he lacked"? (49)

2. Why won't Julie reconcile with Imogene, despite her pleas?

3. Why does Julie refuse to talk to the Lissaks, as Spogel wants him to, but call Ronnie Fitts and beg him to invest in the film?

4. Why does the story end with Mrs. Vencie saying, "It's like a fairyland, David. It's like magic!" (69)

FOR FURTHER REFLECTION

1. Is it worth pursuing a dream even if it is not achievable?

2. Does California still represent a "fairyland" in popular culture?

3. How does westward migration affect American identity?

4. How do Whitman and Fuchs define the American dream?

Equality is a principle that enters into virtually all political thinking. Either as a central focus of discussion or as a background concept, it informs matters relating to legislation, social and economic policy, judicial proceedings, the scope of liberty, and numerous other issues having to do with society's meting out of goods and services. More narrowly, considerations of what can and should constitute equality pervade many characterizations of political positions—whether they are called liberal, conservative, libertarian, or something else. The following selections examine the notion of equality from the perspectives of two writers who fundamentally differ in their understanding of the relation of political and economic equality.

Austrian-born British writer **Friedrich A. Hayek** (1899–1992) was a strong supporter of a free market economy. The topics discussed in his 1960 book *The Constitution of Liberty*, from which the following selection is taken, are largely concerned with the relation of economics to political philosophy. In the chapter "Equality, Value, and Merit," Hayek argues that political equality is irreconcilable with government-instituted economic equality. Although he concedes that narrowing the gap between the rich and poor is to be preferred, Hayek strongly disagrees that there is anything we can do to institute redistribution without infringing on freedom.

American legal philosopher **Ronald Dworkin** (1931–2013) begins this selection from his essay "Liberalism," first published in *Public and Private Morality* (1978), by describing the tension between equality and liberty. Dworkin's concern is to identify the unifying characteristics of the often diffusely defined liberal position in the United States. By examining the distinction between equality and liberty, he makes the argument that all political alignments can be identified through their unique approaches to equality.

Equality, Value, and Merit

Friedrich A. Hayek

I have no respect for the passion for equality,
which seems to me merely idealizing envy.
OLIVER WENDELL HOLMES JR.

The great aim of the struggle for liberty has been equality before the law. This equality under the rules which the state enforces may be supplemented by a similar equality of the rules that men voluntarily obey in their relations with one another. This extension of the principle of equality to the rules of moral and social conduct is the chief expression of what is commonly called the democratic spirit—and probably that aspect of it that does most to make inoffensive the inequalities that liberty necessarily produces.

Equality of the general rules of law and conduct, however, is the only kind of equality conducive to liberty and the only equality which we can secure without destroying liberty. Not only has liberty nothing to do with any other sort of equality, but it is even bound to produce inequality in many respects. This is the necessary result and part of the justification of individual liberty: if the result of individual liberty did not demonstrate that some manners of living are more successful than others, much of the case for it would vanish.

It is neither because it assumes that people are in fact equal nor because it attempts to make them equal that the argument for liberty demands that government treat them equally. This argument not only recognizes that individuals are very different but in a great measure rests on that assumption. It insists that these individual differences provide no justification for government to treat them differently. And it objects to the differences in treatment by the state that would be necessary if persons who are in fact very different were to be assured equal positions in life.

Modern advocates of a more far-reaching material equality usually deny that their demands are based on any assumption of the factual equality of all men. It is nevertheless still widely believed that this is the main justification for such demands. Nothing, however, is more damaging to the demand for equal treatment than to base it on so obviously untrue an assumption as that of the factual equality of all men. To rest the case for equal treatment of national or racial minorities on the assertion that they do not differ from other men is implicitly to admit that factual inequality would justify unequal treatment; and the proof that some differences do, in fact, exist would not be long in forthcoming. It is of the essence of the demand for equality before the law that people should be treated alike in spite of the fact that they are different.

The boundless variety of human nature—the wide range of differences in individual capacities and potentialities—is one of the most distinctive facts about the human species. Its evolution has made it probably the most variable among all kinds of creatures. It has been well said that

> biology, with variability as its cornerstone, confers on every
> human individual a unique set of attributes which give him a
> dignity he could not otherwise possess. Every newborn baby is an
> unknown quantity so far as potentialities are concerned because
> there are many thousands of unknown interrelated genes and
> gene patterns which contribute to his make-up. As a result of
> nature and nurture the newborn infant may become one of the
> greatest of men or women ever to have lived. In every case he or
> she has the making of a distinctive individual. . . . If the differ-
> ences are not very important, then freedom is not very important
> and the idea of individual worth is not very important.[1]

1. [R. J. Williams, *Free and Unequal: The Biological Basis of Individual Liberty* (1953), 23, 70.]

The writer justly adds that the widely held uniformity theory of human nature, "which on the surface appears to accord with democracy . . . would in time undermine the very basic ideals of freedom and individual worth and render life as we know it meaningless."[2]

It has been the fashion in modern times to minimize the importance of congenital differences between men and to ascribe all the important differences to the influence of environment. However important the latter may be, we must not overlook the fact that individuals are very different from the outset. The importance of individual differences would hardly be less if all people were brought up in very similar environments. As a statement of fact, it just is not true that "all men are born equal." We may continue to use this hallowed phrase to express the ideal that legally and morally all men ought to be treated alike. But if we want to understand what this ideal of equality can or should mean, the first requirement is that we free ourselves from the belief in factual equality.

From the fact that people are very different it follows that, if we treat them equally, the result must be inequality in their actual position, and that the only way to place them in an equal position would be to treat them differently. Equality before the law and material equality are therefore not only different but are in conflict with each other; and we can achieve either the one or the other, but not both at the same time. The equality before the law which freedom requires leads to material inequality. Our argument will be that, though where the state must use coercion for other reasons, it should treat all people alike, the desire of making people more alike in their condition cannot be accepted in a free society as a justification for further and discriminatory coercion.

We do not object to equality as such. It merely happens to be the case that a demand for equality is the professed motive of most of those who desire to impose upon society a preconceived pattern of distribution. Our objection is against all attempts to impress upon society a deliberately chosen pattern of distribution, whether it be an order of equality or of inequality. We shall indeed see that many of those who demand an extension of equality do not really demand

2. [Williams, 152.]

equality but a distribution that conforms more closely to human conceptions of individual merit and that their desires are as irreconcilable with freedom as the more strictly egalitarian demands.

If one objects to the use of coercion in order to bring about a more even or a more just distribution, this does not mean that one does not regard these as desirable. But if we wish to preserve a free society, it is essential that we recognize that the desirability of a particular object is not sufficient justification for the use of coercion. One may well feel attracted to a community in which there are no extreme contrasts between rich and poor and may welcome the fact that the general increase in wealth seems gradually to reduce those differences. I fully share these feelings and certainly regard the degree of social equality that the United States has achieved as wholly admirable.

There also seems no reason why these widely felt preferences should not guide policy in some respects. Wherever there is a legitimate need for government action and we have to choose between different methods of satisfying such a need, those that incidentally also reduce inequality may well be preferable. If, for example, in the law of intestate succession one kind of provision will be more conducive to equality than another, this may be a strong argument in its favor. It is a different matter, however, if it is demanded that, in order to produce substantive equality, we should abandon the basic postulate of a free society, namely, the limitation of all coercion by equal law. Against this we shall hold that economic inequality is not one of the evils which justify our resorting to discriminatory coercion or privilege as a remedy.

Our contention rests on two basic propositions which probably need only be stated to win fairly general assent. The first of them is an expression of the belief in a certain similarity of all human beings: it is the proposition that no man or group of men possesses the capacity to determine conclusively the potentialities of other human beings and that we should certainly never trust anyone invariably to exercise such a capacity. However great the differences between men may be, we have no ground for believing that they will ever be so great as to enable one man's mind in a particular instance to comprehend fully all that another responsible man's mind is capable of.

The second basic proposition is that the acquisition by any member of the community of additional capacities to do things which may be valuable must always be regarded as a gain for that community. It is true that particular people may be worse off because of the superior ability of some new competitor in their field; but any such additional ability in the community is likely to benefit the majority. This implies that the desirability of increasing the abilities and opportunities of any individual does not depend on whether the same can also be done for the others—provided, of course, that others are not thereby deprived of the opportunity of acquiring the same or other abilities which might have been accessible to them had they not been secured by that individual.

Egalitarians generally regard differently those differences in individual capacities which are inborn and those which are due to the influences of environment, or those which are the result of "nature" and those which are the result of "nurture." Neither, be it said at once, has anything to do with moral merit. Though either may greatly affect the value which an individual has for his fellows, no more credit belongs to him for having been born with desirable qualities than for having grown up under favorable circumstances. The distinction between the two is important only because the former advantages are due to circumstances clearly beyond human control, while the latter are due to factors which we might be able to alter. The important question is whether there is a case for so changing our institutions as to eliminate as much as possible those advantages due to environment. Are we to agree that "all inequalities that rest on birth and inherited property ought to be abolished and none remain unless it is an effect of superior talent and industry"?

The fact that certain advantages rest on human arrangements does not necessarily mean that we could provide the same advantages for all or that, if they are given to some, somebody else is thereby deprived of them. The most important factors to be considered in this connection are the family, inheritance, and education, and it is against the inequality which they produce that criticism is mainly directed. They are, however, not the only important factors of environment. Geographic conditions such as climate and landscape, not to speak of local and sectional differences in cultural and moral traditions, are scarcely less important. We can, however, consider here only the three factors whose effects are most commonly impugned.

So far as the family is concerned, there exists a curious contrast between the esteem most people profess for the institution and their dislike of the fact that being born into a particular family should confer on a person special advantages. It seems to be widely believed that, while useful qualities which a person acquires because of his native gifts under conditions which are the same for all are socially beneficial, the same qualities become somehow undesirable if they are the result of environmental advantages not available to others. Yet it is difficult to see why the same useful quality which is welcomed when it is the result of a person's natural endowment should be less valuable when it is the product of such circumstances as intelligent parents or a good home.

The value which most people attach to the institution of the family rests on the belief that, as a rule, parents can do more to prepare their children for a satisfactory life than anyone else. This means not only that the benefits which particular people derive from their family environment will be different but also that these benefits may operate cumulatively through several generations. What reason can there be for believing that a desirable quality in a person is less valuable to society if it has been the result of family background than if it has not? There is, indeed, good reason to think that there are some socially valuable qualities which will be rarely acquired in a single generation but which will generally be formed only by the continuous efforts of two or three. This means simply that there are parts of the cultural heritage of a society that are more effectively transmitted through the family. Granted this, it would be unreasonable to deny that a society is likely to get a better elite if ascent is not limited to one generation, if individuals are not deliberately made to start from the same level, and if children are not deprived of the chance to benefit from the better education and material environment which their parents may be able to provide. To admit this is merely to recognize that belonging to a particular family is part of the individual personality, that society is made up as much of families as of individuals, and that the transmission of the heritage of civilization within the family is as important a tool in man's striving toward better things as is the heredity of beneficial physical attributes.

Many people who agree that the family is desirable as an instrument for the transmission of morals, tastes, and knowledge still question the desirability of the transmission of material property. Yet there can be little doubt that, in order that the former may be possible, some continuity of standards, of the external forms of life, is essential, and that this will be achieved only if it is possible to transmit not only immaterial but also material advantages. There is, of course, neither greater merit nor any greater injustice involved in some people being born to wealthy parents than there is in others being born to kind or intelligent parents. The fact is that it is no less of an advantage to the community if at least some children can start with the advantages which at any given time only wealthy homes can offer than if some children inherit great intelligence or are taught better morals at home.

We are not concerned here with the chief argument for private inheritance, namely, that it seems essential as a means to preserve the dispersal in the control of capital and as an inducement for its accumulation. Rather, our concern here is whether the fact that it confers unmerited benefits on some is a valid argument against the institution. It is unquestionably one of the institutional causes of inequality. In the present context we need not inquire whether liberty demands unlimited freedom of bequest. Our problem here is merely whether people ought to be free to pass on to children or others such material possessions as will cause substantial inequality.

Once we agree that it is desirable to harness the natural instincts of parents to equip the new generation as well as they can, there seems no sensible ground for limiting this to nonmaterial benefits. The family's function of passing on standards and traditions is closely tied up with the possibility of transmitting material goods. And it is difficult to see how it would serve the true interest of society to limit the gain in material conditions to one generation.

There is another consideration which, though it may appear somewhat cynical, strongly suggests that if we wish to make the best use of the natural partiality of parents for their children, we ought not to preclude the transmission of property. It seems certain that among the many ways in which those who have gained power and influence might provide for their children, the bequest of a fortune is socially by far the cheapest. Without this outlet, these men would look for other ways of providing for their children, such as placing them in positions which might bring them the income and the prestige that a fortune would have done; and this would cause a waste of resources and an injustice much greater than is caused by the inheritance of property. Such is the case with all societies in which inheritance of property does not exist, including the Communist. Those who dislike the inequalities caused by inheritance should therefore recognize that, men being what they are, it is the least of evils, even from their point of view.

Though inheritance used to be the most widely criticized source of inequality, it is today probably no longer so. Egalitarian agitation now tends to concentrate on the unequal advantages due to differences in education. There is a growing tendency to express the desire to secure equality of conditions in the claim that the best education we have learned to provide for some should be made gratuitously available for all and that, if this is not possible, one should not be allowed to get a better education than the rest merely because one's parents are able to pay for it, but only those and all those who can pass a uniform test of ability should be admitted to the benefits of the limited resources of higher education.

The problem of educational policy raises too many issues to allow of their being discussed incidentally under the general heading of equality. We shall have to devote a separate chapter to them at the end of this book. For the present we shall only point out that enforced equality in this field can hardly avoid preventing some from getting the education they otherwise might. Whatever we might do, there is no way of preventing those advantages which only some can have, and which it is desirable that some should have, from going to people who neither individually merit them nor will make as good a use of them as some other person might have done. Such a problem cannot be satisfactorily solved by the exclusive and coercive powers of the state.

It is instructive at this point to glance briefly at the change that the ideal of equality has undergone in this field in modern times. A hundred years ago, at the height of the classical liberal movement, the demand was generally expressed by the phrase *la carrière ouverte aux talents*. It was a demand that all man-made obstacles to the rise of some should be removed, that all privileges of individuals should be abolished, and that what the state contributed to the chance of improving one's conditions should be the same for all. That so long as people were different and grew up in different families this could not assure an equal start was fairly generally accepted. It was understood that the duty of government was not to ensure that everybody had the same prospect of reaching a given position but merely to make available to all on equal terms those facilities which in their nature depended on government action. That the results were bound to be different, not only because the individuals were different, but also because only a small part of the relevant circumstances depended on government action, was taken for granted.

This conception that all should be allowed to try has been largely replaced by the altogether different conception that all must be assured an equal start and the same prospects. This means little less than that the government, instead of providing the same circumstances for all, should aim at controlling all conditions relevant to a particular individual's prospects and so adjust them to his capacities as to assure him of the same prospects as everybody else. Such deliberate adaptation of opportunities to individual aims and capacities would, of course, be the opposite of freedom. Nor could it be justified as a means of making the best use of all available knowledge except on the assumption that government knows best how individual capacities can be used.

When we inquire into the justification of these demands, we find that they rest on the discontent that the success of some people often produces in those that are less successful, or, to put it bluntly, on envy. The modern tendency to gratify this passion and to disguise it in the respectable garment of social justice is developing into a serious threat to freedom. Recently an attempt was made to base these demands on the argument that it ought to be the aim of politics to remove all sources of discontent. This would, of course, necessarily mean that it is the responsibility of government to see that nobody is healthier or possesses a happier temperament, a better-suited spouse or more prospering children, than anybody else. If really all unfulfilled desires have a claim on the community, individual responsibility is at an end. However human, envy is certainly not one of the sources of discontent that a free society can eliminate. It is probably one of the essential conditions for the preservation of such a society that we do not countenance envy, not sanction its demands by camouflaging it as social justice, but treat it, in the words of John Stuart Mill, as "the most anti-social and evil of all passions."

While most of the strictly egalitarian demands are based on nothing better than envy, we must recognize that much that on the surface appears as a demand for greater equality is in fact a demand for a juster distribution of the good things of this world and springs therefore from much more creditable motives. Most people will object not to the bare fact of inequality but to the fact that the differences in reward do not correspond to any recognizable differences in the merits of those who receive them. The answer commonly given to this is that a free society on the whole achieves this kind of justice. This, however, is an indefensible contention if by justice is meant proportionality of reward to moral merit. Any attempt to found the case for freedom on this argument is very damaging to it, since it concedes that material rewards ought to be made to correspond to recognizable merit and then opposes the conclusion that most people will draw from this by an assertion which is untrue. The proper answer is that in a free system it is neither desirable nor practicable that material rewards should be made generally to correspond to what men recognize as merit and that it is an essential characteristic of a free society that an individual's position should not necessarily depend on the views that his fellows hold about the merit he has acquired.

This contention may appear at first so strange and even shocking that I will ask the reader to suspend judgment until I have further explained the distinction between value and merit. The difficulty in making the point clear is due to the fact that the term "merit," which is the only one available to describe what I mean, is also used in a wider and vaguer sense. It will be used here exclusively to describe the attributes of conduct that make it deserving of praise, that is, the moral character of the action and not the value of the achievement.

As we have seen throughout our discussion, the value that the performance or capacity of a person has to his fellows has no necessary connection with its ascertainable merit in this sense. The inborn as well as the acquired gifts of a person clearly have a value to his fellows which does not depend on any credit due to him for possessing them. There is little a man can do to alter the fact that his special talents are very common or exceedingly rare. A good mind or a fine voice, a beautiful face or a skillful hand, and a ready wit or an attractive personality are in a large measure as independent of a person's efforts as the opportunities or the experiences he has had. In all these instances the value which a person's capacities or services have for us and for which he is recompensed has little relation to anything that we can call moral merit or deserts. Our problem is whether it is desirable that people should enjoy advantages in proportion to the benefits which their fellows derive from their activities or whether the distribution of these advantages should be based on other men's views of their merits.

Reward according to merit must in practice mean reward according to assessable merit, merit that other people can recognize and agree upon and not merit merely in the sight of some higher power. Assessable merit in this sense presupposes that we can ascertain that a man has done what some accepted rule of conduct demanded of him and that this has cost him some pain and effort. Whether this has been the case cannot be judged by the result: merit is not a matter of the objective outcome but of subjective effort. The attempt to achieve a valuable result may be highly meritorious but a complete failure, and full success may be entirely the result of accident and thus without merit. If we know that a man has done his best, we will often wish to see him rewarded irrespective of the result; and if we know that a most valuable achievement is almost entirely due to luck or favorable circumstances, we will give little credit to the author.

We may wish that we were able to draw this distinction in every instance. In fact, we can do so only rarely with any degree of assurance. It is possible only where we possess all the knowledge which was at the disposal of the acting person, including a knowledge of his skill and confidence, his state of mind and his feelings, his capacity for attention, his energy and persistence, etc. The possibility of a true judgment of merit thus depends on the presence of precisely those conditions whose general absence is the main argument for liberty. It is because we want people to use knowledge which we do not possess that we let them decide for themselves. But insofar as we want them to be free to use capacities and knowledge of facts which we do not have, we are not in a position to judge the merit of their achievements. To decide on merit presupposes that we can judge whether people have made such use of their opportunities as they ought to have made and how much effort of will or self-denial this has cost them; it presupposes also that we can distinguish between that part of their achievement which is due to circumstances within their control and that part which is not.

The incompatibility of reward according to merit with freedom to choose one's pursuit is most evident in those areas where the uncertainty of the outcome is particularly great and our individual estimates of the chances of various kinds of effort very different. In those speculative efforts which we call "research" or "exploration," or in economic activities which we commonly describe as "speculation," we cannot expect to attract those best qualified for them unless we give the successful ones all the credit or gain, though many others may have striven as meritoriously. For the same reason that nobody can know beforehand who will be the successful ones, nobody can say who has earned greater merit. It would clearly not serve our purpose if we let all who have honestly striven share in the prize. Moreover, to do so would make it necessary that somebody have the right to decide who is to be allowed to strive for it. If in their pursuit of uncertain goals people are to use their own knowledge and capacities, they must be guided, not by what other people think they ought to do, but by the value others attach to the result at which they aim.

What is so obviously true about those undertakings which we commonly regard as risky is scarcely less true of any chosen object we decide to pursue. Any such decision is beset with uncertainty, and if the choice is to be as wise as it is humanly possible to make it, the alternative results anticipated must be labeled according to their value. If the remuneration did not correspond to the value that the product of a man's efforts has for his fellows, he would have no basis for deciding whether the pursuit of a given object is worth the effort and risk. He would necessarily have to be told what to do, and some other person's estimate of what was the best use of his capacities would have to determine both his duties and his remuneration.

The fact is, of course, that we do not wish people to earn a maximum of merit but to achieve a maximum of usefulness at a minimum of pain and sacrifice and therefore a minimum of merit. Not only would it be impossible for us to reward all merit justly, but it would not even be desirable that people should aim chiefly at earning a maximum of merit. Any attempt to induce them to do this would necessarily result in people being rewarded differently for the same service. And it is only the value of the result that we can judge with any degree of confidence, not the different degrees of effort and care that it has cost different people to achieve it.

The prizes that a free society offers for the result serve to tell those who strive for them how much effort they are worth. However, the same prizes will go to all those who produce the same result, regardless of effort. What is true here of the remuneration for the same services rendered by different people is even more true of the relative remuneration for different services requiring different gifts and capacities: they will have little relation to merit. The market will generally offer for services of any kind the value they will have for those who benefit from them; but it will rarely be known whether it was necessary to offer so much in order to obtain these services, and often, no doubt, the community could have had them for much less. The pianist who was reported not long ago to have said that he would perform even if he had to pay for the privilege probably described the position of many who earn large incomes from activities which are also their chief pleasure.

Though most people regard as very natural the claim that nobody should be rewarded more than he deserves for his pain and effort, it is nevertheless based on a colossal presumption. It presumes that we are able to judge in every individual instance how well people use the different opportunities and talents given to them and how meritorious their achievements are in the light of all the circumstances which have made them possible. It presumes that some human beings are in a position to determine conclusively what a person is worth and are entitled to determine what he may achieve. It presumes, then, what the argument for liberty specifically rejects: that we can and do know all that guides a person's action.

A society in which the position of the individuals was made to correspond to human ideas of moral merit would therefore be the exact opposite of a free society. It would be a society in which people were rewarded for duty performed instead of for success, in which every move of every individual was guided by what other people thought he ought to do, and in which the individual was thus relieved of the responsibility and the risk of decision. But if nobody's knowledge is sufficient to guide all human action, there is also no human being who is competent to reward all efforts according to merit.

In our individual conduct we generally act on the assumption that it is the value of a person's performance and not his merit that determines our obligation to him. Whatever may be true in more intimate relations, in the ordinary business of life we do not feel that, because a man has rendered us a service at a great sacrifice, our debt to him is determined by this, so long as we could have had the same service provided with ease by somebody else. In our dealings with other men we feel that we are doing justice if we recompense value rendered with equal value, without inquiring what it might have cost the particular individual to supply us with these services. What determines our responsibility is the advantage we derive from what others offer us, not their merit in providing it. We also expect in our dealings with others to be remunerated not according to our subjective merit but according to what our services are worth to them. Indeed, so long as we think in terms of our relations to particular people, we are generally quite aware that the mark of the free man is to be dependent for his livelihood not on other people's views of his merit but solely on what he has to offer them. It is only when we think of our position or our income as determined by "society" as a whole that we demand reward according to merit.

Though moral value or merit is a species of value, not all value is moral value, and most of our judgments of value are not moral judgments. That this must be so in a free society is a point of cardinal importance; and the failure to distinguish between value and merit has been the source of serious confusion. We do not necessarily admire all activities whose product we value; and in most instances where we value what we get, we are in no position to assess the merit of those who have provided it for us. If a man's ability in a given field is more valuable after thirty years' work than it was earlier, this is independent of whether these thirty years were most profitable and enjoyable or whether they were a time of unceasing sacrifice and worry. If the pursuit of a hobby produces a special skill or an accidental invention turns out to be extremely useful to others, the fact that there is little merit in it does not make it any less valuable than if the result had been produced by painful effort.

This difference between value and merit is not peculiar to any one type of society—it would exist anywhere. We might, of course, attempt to make rewards correspond to merit instead of value, but we are not likely to succeed in this. In attempting it, we would destroy the incentives which enable people to decide for themselves what they should do. Moreover, it is more than doubtful whether even a fairly successful attempt to make rewards correspond to merit would produce a more attractive or even a tolerable social order. A society in which it was generally presumed that a high income was proof of merit and a low income of the lack of it, in which it was universally believed that position and remuneration corresponded to merit, in which there was no other road to success than the approval of one's conduct by the majority of one's fellows, would probably be much more unbearable to the unsuccessful ones than one in which it was frankly recognized that there was no necessary connection between merit and success.

It would probably contribute more to human happiness if, instead of trying to make remuneration correspond to merit, we made clearer how uncertain is the connection between value and merit.

91

We are probably all much too ready to ascribe personal merit where there is, in fact, only superior value. The possession by an individual or a group of a superior civilization or education certainly represents an important value and constitutes an asset for the community to which they belong; but it usually constitutes little merit. Popularity and esteem do not depend more on merit than does financial success. It is, in fact, largely because we are so used to assuming an often nonexistent merit wherever we find value that we balk when, in particular instances, the discrepancy is too large to be ignored.

There is every reason why we ought to endeavor to honor special merit where it has gone without adequate reward. But the problem of rewarding action of outstanding merit which we wish to be widely known as an example is different from that of the incentives on which the ordinary functioning of society rests. A free society produces institutions in which, for those who prefer it, a man's advancement depends on the judgment of some superior or of the majority of his fellows. Indeed, as organizations grow larger and more complex, the task of ascertaining the individual's contribution will become more difficult; and it will become increasingly necessary that, for many, merit in the eyes of the managers rather than the ascertainable value of the contribution should determine the rewards. So long as this does not produce a situation in which a single comprehensive scale of merit is imposed upon the whole society, so long as a multiplicity of organizations compete with one another in offering different prospects, this is not merely compatible with freedom but extends the range of choice open to the individual.

Justice, like liberty and coercion, is a concept which, for the sake of clarity, ought to be confined to the deliberate treatment of men by other men. It is an aspect of the intentional determination of those conditions of people's lives that are subject to such control. Insofar as we want the efforts of individuals to be guided by their own views about prospects and chances, the results of the individual's efforts are necessarily unpredictable, and the question as to whether the resulting distribution of incomes is just has no meaning. Justice does require that those conditions of people's lives that are determined by government be provided equally for all. But equality of those conditions must lead to inequality of results. Neither the equal provision of particular public facilities nor the equal treatment of different partners in our voluntary dealings with one another will secure reward that is proportional to merit. Reward for merit is reward for obeying the wishes of others in what we do, not compensation for the benefits we have conferred upon them by doing what we thought best.

It is, in fact, one of the objections against attempts by government to fix income scales that the state must attempt to be just in all it does. Once the principle of reward according to merit is accepted as the just foundation for the distribution of incomes, justice would require that all who desire it should be rewarded according to that principle. Soon it would also be demanded that the same principle be applied to all and that incomes not in proportion to recognizable merit not be tolerated. Even an attempt merely to distinguish between those incomes or gains which are "earned" and those which are not will set up a principle which the state will have to try to apply but cannot in fact apply generally. And every such attempt at deliberate control of some remunerations is bound to create further demands for new controls. The principle of distributive justice, once introduced, would not be fulfilled until the whole of society was organized in accordance with it. This would produce a kind of society which in all essential respects would be the opposite of a free society—a society in which authority decided what the individual was to do and how he was to do it.

In conclusion we must briefly look at another argument on which the demands for a more equal distribution are frequently based, though it is rarely explicitly stated. This is the contention that membership in a particular community or nation entitles the individual to a particular material standard that is determined by the general wealth of the group to which he belongs. This demand is in curious conflict with the desire to base distribution on personal merit. There is clearly no merit in being born into a particular community, and no argument of justice can be based on the accident of a particular individual's being born in one place rather than another. A relatively wealthy community in fact regularly confers advantages on its poorest members unknown to those born in poor communities. In a wealthy community the only justification its members can have for insisting on further advantages is that there is much private wealth that the government can confiscate and redistribute and that men who constantly see such wealth being enjoyed by others will have a stronger desire for it than those who know of it only abstractly, if at all.

There is no obvious reason why the joint efforts of the members of any group to ensure the maintenance of law and order and to organize the provision of certain services should give the members a claim to a particular share in the wealth of this group. Such claims would be especially difficult to defend where those who advanced them were unwilling to concede the same rights to those who did not belong to the same nation or community. The recognition of such claims on a national scale would in fact only create a new kind of collective (but not less exclusive) property right in the resources of the nation that could not be justified on the same grounds as individual property. Few people would be prepared to recognize the justice of these demands on a world scale. And the bare fact that within a given nation the majority had the actual power to enforce such demands, while in the world as a whole it did not yet have it, would hardly make them more just.

There are good reasons why we should endeavor to use whatever political organization we have at our disposal to make provision for the weak or infirm or for the victims of unforeseeable disaster. It may well be true that the most effective method of providing against certain risks common to all citizens of a state is to give every citizen protection against those risks. The level on which such provisions against common risks can be made will necessarily depend on the general wealth of the community.

It is an entirely different matter, however, to suggest that those who are poor, merely in the sense that there are those in the same community who are richer, are entitled to a share in the wealth of the latter or that being born into a group that has reached a particular level of civilization and comfort confers a title to a share in all its benefits. The fact that all citizens have an interest in the common provision of some services is no justification for anyone's claiming as a right a share in all the benefits. It may set a standard for what some ought to be willing to give, but not for what anyone can demand.

National groups will become more and more exclusive as the acceptance of this view that we have been contending against spreads. Rather than admit people to the advantages that living in their country offers, a nation will prefer to keep them out altogether; for, once admitted, they will soon claim as a right a particular share in its wealth. The conception that citizenship or even residence in a country confers a claim to a particular standard of living is becoming a serious source of international friction. And since the only justification for applying the principle within a given country is that its government has the power to enforce it, we must not be surprised if we find the same principle being applied by force on an international scale. Once the right of the majority to the benefits that minorities enjoy is recognized on a national scale, there is no reason why this should stop at the boundaries of the existing states.

Liberalism
(selection)

Ronald Dworkin

What does it mean for the government to treat its citizens as equals? That is, I think, the same question as the question of what it means for the government to treat all its citizens as free, or as independent, or with equal dignity. In any case, it is a question that has been central to political theory at least since Kant.

It may be answered in two fundamentally different ways. The first supposes that government must be neutral on what might be called the question of the good life. The second supposes that government cannot be neutral on that question, because it cannot treat its citizens as equal human beings without a theory of what human beings ought to be. I must explain that distinction further. Each person follows a more-or-less articulate conception of what gives value to life. The scholar who values a life of contemplation has such a conception; so does the television-watching, beer-drinking citizen who is fond of saying "This is the life," though of course he has thought less about the issue and is less able to describe or defend his conception.

The first theory of equality supposes that political decisions must be, so far as is possible, independent of any particular conception of the good life, or of what gives value to life. Since the citizens of a society differ in their conceptions, the government does not treat them as equals if it prefers one conception to another, either because the officials believe that one is intrinsically superior, or because one is held by the more numerous or more powerful group. The second theory argues, on the contrary, that the content of equal treatment cannot be independent of some theory about the good for man or the good of life, because treating a person as an equal means treating him the way the good or truly wise person would wish to be treated. Good government consists in fostering or at least recognizing good lives; treatment as an equal consists in treating each person as if he were desirous of leading the life that is in fact good, at least so far as this is possible.

This distinction is very abstract, but it is also very important. I shall now argue that liberalism takes, as its constitutive political morality, the first conception of equality. I shall try to support that claim in this way. In the next section of this essay I shall show how it is plausible, and even likely, that a thoughtful person who accepted the first conception of equality would, given the economic and political circumstances of the United States in the last several decades, reach the positions I identified as the familiar core of liberal positions. If so, then the hypothesis satisfies the second of the conditions I described for a successful theory. In the following section I shall try to satisfy the third condition by showing how it is plausible and even likely that someone who held a particular version of the second theory of equality would reach what are normally regarded as the core of American conservative positions. I say "a particular version of" because American conservatism does not follow automatically from rejecting the liberal theory of equality. The second (or nonliberal) theory of equality holds merely that the treatment government owes citizens is at least partly determined by some conception of the good life. Many political theories share that thesis, including theories as far apart as, for example, American conservatism and various forms of socialism or Marxism, though these will of course differ in the conception of the good life they adopt, and hence in the political institutions and decisions they endorse. In this respect, liberalism is decidedly not some compromise or halfway house between more forceful positions, but stands on one side of an important line that distinguishes it from all competitors taken as a group.

I shall not provide arguments in this essay that my theory of liberalism meets the first condition I described—that the theory must provide a political morality that it makes sense to suppose people in our culture hold—though I think it plain that the theory does meet this condition. The fourth condition requires that a theory be as abstract and general as the first three conditions allow. I doubt there will be objections to my theory on that account.

I now define a liberal as someone who holds the first, or liberal, theory of what equality requires. Suppose that a liberal is asked to found a new state. He is required to dictate its constitution and fundamental institutions. He must propose a general theory of political distribution, that is, a theory of how whatever the community has to assign, by way of goods or resources or opportunities, should be assigned. He will arrive initially at something like this principle of rough equality: resources and opportunities should be distributed, so far as possible, equally, so that roughly the same share of whatever is available is devoted to satisfying the ambitions of each. Any other general aim of distribution will assume either that the fate of some people should be of greater concern than that of others, or that the ambitions or talents of some are more worthy, and should be supported more generously on that account.

Someone may object that this principle of rough equality is unfair because it ignores the fact that people have different tastes, and that some of these are more expensive to satisfy than others, so that, for example, the man who prefers champagne will need more funds if he is not to be frustrated than the man satisfied with beer. But the liberal may reply that tastes as to which people differ are, by and large, not afflictions, like diseases, but are rather cultivated, in accordance with each person's theory of what his life should be like. The most effective neutrality, therefore, requires that the same share be devoted to each, so that the choice between expensive and less expensive tastes can be made by each person for himself, with no sense that his overall share will be enlarged by choosing a more expensive life, or that, whatever he chooses, his choice will subsidize those who have chosen more expensively.

But what does the principle of rough equality of distribution require in practice? If all resources were distributed directly by the government through grants of food, housing, and so forth; if every opportunity citizens have were provided directly by the government

99

through the provisions of civil and criminal law; if every citizen had exactly the same talents; if every citizen started his life with no more than what any other citizen had at the start; and if every citizen had exactly the same theory of the good life and hence exactly the same scheme of preferences as every other citizen, including preferences between productive activity of different forms and leisure, then the principle of rough equality of treatment could be satisfied simply by equal distributions of everything to be distributed and by civil and criminal laws of universal application. Government would arrange for production that maximized the mix of goods, including jobs and leisure, that everyone favored, distributing the product equally.

Of course, none of these conditions of similarity holds. But the moral relevance of different sorts of diversity are very different, as may be shown by the following exercise. Suppose all the conditions of similarity I mentioned did hold except the last: citizens have different theories of the good and hence different preferences. They therefore disagree about what product the raw materials and labor and savings of the community should be used to produce, and about which activities should be prohibited or regulated so as to make others possible or easier. The liberal, as lawgiver, now needs mechanisms to satisfy the principles of equal treatment in spite of these disagreements. He will decide that there are no better mechanisms available, as general political institutions, than the two main institutions of our own political economy: the economic market, for decisions about what goods shall be produced and how they shall be distributed, and representative democracy, for collective decisions about what conduct shall be prohibited or regulated so that other conduct might be made possible or convenient. Each of these familiar institutions may be expected to provide a more egalitarian division than any other general arrangement. The market, if it can be made to function efficiently, will determine for each product a price that reflects the cost in resources of material, labor, and capital that might have been applied to produce something different that someone else wants. That cost determines, for anyone who consumes that product, how much his account should be charged in computing the egalitarian division of social resources. It provides a measure of how much more his account should be charged for a house than a book, and for one book rather than another. The market will also provide, for the laborer, a measure of how much should be credited to his account for his choice of productive activity over leisure, and for one activity rather than another. It will tell us, through the price it puts on his labor, how much he should gain or lose by his decision to pursue one career rather than another. These measurements make a citizen's own distribution a function of the personal preferences of others as well as of his own, and it is the sum of these personal preferences that fixes the true cost to the community of meeting his own preferences for goods and activities. The egalitarian distribution, which requires that the cost of satisfying one person's preferences should as far as is possible be equal to the cost of satisfying another's, cannot be enforced unless those measurements are made.

We are familiar with the anti-egalitarian consequences of free enterprise in practice; it may therefore seem paradoxical that the liberal as lawgiver should choose a market economy for reasons of equality rather than efficiency. But, under the special condition that people differ only in preferences for goods and activities, the market is more egalitarian than any alternative of comparable generality. The most plausible alternative would be to allow decisions of production, investment, price, and wage to be made by elected officials in a socialist economy. But what principles should officials use in making those decisions? The liberal might tell them to mimic the decisions that a market would make it if was working efficiently under proper competition and full knowledge. This mimicry would be, in practice, much less efficient than an actual market would be. In any case, unless the liberal had reason to think it would be much more efficient, he would have good reason to reject it. Any minimally efficient mimicking of a hypothetical market would require invasions of privacy to determine what decisions individuals would make if forced actually to pay for their investment, consumption, and employment decisions at market rates, and this information gathering would be, in many other ways, much more expensive than an actual market. Inevitably, moreover, the assumptions officials make about how people would behave in a hypothetical market reflect the officials' own beliefs about how people should behave.

So there would be, for the liberal, little to gain and much to lose in a socialist economy in which officials were asked to mimic a hypothetical market.

But any other instructions would be a direct violation of the liberal theory of what equality requires, because if a decision is made to produce and sell goods at a price below the price a market would fix, then those who prefer those goods are, *pro tanto*, receiving more than an equal share of the resources of the community at the expense of those who would prefer some other use of the resources. Suppose the limited demand for books, matched against the demand for competing uses for wood pulp, would fix the price of books at a point higher than the socialist managers of the economy will charge; those who want books are having less charged to their account than the egalitarian principle would require. It might be said that in a socialist economy books are simply valued more, because they are inherently more worthy uses of social resources, quite apart from the popular demand for books. But the liberal theory of equality rules out that appeal to the inherent value of one theory of what is good in life.

In a society in which people differed only in preferences, then, a market would be favored for its egalitarian consequences. Inequality of monetary wealth would be the consequence only of the fact that some preferences are more expensive than others, including the preference for leisure time rather than the most lucrative productive activity. But we must now return to the real world. In the actual society for which the liberal must construct political institutions, there are all the other differences. Talents are not distributed equally, so the decision of one person to work in a factory rather than a law firm, or not to work at all, will be governed in large part by his abilities rather than his preferences for work or between work and leisure. The institutions of wealth, which allow people to dispose of what they receive by gift, means that children of the successful will start with more wealth than the children of the unsuccessful. Some people have special needs, because they are handicapped; their handicap will not only disable them from the most productive and lucrative employment, but will incapacitate them from using the proceeds of whatever employment they find as efficiently, so that they will need more than those who are not handicapped to satisfy identical ambitions.

These inequalities will have great, often catastrophic, effects on the distribution that a market economy will provide. But, unlike differences in preferences, the differences these inequalities make are indefensible according to the liberal conception of equality. It is obviously obnoxious to the liberal conception, for example, that someone should have more of what the community as a whole has to distribute because he or his father had superior skill or luck. The liberal lawgiver therefore faces a difficult task. His conception of equality requires an economic system that produces certain inequalities (those that reflect the true differential costs of goods and opportunities) but not others (those that follow from differences in ability, inheritance, and etc.). The market produces both the required and the forbidden inequalities, and there is no alternative system that can be relied upon to produce the former without the latter.

The liberal must be tempted, therefore, to a reform of the market through a scheme of redistribution that leaves its pricing system relatively intact but sharply limits, at least, the inequalities in welfare that his initial principle prohibits. No solution will seem perfect. The liberal may find the best answer in a scheme of welfare rights financed through redistributive income and inheritance taxes of the conventional sort, which redistributes just to the Rawlsian point, that is, to the point at which the worst-off group would be harmed rather than benefited by further transfers. In that case, he will remain a reluctant capitalist, believing that a market economy so reformed is superior, from the standpoint of his conception of equality, to any practical socialist alternative. Or he may believe that the redistribution that is possible in a capitalist economy will be so inadequate, or will be purchased at the cost of such inefficiency, that it is better to proceed in a more radical way, by substituting socialist for market decisions over a large part of the economy, and then relying on the political process to insure that prices are set in a manner at least roughly consistent with his conception of equality. In that case he will be a reluctant socialist, who acknowledges the egalitarian defects of socialism but counts them as less severe than the practical alternatives. In either case, he chooses a mixed economic system—either redistributive capitalism or limited socialism—not in order to compromise antagonistic ideals of efficiency and equality, but to achieve the best practical realization of the demands of equality itself.

Let us assume that in this manner the liberal either refines or partially retracts his original selection of a market economy. He must now consider the second of the two familiar institutions he first selected, which is representative democracy. Democracy is justified because it enforces the right of each person to respect and concern as an individual; but in practice the decisions of a democratic majority may often violate that right, according to the liberal theory of what the right requires. Suppose a legislature elected by a majority decides to make criminal some act (like speaking in favor of an unpopular political position, or participating in eccentric sexual practices) not because the act deprives others of opportunities they want, but because the majority disapproves of those views or that sexual morality. The political decision, in other words, reflects not simply some accommodation of the *personal* preferences of everyone, in such a way as to make the opportunities of all as nearly equal as may be, but the domination of one set of *external* preferences, that is, preferences people have about what others shall do or have. The decision invades rather than enforces the right of citizens to be treated as equals.

How can the liberal protect citizens against that sort of violation of their fundamental right? It will not do for the liberal simply to instruct legislators, in some constitutional exhortation, to disregard the external preferences of their constituents. Citizens will vote these preferences in electing their representatives, and a legislator who chooses to ignore them will not survive. In any case, it is sometimes impossible to distinguish, even by introspection, the external and personal components of a political position: this is the case, for example, with associational preferences, which are the preferences some people have for opportunities, like the opportunity to attend public schools, but only with others of the same "background."

The liberal, therefore, needs a scheme of civil rights, whose effect will be to determine those political decisions that are antecedently likely to reflect strong external preferences, and to remove those decisions from majoritarian political institutions altogether. Of course the scheme of rights necessary to do this will depend on general facts about the prejudices and other external preferences of the majority at any given time, and different liberals will disagree about what is needed at any particular time. But the rights encoded in the Bill of Rights of the United States Constitution, as interpreted (on the whole) by the Supreme Court, are those that a substantial number of liberals would think reasonably well suited to what the United States now requires (though most would think that the protection of the individual in certain important areas, including sexual publication and practice, are much too weak).

The main parts of the criminal law, however, present a special problem not easily met by a scheme of civil rights that disable the legislature from taking certain political decisions. The liberal knows that many of the most important decisions required by an effective criminal law are not made by legislators at all, but by prosecutors deciding whom to prosecute for what crime, and by juries and judges deciding whom to convict and what sentences to impose. He also knows that these decisions are antecedently very likely to be corrupted by the external preferences of those who make these decisions because those they judge, typically, have attitudes and ways of life very different from their own. The liberal does not have available, as protection against these decisions, any strategy comparable to the strategy of civil rights that simply remove a decision from an institution. Decisions to prosecute, convict, and sentence must be made by someone. But he has available, in the notion of procedural rights, a different device to protect equality in a different way. He will insist that criminal procedure be structured to achieve a margin of safety in decisions, so that the process is biased strongly against the conviction of the innocent. It would be a mistake to suppose that the liberal thinks that these procedural rights will improve the *accuracy* of the criminal process, that is, the probability that any particular decision about guilt or innocence will be the right one. Procedural rights intervene in the process, even at the cost of inaccuracy, to compensate in a rough way for the antecedent risk that a criminal process, especially if it is largely administered by one class against another, will be corrupted by the impact of external preferences that cannot be eliminated directly. This is, of course, only the briefest sketch of how various substantive and procedural civil rights follow from the liberal's initial conception of equality; it is meant to suggest, rather than demonstrate, the more precise argument that would be available for more particular rights.

So the liberal, drawn to the economic market and to political democracy for distinctly egalitarian reasons, finds that these institutions will produce inegalitarian results unless he adds to his scheme different sorts of individual rights. These rights will function as trump cards held by individuals; they will enable individuals to resist particular decisions in spite of the fact that these decisions are or would be reached through the normal workings of general institutions that are not themselves challenged. The ultimate justification for these rights is that they are necessary to protect equal concern and respect; but they are not to be understood as representing equality in contrast to some other goal or principle served by democracy or the economic market. The familiar idea, for example, that rights of redistribution are justified by an ideal of equality that overrides the efficiency ideals of the market in certain cases, has no place in liberal theory. For the liberal, rights are justified, not by some principle in competition with an independent justification of the political and economic institutions they qualify, but in order to make more perfect the only justification on which these other institutions may themselves rely. If the liberal arguments for a particular right are sound, then the right is an unqualified improvement in political morality, not a necessary but regrettable compromise of some other independent goal, like economic efficiency.

I said that the conservative holds one among a number of possible alternatives to the liberal conception of equality. Each of these alternatives shares the opinion that treating a person with respect requires treating him as the good man would wish to be treated. The conservative supposes that the good man would wish to be treated in accordance with the principles of a special sort of society, which I shall call the virtuous society. A virtuous society has these general features. Its members share a sound conception of virtue, that is, of the qualities and dispositions people should strive to have and exhibit. They share this conception of virtue not only privately, as individuals, but publicly: they believe their community, in its social and political activity, exhibits virtues, and that they have a responsibility, as citizens, to promote these virtues. In that sense they treat the lives of other members of their community as part of their own lives. The conservative position is not the only position that relies on this ideal of the virtuous society (some forms of socialism rely on it as well). But the conservative is distinct in believing that his own society, with its present institutions, is a virtuous society for the special reason that its history and common experience are better guides to sound virtue than any nonhistorical and therefore abstract deduction of virtue from first principles could provide.

Suppose a conservative is asked to draft a constitution for a society generally like ours, which he believes to be virtuous. Like the liberal, he will see great merit in the familiar institutions of political democracy and an economic market. The appeal of these institutions will be very different for the conservative, however. The economic market, in practice, assigns greater rewards to those who, because they have the virtues of talent and industry, supply more of what is wanted by the other members of the virtuous society; and that is, for the conservative, the paradigm of fairness in distribution. Political democracy distributes opportunities, through the provisions of the civil and criminal law, as the citizens of a virtuous society wish it to be distributed, and that process will provide more scope for virtuous activity and less for vice than any less democratic technique. Democracy has a further advantage, moreover, that no other technique could have. It allows the community to use the processes of legislation to reaffirm, as a community, its public conception of virtue.

The appeal of the familiar institutions to the conservative is, therefore, very different from their appeal to the liberal. Since the conservative and the liberal both find the familiar institutions useful, though for different reasons, the existence of these institutions, as institutions, will not necessarily be a point of controversy between them. But they will disagree sharply over which corrective devices, in the form of individual rights, are necessary in order to maintain justice, and the disagreement will not be a matter of degree. The liberal, as I said, finds the market defective principally because it allows morally irrelevant differences, like differences in talent, to affect distribution, and he therefore considers that those who have less talent, as the market judges talent, have a right to some form of redistribution in the name of justice. But the conservative prizes just the feature of the market that puts a premium on talents prized in the community, because these are, in a virtuous community, virtues. So he will find no genuine merit, but only expediency, in the idea of redistribution. He will allow room of course, for the virtue of charity, for it is a virtue that is part of the public catalog; but he will prefer private charity to public, because it is a purer expression of that virtue. He may accept public charity as well, particularly when it seems necessary to retain the political allegiance of those who would otherwise suffer too much to tolerate a capitalist society at all. But public charity, justified either on grounds of virtue or expediency, will seem to the conservative a compromise with the primary justification of the market, rather than, as redistribution seems to the liberal, an improvement in that primary justification.

Nor will the conservative find the same defects in representative democracy that the liberal finds there. The conservative will not aim to exclude moralistic or other external preferences from the democratic process by any scheme of civil rights; on the contrary, it is the pride of democracy, for him, that external preferences are legislated into a public morality. But the conservative will find different defects in democracy, and he will contemplate a different scheme of rights to diminish the injustice they work.

The economic market distributes rewards for talents valued in the virtuous society, but since these talents are unequally distributed, wealth will be concentrated, and the wealthy will be at the mercy of an envious political majority anxious to take by law what it cannot take by talent. Justice requires some protection for the successful. The conservative will be (as historically he has been) anxious to hold some line against extensions of the vote to those groups most likely to be envious, but there is an apparent conflict between the ideals of abstract equality, even in the conservative conception, and disenfranchisement of large parts of the population. In any case, if conservatism is to be politically powerful, it must not threaten to exclude from political power those who would be asked to consent, formally or tacitly, to their own exclusion. The conservative will find more appeal in the different, and politically much more feasible, idea of rights to property.

These rights have the same force, though of course radically different content, as the liberal's civil rights. The liberal will, for his own purposes, accept some right to property, because he will count some sovereignty over a range of personal possessions essential to dignity. But the conservative will strive for rights to property of a very different order; he will want rights that protect, not some minimum dominion over a range of possessions independently shown to be desirable, but an unlimited dominion over whatever has been acquired through an institution that defines and rewards talent.

The conservative will not, of course, follow the liberal in the latter's concern for procedural rights in the criminal process. He will accept the basic institutions of criminal legislation and trial as proper; but he will see, in the possible acquittal of the guilty, not simply an inefficiency in the strategy of deterrence, but an affront to the basic principle that the censure of vice is indispensable to the honor of virtue. He will believe, therefore, that just criminal procedures are those that improve the antecedent probability that particular decisions of guilt or innocence will be accurate. He will support rights against interrogation or self-incrimination, for example, when such rights seem necessary to protect against torture or other means likely to elicit a confession from the innocent; but he will lose his concern for such rights when noncoercion can be guaranteed in other ways.

The fair-minded conservative will be concerned about racial discrimination, but his concern will differ from the concern of the liberal, and the remedies he will countenance will also be different. The distinction between equality of opportunity and equality of result is crucial to the conservative: the institutions of the economic market and representative democracy cannot achieve what he supposes they do unless each citizen has an equal opportunity to capitalize on his genuine talents and other virtues in the contest these institutions provide. But since the conservative knows that these virtues are unequally distributed, he also knows that equality of opportunity must have been denied if the outcome of the contest is equality of result.

The fair conservative must, therefore, attend to the charge that prejudice denies equality of opportunity between members of different races, and he must accept the justice of remedies designed to reinstate that equality, so far as this may be possible. But he will steadily oppose any form of "affirmative action" that offers special opportunities, like places in medical school or jobs, on criteria other than some proper conception of the virtue appropriate to the reward.

The issue of gun control, which I have thus far not mentioned, is an excellent illustration of the power of the conservative's constitutive political morality. He favors strict control of sexual publication and practice, but he opposes parallel control of the ownership or use of guns, though of course guns are more dangerous than sex. President Ford, in the second Carter–Ford debate, put the conservative position of gun control especially clearly. Sensible conservatives do not dispute that private and uncontrolled ownership of guns leads to violence, because it puts guns in circulation that bad men may use badly. But (President Ford said) if we meet that problem by not allowing good men to have guns, we are punishing the wrong people. It is, of course, distinctive to the conservative's position to regard regulation as condemnation and hence as punishment. But he must regard regulation that way, because he believes that opportunities should be distributed, in a virtuous society, so as to promote virtuous acts at the expense of vicious ones.

QUESTIONS FOR DISCUSSION

Why does Hayek advocate equality before the law in social interactions, but reject the idea of redistributing society's goods in the name of equality?

1. Why does Hayek believe that equality before the law and material equality are "not only different but are in conflict with each other"? (79)

2. Why does Hayek argue that a society that rewards individuals for the moral merit of their actions is "the exact opposite of a free society"? (90)

3. According to Hayek, why is justice "a concept which, for the sake of clarity, ought to be confined to the deliberate treatment of men by other men"? (92)

4. Why does Hayek make a distinction between merit and value in discussing how the contributions of individuals to a free society should be assessed?

According to Dworkin, why should liberal thinkers supplement efficient markets and representative democracy with "different sorts of individual rights"? (106)

1. What principles does Dworkin think a liberal thinker should appeal to in devising "a scheme of civil rights"? (104)

2. Why does Dworkin believe that liberals' and conservatives' disagreement over individual rights "will not be a matter of degree"? (108)

3. Why does Dworkin think that conservatives' support for property rights entails "an unlimited dominion over whatever has been acquired through an institution that defines and rewards talent"? (109)

4. According to Dworkin, why is "the distinction between equality of opportunity and equality of result" crucial to the conservative? (109)

FOR FURTHER REFLECTION

1. Would you rather live in a society governed by Hayek's or Dworkin's principles?

2. In a representative democracy, is it ever legitimate for the government to override majority decisions in order to further civil rights?

3. Is it right for a government to legislate on issues of private morality?

4. Should a government be neutral on the question of what makes a good life?

FIDELITY

FIDELITY

The nature of commitment and faithfulness has preoccupied writers of all eras. Explored variously through prisms of monogamy, passion, friendship, and romance, the interpretation of fidelity is as varied as the individuals who experience it. Across the broadest range of emotional, physical, and social situations, faithfulness has preoccupied artists from ancient times to the modern day. The following selections reflect two differing interpretations of fidelity and its perceived value in marriage and in memory.

British poet **Philip Larkin** (1922–1985) appears to portray a traditional conception of marital loyalty in his poem "An Arundel Tomb" (1956). He explores cultural ideas of love and fidelity in his description of the medieval stone tomb of a knight and his wife in Chichester Cathedral. Yet the changing response to the tomb by the public over the centuries lends an ambivalence to easy assumptions of loving devotion. The final claim that the tomb stands as a testament to the enduring nature of love seems uncertain given the shifting and cynical tone of the poem.

American author and therapist **Amy Bloom** (1953–) describes a range of loving relationships in her short story "Love Is Not a Pie," which is included in her 1993 collection *Come to Me*. The narrator, Ellen, reflects on her relationship with her fiancé and questions her commitment to their forthcoming marriage. Childhood memories of the unconventional relationship between her own parents and another man, Mr. DeCuervo, steer Ellen's feelings beyond conventional narratives of fidelity, and toward a different, more inclusive sense of the possibilities of love. Bloom's story does not espouse generalities, but instead focuses on the nuance of individual experience. As she says in a 2004 *Ploughshares* article, "There is no big picture. There is only this particular moment, in this particular life."

An Arundel Tomb

Philip Larkin

Side by side, their faces blurred,
The earl and countess lie in stone,
Their proper habits vaguely shown
As jointed armour, stiffened pleat,
And that faint hint of the absurd—
The little dogs under their feet.

Such plainness of the pre-baroque
Hardly involves the eye, until
It meets his left-hand gauntlet, still
Clasped empty in the other; and
One sees, with a sharp tender shock,
His hand withdrawn, holding her hand.

They would not think to lie so long.
Such faithfulness in effigy
Was just a detail friends would see:
A sculptor's sweet commissioned grace
Thrown off in helping to prolong
The Latin names around the base.

They would not guess how early in
Their supine stationary voyage
The air would change to soundless damage,
Turn the old tenantry away;
How soon succeeding eyes begin
To look, not read. Rigidly they

Persisted, linked, through lengths and breadths
Of time. Snow fell, undated. Light
Each summer thronged the glass. A bright
Litter of birdcalls strewed the same
Bone-riddled ground. And up the paths
The endless altered people came,

Washing at their identity.
Now, helpless in the hollow of
An unarmorial age, a trough
Of smoke in slow suspended skeins
Above their scrap of history,
Only an attitude remains:

Time has transfigured them into
Untruth. The stone fidelity
They hardly meant has come to be
Their final blazon, and to prove
Our almost-instinct almost true:
What will survive of us is love.

Love Is Not a Pie

Amy Bloom

In the middle of the eulogy at my mother's boring and heart-breaking funeral, I began to think about calling off the wedding. August 21 did not seem like a good date, John Wescott did not seem like a good person to marry, and I couldn't see myself in the long white silk gown Mrs. Wescott had offered me. We had gotten engaged at Christmas, while my mother was starting to die; she died in May, earlier than we had expected. When the minister said, "She was a rare spirit, full of the kind bravery and joy which inspires others," I stared at the pale blue ceiling and thought, "My mother would not have wanted me to spend my life with this man." He had asked me if I wanted him to come to the funeral from Boston, and I said no. And so he didn't, respecting my autonomy and so forth. I think he should have known that I was just being considerate.

After the funeral, we took the little box of ashes back to the house and entertained everybody who came by to pay their respects. Lots of my father's law school colleagues, a few of his former students, my uncle Steve and his new wife, my cousins (whom my sister Lizzie and I always referred to as Thing One and Thing Two), friends from the old neighborhood, before my mother's sculpture started selling, her art world friends, her sisters, some of my friends from high school, some people I used to babysit for, my best friend from college, some friends of Lizzie's, a lot of people I didn't recognize. I'd been living away from home for a long time, first at college, now at law school.

My sister, my father, and I worked the room. And everyone who came in my father embraced. It didn't matter whether they started to pat him on the back or shake his hand, he pulled them to him and hugged them so hard I saw people's feet lift right off the floor. Lizzie and I took the more passive route, letting people do whatever they wanted to us, patting, stroking, embracing, cupping our faces in their hands.

My father was in the middle of squeezing Mrs. Ellis, our cleaning lady, when he saw Mr. DeCuervo come in, still carrying his suitcase. He about dropped Mrs. Ellis and went charging over to Mr. De-Cuervo, wrapped his arms around him, and the two of them moaned and rocked together in a passionate, musicless waltz. My sister and I sat down on the couch, pressed against each other, watching our father cry all over his friend, our mother's lover.

When I was eleven and Lizzie was eight, her last naked summer, Mr. DeCuervo and his daughter, Gisela, who was just about to turn eight, spent part of the summer with us at the cabin in Maine. The cabin was from the Spencer side, my father's side of the family, and he and my uncle Steve were co-owners. We went there every July (colder water, better weather), and they came in August. My father felt about his brother the way we felt about our cousins, so we would only overlap for lunch on the last day of our stay.

That July, the DeCuervos came, but without Mrs. DeCuervo, who had to go visit a sick someone in Argentina, where they were from. That was okay with us. Mrs. DeCuervo was a professional mother, a type that made my sister and me very uncomfortable. She told us to wash the berries before we ate them, to rest after lunch, to put on more suntan lotion, to make our beds. She was a nice lady, she was just always in our way. My mother had a few very basic summer rules: don't eat food with mold or insects on it; don't swim alone; don't even think about waking your mother before 8:00 a.m. unless you are fatally injured or ill. That was about it, but Mrs. DeCuervo was always amending and adding to the list, one apologetic eye on our mother, who was pleasant and friendly as usual and did things the way she always did. She made it pretty clear that if we were cowed by the likes of Mrs. DeCuervo, we were on our own. They got divorced when Gisela was a sophomore at Mount Holyoke.

We liked pretty, docile Gisela, and bullied her a little bit, and liked her even more because she didn't squeal on us, on me in particular. We liked her father, too. We saw the two of them, sometimes the three of them, at occasional picnics and lesser holidays. He always complimented us, never made stupid jokes at our expense, and brought us unusual, perfect little presents. Silver barrettes for me the summer I was letting my hair grow out from my pixie cut; a leather bookmark for Lizzie, who learned to read when she was three. My mother would stand behind us as we unwrapped the gifts, smiling and shaking her head at his extravagance.

When they drove up, we were all sitting on the porch. Mr. De-Cuervo got out first, his curly brown hair making him look like a giant dandelion, with his yellow T-shirt and brown jeans. Gisela looked just like him, her long, curly brown hair caught up in a bun, wisps flying around her tanned little face. As they walked toward us, she took his hand and I felt a rush of warmth for her, for showing how much she loved her daddy, like I loved mine, and for showing that she was a little afraid of us, of me, probably. People weren't often frightened of Lizzie; she never left her books long enough to bother anyone.

My parents came down from the porch; my big father, in his faded blue trunks, drooping below his belly, his freckled back pink and moist in the sun, as it was every summer. The sun caught the red hair on his head and shoulders and chest, and he shone. The Spencers were half-Viking, he said. My mother was wearing her summer outfit, a black two-piece bathing suit. I don't remember her ever wearing a different suit. At night, she'd add one of my father's shirts and wrap it around her like a kimono. Some years, she looked great in her suit, waist nipped in, skin smooth and tan; other years, her skin looked burnt and crumpled, and the suit was too big in some places and too small in others. Those years, she smoked too much and went out on the porch to cough. But that summer the suit fit beautifully, and when she jumped off the porch into my father's arms, he whirled her around and let her black hair whip his face while he smiled and smiled.

They both hugged Mr. DeCuervo and Gisela; my mother took her flowered suitcase and my father took his duffel bag and they led them into the cabin.

The cabin was our palace; Lizzie and I would say very grandly, "We're going to the cabin for the summer, come visit us there, if it's okay with your parents." And we loved it and loved to act as though it was nothing special, when we knew, really, that it was magnificent. The pines and birches came right down to the lake, with just a thin lacing of mossy rocks before you got to the smooth cold water, and little gray fish swam around the splintery dock and through our legs, or out of reach of our oars when we took out the old blue rowboat.

The cabin itself was three bedrooms and a tiny kitchen and a living room that took up half the house. The two small bedrooms had big beds with pastel chenille spreads; yellow with red roses in my parents' room, white with blue pansies in the other. The kids' room was much bigger, like a dormitory, with three sets of bunk beds, each with its own mismatched sheets and pillowcases. The pillows were always a little damp and smelled like salt and pine, and mine smelled of Ma Griffe as well, because I used to sleep with my mother's scarf tucked under it. The shower was outside, with a thin green plastic curtain around it, but there was a regular bathroom inside, next to my parents' room.

Mr. DeCuervo and Gisela fit into our routine as though they'd been coming to the cabin for years, instead of just last summer. We had the kind of summer cabin routine that stays with you forever as a model of leisure, of life being enjoyed. We'd get up early, listening to the birds screaming and trilling, and make ourselves some breakfast; cereal or toast if the parents were up, cake or cold spaghetti or marshmallows if they were still asleep. My mother got up first, usually. She'd make a cup of coffee and brush and braid our hair and set us loose. If we were going exploring, she'd put three sandwiches and three pieces of fruit in a bag, with an army blanket. Otherwise, she'd just wave to us as we headed down to the lake.

We'd come back at lunchtime and eat whatever was around and then go out to the lake or the forest, or down the road to see if the townie kids were in a mood to play with us. I don't know what the grownups did all day; sometimes they'd come out to swim for a while, and sometimes we'd find my mother in the shed she used for a studio. But when we came back at five or six, they all seemed happy and relaxed, drinking gin and tonics on the porch, watching us run toward the house. It was the most beautiful time.

At night, after dinner, the fathers would wash up and my mother would sit on the porch, smoking a cigarette, listening to Aretha Franklin or Billie Holiday or Sam Cooke, and after a little while she'd stub out her cigarette and the four of us would dance. We'd twist and lindy and jitterbug and stomp, all of us copying my mother. And pretty soon the daddies would drift in with their dish towels and their beers, and they'd lean in the doorway and watch. My mother would turn first to my father, always to him, first.

"What about it, Danny? Care to dance?" And she'd put her hand on his shoulder and he'd smile, tossing his dish towel to Mr. De-Cuervo, resting his beer on the floor. My father would lumber along gamely, shuffling his feet and smiling. Sometimes he'd wave his arms around and pretend to be a fish or a bear while my mother swung her body easily and dreamily, sliding through the music. They'd always lindy together to Fats Domino. That was my father's favorite, and then he'd sit down, puffing a little.

My mother would stand there, snapping her fingers, shifting back and forth.

"Gaucho, you dance with her, before I have a coronary," said my father.

Mr. DeCuervo's real name was Bolivar, which I didn't know until Lizzie told me after the funeral. We always called him Mr. DeCuervo because we felt embarrassed to call him by a nickname.

So Mr. DeCuervo would shrug gracefully and toss the two dish towels back to my father. And then he'd bop toward my mother, his face still turned toward my father.

"We'll go running tomorrow, Dan, get you back into shape so you can dance all night."

"What do you mean, 'back'? I've been exactly this same svelte shape for twenty years. Why fix it if it ain't broke?"

And they all laughed, and Mr. DeCuervo and my mother rolled their eyes at each other, and my mother walked over and kissed my father where the sweat was beading up at his temples. Then she took Mr. DeCuervo's hand and they walked to the center of the living room.

When she and my father danced, my sister and I giggled and interfered and treated it like a family badminton game in which they were the core players but we were welcome participants. When she danced with Mr. DeCuervo, we'd sit on the porch swing or lean on the windowsill and watch, not even looking at each other.

They only danced the fast dances, and they danced as though they'd been waiting all their lives for each song. My mother's movements got deeper and smoother, and Mr. DeCuervo suddenly came alive, as though a spotlight had hit him. My father danced the way he was, warm, noisy, teasing, a little overpowering; but Mr. DeCuervo, who was usually quiet and thoughtful and serious, became a different man when he danced with my mother. His dancing was light and happy and soulful, edging up on my mother, turning her, matching her every step. They would smile at all of us, in turn, and then face each other, too transported to smile.

"Dance with Daddy some more," my sister said, speaking for all three of us. They had left us too far behind.

My mother blew Lizzie a kiss. "Okay, sweetheart."

She turned to both men, laughing, and said, "That message was certainly loud and clear. Let's take a little break, Gauch, and get these monkeys to bed. It's getting late, girls."

And the three of them shepherded the three of us through the bedtime rituals, moving us in and out of the kitchen for milk, the bathroom for teeth, toilet, and calamine lotion, and finally to our big bedroom. We slept in our underwear and T-shirts, which impressed Gisela.

"No pajamas?" she had said the first night.

"Not necessary," I said smugly.

We would lie there after they kissed us, listening to our parents talk and crack peanuts and snap cards; they played gin and poker while they listened to Dinah Washington and Odetta.

One night, I woke up around midnight and crossed the living room to get some water in the kitchen and see if there was any strawberry shortcake left. I saw my mother and Mr. DeCuervo hugging, and I remember being surprised, and puzzled. I had seen movies; if you hugged someone like you'd never let them go, surely you were supposed to be kissing, too. It wasn't a Mommy-Daddy hug, partly because their hugs were defined by the fact that my father was eight inches taller and a hundred pounds heavier than my mother. These two looked all wrong to me; embraces were a big pink-and-orange man enveloping a small, lean black-and-white woman who gazed up at him. My mother and Mr. DeCuervo looked like sister and brother, standing cheek-to-cheek, with their broad shoulders and long, tanned, bare legs. My mother's hands were under Mr. DeCuervo's white T-shirt.

She must have felt my eyes on her, because she opened hers slowly.

"Oh, honey, you startled us. Mr. DeCuervo and I were just saying good night. Do you want me to tuck you in after you go to the bathroom?" Not quite a bribe, certainly a reminder that I was more important to her than he was. They had moved apart so quickly and smoothly I couldn't even remember how they had looked together. I nodded to my mother; what I had seen was already being transformed into a standard good-night embrace, the kind my mother gave to all of her close friends.

When I came back from the bathroom, Mr. DeCuervo had disappeared and my mother was waiting, looking out at the moon. She walked me to the bedroom and kissed me, first on the forehead, then on my lips.

"Sleep well, pumpkin pie. See you in the morning."

"Will you make blueberry pancakes tomorrow?" It seemed like a good time to ask.

"We'll see. Go to sleep."

"Please, Mommy."

"Okay, we'll have a blueberry morning. Go to sleep now. Good night, nurse." And she watched me for a moment from the doorway, and then she was gone.

My father got up at five to go fishing with some men at the other side of the lake. Every Saturday in July he'd go off with a big red bandanna tied over his bald spot, his Mets T-shirt, and his tackle box, and he'd fish until around three. Mr. DeCuervo said that he'd clean them, cook them, and eat them but he wouldn't spend a day with a bunch of guys in baseball caps and white socks to catch them.

I woke up smelling coffee and butter. Gisela and Lizzie were already out of bed, and I was aggrieved; I was the one who had asked for the pancakes, and they were probably all eaten by now.

Mr. DeCuervo and Lizzie were sitting at the table, finishing their pancakes. My mother and Gisela were sitting on the blue couch in the living room while my mother brushed Gisela's hair. She was brushing it more gently than she brushed mine, not slapping her on the shoulder to make her sit still. Gisela didn't wiggle, and she didn't scream when my mother hit a knot.

I was getting ready to be mad when my mother winked at me over Gisela's head and said, "There's a stack of pancakes for you on top of the stove, bunny. Gauch, would you please lift them for Ellen? The plate's probably hot."

Mr. DeCuervo handed me my pancakes, which were huge brown wheels studded with smashed purpley berries; he put my fork and knife on top of a folded paper towel and patted my cheek. His hand smelled like coffee and cinnamon. He knew what I liked and pushed the butter and the honey and the syrup towards me.

"Juice?" he said.

I nodded, trying to watch him when he wasn't looking; he didn't seem like the man I thought I saw in the moonlight, giving my mother a funny hug.

"Great pancakes, Lila," he said.

"Great, Mom." I didn't want to be outclassed by the DeCuervos' habitual good manners. Gisela remembered her "please" and "thank you" for every little thing.

My mother smiled and put a barrette in Gisela's hair. It was starting to get warm, so I swallowed my pancakes and kicked Lizzie to get her attention.

"Let's go," I said.

"Wash your face, then go," my mother said.

I stuck my face under the kitchen tap, and my mother and Mr. DeCuervo laughed. Triumphantly, I led the two little girls out of the house, snatching our towels off the line as we ran down to the water, suddenly filled with longing for the lake.

"Last one in's a fart," I screamed, cannonballing off the end of the dock. I hit the cold blue water, shattering its surface. Lizzie and Gisela jumped in beside me, and we played water games until my father drove up in the pickup with a bucket of fish. He waved to us and told us we'd be eating fish for the next two days, and we groaned and held our noses as he went into the cabin, laughing.

There was a string of sunny days like that one: swimming, fishing with Daddy off the dock, eating peanut butter and jelly sandwiches in the rowboat, drinking Orange Crush on the porch swing.

And then it rained for a week. We woke up the first rainy morning, listening to it tap and dance on the roof. My mother stuck her head into our bedroom.

"It's monsoon weather, honeys. How about cocoa and cinnamon toast?"

We pulled on our overalls and sweaters and went into the kitchen, where my mother had already laid our mugs and plates. She was engaged in her rainy day ritual: making sangria. First she poured the orange juice out of the big white plastic pitcher into three empty peanut butter jars. Then she started chopping up all the oranges, lemons, and limes we had in the house. She let me pour the brandy over the fruit, Gisela threw in the sugar, and Lizzie came up for air long enough to pour the big bottle of red wine over everything. I cannot imagine drinking anything else on rainy days.

My mother went out onto the porch for her morning cigarette, and when my father came down he joined her while we played Go Fish; I could see them snuggling on the wicker settee. A few minutes later Mr. DeCuervo came down, looked out to the porch, and picked up an old magazine and started reading.

We decided to go play Monopoly in our room since the grown-ups didn't want to entertain us. After two hours, in which I rotted in jail and Lizzie forgot to charge rent, little Gisela beat us and the three of us went back to the kitchen for a snack. Rainy days were basically a series of snacks, more and less elaborate, punctuated by board games, card games, and whining. We drank soda and juice all day, ate cheese, bananas, cookies, bologna, graham crackers, Jiffy popcorn, hard-boiled eggs. The grownups ate cheese and crackers and drank sangria.

The daddies were reading in the two big armchairs, my mother had gone off to her room to sketch, and we were getting bored. When my mother came downstairs for a cigarette, I was writing my name in the honey that had spilled on the kitchen table, and Gisela and Lizzie were pulling the stuffing out of the hole in the bottom of the blue couch.

"Jesus Christ, Ellen, get your hands out of the goddamn honey. Liz, Gisela, that's absolutely unacceptable, you know that. Leave the poor couch alone. If you're so damn stir-crazy, go outside and dance in the rain."

The two men looked up, slowly focusing, as if from a great distance.

"Lila, really . . . ," said my father.

"Lila, it's pouring. We'll keep an eye on them now," said Mr. DeCuervo.

"Right. Like you were." My mother was grinning.

"Can we, Mommy, can we go in the rain? Can we take off our clothes and go in the rain?"

"Sure, go naked, there's no point in getting your clothes wet and no point in suits. There's not likely to be a big crowd in the yard."

We raced to the porch before my mother could get rational, stripped and ran whooping into the rain, leaping off the porch onto the muddy lawn, shouting and feeling superior to every child in Maine who had to stay indoors.

We played Goddessess-in-the-Rain, which consisted of caressing our bodies and screaming the names of everyone we knew, and we played ring-around-the-rosy and tag and red light/green light and catch, all deliciously slippery and surreal in the sheets of gray rain. Our parents watched us from the porch.

When we finally came in, thrilled with ourselves and the extent to which we were completely, profoundly wet, in every pore, they bundled us up and told us to dry our hair and get ready for dinner.

My mother brushed our hair, and then she made spaghetti sauce while my father made a salad and Mr. DeCuervo made a strawberry tart, piling the berries into a huge, red, shiny pyramid in the center of the pastry. We were in heaven. The grownups were laughing a lot, sipping their rosy drinks, tossing vegetables back and forth.

After dinner, my mother took us into the living room to dance, and then the power went off.

"Shit," said my father in the kitchen.

"Double shit," said Mr. DeCuervo, and we heard them stumbling around in the dark, laughing and cursing, until they came in with two flashlights.

"The cavalry is here, ladies," said Daddy, bowing to us all, twirling his flashlight.

"American and Argentine divisions, señora y señoritas."

I had never heard Mr. DeCuervo speak Spanish before, not even that little bit.

"Well then, I know I'm safe—from the bad guys, anyway. On the other hand . . . " My mother laughed, and the daddies put their arms around each other and they laughed too.

"On the other hand, what? What, Mommy?" I tugged at her the way I did when I was afraid of losing her in a big department store.

"Nothing, honey. Mommy was just being silly. Let's get ready for bed, munchkins. Then you can all talk for a while. We're shut down for the night, I'm sure."

The daddies accompanied us to the bathroom and whispered that we could skip everything except peeing, since there was no electricity. The two of them kissed us good night, my father's mustache tickling, Mr. DeCuervo's sliding over my cheek. My mother came into the room a moment later, and her face was as smooth and warm as a velvet cushion. We didn't stay awake for long. The rain dance and the eating and the storm had worn us out.

It was still dark when I woke up, but the rain had stopped and the power had returned and the light was burning in our hallway. It made me feel very grown-up and responsible, getting out of bed and going around the house, turning out the lights that no one else knew were on; I was conserving electricity.

I went into the bathroom and was squeezed by stomach cramps, probably from all the burnt popcorn kernels I had eaten. I sat on the toilet for a long time, watching a brown spider crawl along the wall; I'd knock him down and then watch him climb back up again, towards the towels. My cramps were better but not gone, so I decided to wake my mother. My father would have been more sympathetic, but he was the heavier sleeper, and by the time he understood what I was telling him, my mother would have her bathrobe on and be massaging my stomach kindly, though without the excited concern I felt was my due as a victim of illness.

I walked down to my parents' room, turning the hall light back on. I pushed open the creaky door and saw my mother spooned up against my father's back, as she always was, and Mr. DeCuervo spooned up against her, his arm over the covers, his other resting on top of her head.

I stood and looked and then backed out of the bedroom. They hadn't moved, the three of them breathing deeply, in unison. What was that, I thought, what did I see? I wanted to go back and take another look, to see it again, to make it disappear, to watch them carefully, until I understood.

My cramps were gone. I went back to my own bed, staring at Lizzie and Gisela, who looked in their sleep like little girl-versions of the two men I had just seen. Just sleeping, I thought, the grown-ups were just sleeping. Maybe Mr. DeCuervo's bed had collapsed, like ours did two summers ago. Or maybe it got wet in the storm. I thought I would never be able to fall asleep, but the next thing I remember is waking up to more rain and Lizzie and Gisela begging my mother to take us to the movies in town. We went to see *The Sound of Music*, which had been playing at the Bijou for about ten years.

I don't remember much else about the summer; all of the images run together. We went on swimming and fishing and taking the row-boat out for little adventures, and when the DeCuervos left I hugged Gisela but wasn't going to hug him, until he whispered in my ear, "Next year we'll bring up a motorboat and I'll teach you to water ski," and then I hugged him very hard and my mother put her hand on my head lightly, giving benediction.

The next summer, I went off to camp in July and wasn't there when the DeCuervos came. Lizzie said they had a good time with-out me. Then they couldn't come for a couple of summers in a row, and by the time they came again, Gisela and Lizzie were at camp with me in New Hampshire; the four grownups spent about a week together, and later I heard my father say that another vacation with Elvira DeCuervo would kill him, or he'd kill her. My mother said she wasn't so bad.

We saw them a little less after that. They came, Gisela and Mr. DeCuervo, to my high school graduation, to my mother's opening in Boston, my father's fiftieth birthday party, and then Lizzie's gradua-tion. When my mother went down to New York she'd have dinner with the three of them, she said, but sometimes her plans would change and they'd have to substitute lunch for dinner.

Gisela couldn't come to the funeral. She was in Argentina for the year, working with the architectural firm that Mr. DeCuervo's father had started.

After all the mourners left, Mr. DeCuervo gave us a sympathy note from Gisela, with a beautiful pen-and-ink of our mother inside it. The two men went into the living room and took out a bottle of Scotch and two glasses. It was like we weren't there; they put on Billie Holiday singing "Embraceable You," and they got down to serious drinking and grieving. Lizzie and I went into the kitchen and decided to eat everything sweet that people had brought over: brownies, strudel, pfeffernuesse, sweet potato pie, Mrs. Ellis's chocolate cake with chocolate mousse in the middle. We laid out two plates and two mugs of milk and got to it.

Lizzie said, "You know, when I was home in April, he called every day." She jerked her head toward the living room.

I couldn't tell if she approved or disapproved, and I didn't know what I thought about it either.

"She called him Bolivar."

"What? She always called him Gaucho, and so we didn't call him anything."

"I know, but she called him Bolivar. I heard her talking to him every fucking day, El, she called him Bolivar."

Tears were running down Lizzie's face, and I wished my mother were there to pat her soft fuzzy hair and keep her from choking on her tears. I held her hand across the table, still holding my fork in my other hand. I could feel my mother looking at me, smiling and narrowing her eyes a little, the way she did when I was balking. I dropped the fork onto my plate and went over and hugged Lizzie, who leaned into me as though her spine had collapsed.

"I asked her about it after the third call," she said into my shoulder.

"What'd she say?" I straightened Lizzie up so I could hear her.

"She said, 'Of course he calls at noon. He knows that's when I'm feeling strongest.' And I told her that's not what I meant, that I hadn't known they were so close."

"You said that?"

"Yeah. And she said, 'Honey, nobody loves me more than Bolivar.' And I didn't know what to say, so I just sat there feeling like 'Do I really want to hear this?' and then she fell asleep."

"So what do you think?"

"I don't know. I was getting ready to ask her again—"

"You're amazing, Lizzie," I interrupted. She really is, she's so quiet, but she goes and has conversations I can't even imagine having.

"But I didn't have to ask because she brought it up herself, the next day after he called. She got off the phone, looking just so exhausted, she was sweating but she was smiling. She was staring out at the crab apple trees in the yard, and she said, 'There were apple trees in bloom when I met Bolivar, and the trees were right where the sculpture needed to be in the courtyard, and so he offered to get rid of the trees and I said that seemed arrogant and he said that they'd replant them. So I said, "Okay," and he said, "What's so bad about arrogance?" And the first time he and Daddy met, the two of them drank Scotch and watched soccer while I made dinner. And then they washed up, just like at the cabin. And when the two of them are in the room together and you two girls are with us, I know that I am living in a state of grace.'"

"She said that? She said 'in a state of grace'? Mommy said that?" "Yes, Ellen. Christ, what do you think, I'm making up interesting deathbed statements?" Lizzie hates to be interrupted, especially by me.

"Sorry. Go on."

"Anyway, we were talking and I sort of asked what were we actually talking about. I mean, close friends or very close friends, and she just laughed. You know how she'd look at us like she knew exactly where we were going when we said we were going to a friend's house for the afternoon but we were really going to drink Boone's Farm and skinny-dip at the quarry? Well, she looked just like that and she took my hand. Her hand was so light, El. And she said that the three of them loved each other, each differently, and that they were both amazing men, each special, each deserving love and appreciation. She said that she thought Daddy was the most wonderful husband a woman could have and that she was very glad we had him as a father. And I asked her how she could do it, love them both, and how they could stand it. And she said, 'Love is not a pie, honey. I love you and Ellen differently because you are different people, wonderful people, but not at all the same. And so who I am with each of you is different, unique to us. I don't choose between you. And it's the same way with Daddy and Bolivar. People think that it can't be that way, but it can. You just have to find the right people.' And then she shut her eyes for the afternoon. Your eyes are bugging out, El."

"Well, Jesus, I guess so. I mean, I knew . . . "

"You knew? And you didn't tell me?"

"You were eight or something, Lizzie, what was I supposed to say? I didn't even know what I knew then."

"So, what did you know?" Lizzie was very serious. It was a real breach of our rules not to share inside dirt about our parents, especially our mother; we were always trying to figure her out.

I didn't know how to tell her about the three of them; that was even less normal than her having an affair with Mr. DeCuervo with Daddy's permission. I couldn't even think of the words to describe what I had seen, so I just said, "I saw Mommy and Mr. DeCuervo kissing one night after we were in bed."

"Really? Where was Daddy?"

"I don't know. But wherever he was, obviously he knew what was going on. I mean, that's what Mommy was telling you, right? That Daddy knew and that it was okay with him."

"Yeah. Jesus."

I went back to my chair and sat down. We were halfway through the strudel when the two men came in. There were drunk but not incoherent. They just weren't their normal selves, but I guess we weren't either, with our eyes puffy and red and all this destroyed food around us.

"Beautiful girls," Mr. DeCuervo said to my father. They were hanging in the doorway, one on each side.

"They are, they really are. And smart, couldn't find smarter girls."

My father went on and on about how smart we were. Lizzie and I just looked at each other, embarrassed but not displeased.

"Ellen has Lila's mouth," Mr. DeCuervo said. "You have your mother's mouth, with the right side going up a little more than the left. Exquisite."

My father was nodding his head, like this was the greatest truth ever told. And Daddy turned to Lizzie and said, "And you have your mother's eyes. Since the day you were born and I looked right into them, I thought, 'My God, she's got Lila's eyes, but blue, not green.'"

And Mr. DeCuervo was nodding away, of course. I wondered if they were going to do a complete autopsy, but they stopped.

My father came over to the table and put one hand on each of us. "You girls made your mother incredibly happy. There was nothing she ever created that gave her more pride and joy than you two. And she thought that you were both so special . . . " He started crying, and Mr. DeCuervo put an arm around his waist and picked up for him.

"She did, she had two big pictures of you in her studio, nothing else. And you know, she expected us all to grieve, but you know how much she wanted you to enjoy, too. To enjoy everything, every meal, every drink, every sunrise, every kiss . . . " He started crying too.

"We're gonna lie down for a while, girls. Maybe later we'll have dinner or something." My father kissed us both, wet and rough, and the two of them went down the hall.

Lizzie and I looked at each other again.

"Wanna get drunk?" I said.

"No, I don't think so. I guess I'll go lie down for a while too, unless you want company." She looked like she was about to sleep standing up, so I shook my head. I was planning on calling John anyway.

Lizzie came over and hugged me, hard, and I hugged her back and brushed the chocolate crumbs out of her hair.

Sitting alone in the kitchen, I thought about John, about telling him about my mother and her affair and how the two men were sacked out in my parents' bed, probably snoring. And I could hear John's silence and I knew that he would think my father must not have really loved my mother if he'd let her go with another man; or that my mother must have been a real bitch, forcing my father to tolerate an affair "right in his own home," John would think, maybe even say. I thought I ought to call him before I got myself completely enraged over a conversation that hadn't taken place. Lizzie would say I was projecting anyway.

I called, and John was very sweet, asking how I was feeling, how the memorial service had gone, how my father was. And I told him all that and then I knew I couldn't tell him the rest and that I couldn't marry a man I couldn't tell this story to.

"I'm so sorry, Ellen," he said. "You must be very upset. What a difficult day for you."

I realize that was a perfectly normal response, it just was all wrong for me. I didn't come from a normal family, I wasn't ready to get normal.

I felt terrible, hurting John, but I couldn't marry him just because I didn't want to hurt him, so I said, "And that's not the worst of it, John. I can't marry you, I really can't. I know this is pretty hard to listen to over the phone. . . ." I couldn't think what else to say.

"Ellen, let's talk about this when you get back to Boston. I know what kind of a strain you must be under. I had the feeling that you were unhappy about some of Mother's ideas. We can work something out when you get back."

"I know you think this is because of my mother's death, and it is, but not the way you think. John, I just can't marry you. I'm not going to wear your mother's dress and I'm not going to marry you and I'm very sorry."

He was quiet for a long time, and then he said, "I don't understand, Ellen. We've already ordered the invitations." And I knew that I was right. If he had said, "Fuck this, I'm coming to see you tonight," or even, "I don't know what you're talking about, but I want to marry you anyway," I'd probably have changed my mind before I got off the phone. But as it was, I said goodbye sort of quietly and hung up.

It was like two funerals in one day. I sat at the table, poking the cake into little shapes and then knocking them over. My mother would have sent me out for a walk. I'd started clearing the stuff away when my father and Mr. DeCuervo appeared, looking more together.

"How about some gin rummy, El?" my father said.

"If you're up for it," said Mr. DeCuervo.

"Okay," I said. "I just broke up with John Wescott."

"Oh?"

I couldn't tell which one spoke.

"I told him that I didn't think we'd make each other happy."

Which was what I had meant to say.

My father hugged me and said, "I'm sorry that it's hard for you. You did the right thing." Then he turned to Mr. DeCuervo and said, "Did she know how to call them, or what? Your mother knew that you weren't going to marry that guy."

"She was almost always right, Dan."

"Almost always, not quite," said my father, and the two of them laughed at some private joke and shook hands like a pair of old boxers.

"So, you deal," my father said, leaning back in his chair.

"Penny a point," said Mr. DeCuervo.

QUESTIONS FOR DISCUSSION

Is the speaker in Larkin's poem affirming or denying that "What will survive of us is love"? (118)

1. Why does seeing the earl's ungauntleted hand holding his wife's produce "a sharp tender shock"? (117)

2. What distinction is the speaker making between looking at the tomb and reading it?

3. Why does the speaker believe that time "has transfigured" the figures on the tomb "into / Untruth"? (118)

4. Why does the speaker conclude by saying that the tomb's figures prove, "Our almost-instinct almost true"? (118)

What does Lila mean when she tells Lizzie, "Love is not a pie, honey"? (133)

1. Why does the "summer cabin routine" stay with Ellen "as a model of leisure, of life being enjoyed"? (122)

2. Why do Ellen and Lizzie "watch, not even looking at each other" when their mother dances with Mr. DeCuervo? (124)

3. Why can't Ellen tell Lizzie about seeing their parents and Mr. DeCuervo sharing a bed?

4. At the end of the story, why does Ellen decide not to marry John?

FOR FURTHER REFLECTION

1. Do you agree with Lila that it is possible to have a happy romance among three people?

2. How much explanation of their private lives do parents owe their children?

3. Do you believe that love survives death?

4. What obstacles do we face when we try to understand the lives of previous generations?

ART
ART

One of the perennial debates regarding art—especially literary art that depicts the activities of individuals and their relations in society—concerns whether or not it should provide moral guidance to its audiences. This debate is closely allied with another: whether art has a responsibility to portray the world as it really is, or whether it should only be concerned with skillfully adhering to certain aesthetic standards, the so-called "art for art's sake" position. In the end, these debates ask us to consider the much broader question of art's utility: What purpose does art serve? The following selections by George Eliot and Oscar Wilde directly engage with these concerns.

In her novel *Adam Bede* (1859), British author **George Eliot** (1819–1880) inserts a chapter titled "In Which the Story Pauses a Little," where she explains to the reader why she portrays characters as she does. She rejects the idea that a novel should polish and improve the traits of characters, offering them as exemplary types. Instead, she asserts the realism of her creations, flaws and all. For Eliot, realism in literature is not just a stylistic choice but a fundamental responsibility that has the potential to influence the moral choices of readers.

Vivian, the principal speaker in Irish writer **Oscar Wilde's** (1854–1900) dialogue "The Decay of Lying" (1889), is not concerned with art's ability to influence moral behavior. He rejects the value of art for both human life and the natural world. He argues that art should rely only on itself and operate independently of the real world. Moreover, he states that human life and nature both imitate art, which he sees as the only true source of originality. Wilde's character so thoroughly disputes Eliot's ethical imperative that he even claims that compared to art, humanity offers nothing original or unique.

In Which the Story Pauses a Little

George Eliot

This Rector of Broxton is little better than a pagan!" I hear one of my readers exclaim. "How much more edifying it would have been if you had made him give Arthur some truly spiritual advice. You might have put into his mouth the most beautiful things—quite as good as reading a sermon."

Certainly I could, if I held it the highest vocation of the novelist to represent things as they never have been and never will be. Then, of course, I might refashion life and character entirely after my own liking; I might select the most unexceptionable type of clergyman, and put my own admirable opinions into his mouth on all occasions. But it happens, on the contrary, that my strongest effort is to avoid any such arbitrary picture, and to give a faithful account of men and things as they have mirrored themselves in my mind. The mirror is doubtless defective; the outlines will sometimes be disturbed, the reflection faint or confused; but I feel as much bound to tell you as precisely as I can what that reflection is, as if I were in the witness box narrating my experience on oath.

Sixty years ago—it is a long time, so no wonder things have changed—all clergymen were not zealous; indeed, there is reason to believe that the number of zealous clergymen was small, and it is probable that if one among the small minority had owned the livings of Broxton and Hayslope in the year 1799, you would have liked him no better than you like Mr. Irwine. Ten to one, you would have thought him a tasteless, indiscreet, methodistical man. It is so very rarely that facts hit that nice medium required by our own enlightened opinions and refined taste! Perhaps you will say, "Do improve the facts a little, then; make them more accordant with those correct views which it is our privilege to possess. The world is not just what we like; do touch it up with a tasteful pencil, and make believe it is not quite such a mixed entangled affair. Let all people who hold unexceptionable opinions act unexceptionably. Let your most faulty characters always be on the wrong side, and your virtuous ones on the right. Then we shall see at a glance whom we are to condemn, and whom we are to approve. Then we shall be able to admire, without the slightest disturbance of our prepossessions: we shall hate and despise with that true ruminant relish which belongs to undoubting confidence."

But, my good friend, what will you do then with your fellow parishioner who opposes your husband in the vestry?—with your newly appointed vicar, whose style of preaching you find painfully below that of his regretted predecessor?—with the honest servant who worries your soul with her one failing?—with your neighbour, Mrs. Green, who was really kind to you in your last illness, but has said several ill-natured things about you since your convalescence?—nay, with your excellent husband himself, who has other irritating habits besides that of not wiping his shoes? These fellow mortals, every one, must be accepted as they are: you can neither straighten their noses, nor brighten their wit, nor rectify their dispositions; and it is these people—amongst whom your life is passed—that it is needful you should tolerate, pity, and love: it is these more or less ugly, stupid, inconsistent people, whose movements of goodness you should be able to admire—for whom you should cherish all possible hopes, all possible patience. And I would not, even if I had the choice, be the clever novelist who could create a world so much better than this, in which we get up in the morning to do our daily work, that you would be likely to turn a harder, colder eye on the dusty streets and the common green fields—on the real breathing men and women, who can be chilled by your indifference or injured by your prejudice; who can be cheered and helped onward by your fellow-feeling, your forbearance, your outspoken, brave justice.

So I am content to tell my simple story, without trying to make things seem better than they were; dreading nothing, indeed, but falsity, which in spite of one's best efforts, there is reason to dread. Falsehood is so easy, truth so difficult. The pencil is conscious of a delightful facility in drawing a griffin—the longer the claws, and the larger the wings, the better; but that marvellous facility which we mistook for genius is apt to forsake us when we want to draw a real unexaggerated lion. Examine your words well, and you will find that even when you have no motive to be false, it is a very hard thing to say the exact truth, even about your own immediate feelings—much harder than to say something fine about them which is *not* the exact truth.

It is for this rare, precious quality of truthfulness that I delight in many Dutch paintings, which lofty-minded people despise. I find a source of delicious sympathy in these faithful pictures of a monotonous homely existence, which has been the fate of so many more among my fellow mortals than a life of pomp or of absolute indigence, of tragic suffering or of world-stirring actions. I turn, without shrinking, from cloud-borne angels, from prophets, sibyls, and heroic warriors, to an old woman bending over her flowerpot, or eating her solitary dinner, while the noonday light, softened perhaps by a screen of leaves, falls on her mobcap, and just touches the rim of her spinning wheel, and her stone jug, and all those cheap common things which are the precious necessaries of life to her;—or I turn to that village wedding, kept between four brown walls, where an awkward bridegroom opens the dance with a high-shouldered, broadfaced bride, while elderly and middle-aged friends look on, with very irregular noses and lips, and probably with quart-pots in their hands, but with an expression of unmistakable contentment and goodwill. "Foh!" says my idealistic friend, "what vulgar details! What good is there in taking all these pains to give an exact likeness of old women and clowns? What a low phase of life!—what clumsy, ugly people!"

But bless us, things may be lovable that are not altogether handsome, I hope? I am not at all sure that the majority of the human race have not been ugly, and even among those "lords of their kind," the British, squat figures, ill-shapen nostrils, and dingy complexions are not startling exceptions. Yet there is a great deal of family love amongst us. I have a friend or two whose class of features is such that the Apollo curl on the summit of their brows would be decidedly trying; yet to my certain knowledge tender hearts have beaten for them, and their miniatures—flattering, but still not lovely—are kissed in secret by motherly lips. I have seen many an excellent matron, who could never in her best days have been handsome, and yet she had a packet of yellow love letters in a private drawer, and sweet children showered kisses on her sallow cheeks. And I believe there have been plenty of young heroes, of middle stature and feeble beards, who have felt quite sure they could never love anything more insignificant than a Diana, and yet have found themselves in middle life happily settled with a wife who waddles! Yes! thank God; human feeling is like the mighty rivers that bless the earth: it does not wait for beauty—it flows with resistless force and brings beauty with it.

All honour and reverence to the divine beauty of form! Let us cultivate it to the utmost in men, women, and children—in our gardens and in our houses. But let us love that other beauty too, which lies in no secret of proportion, but in the secret of deep human sympathy. Paint us an angel, if you can, with a floating violet robe, and a face paled by the celestial light; paint us yet oftener a Madonna, turning her mild face upward and opening her arms to welcome the divine glory; but do not impose on us any aesthetic rules which shall banish from the region of Art those old women scraping carrots with their work-worn hands, those heavy clowns taking holiday in a dingy pothouse, those rounded backs and stupid weather-beaten faces that have bent over the spade and done the rough work of the world—those homes with their tin pans, their brown pitchers, their rough curs, and their clusters of onions. In this world there are so many of these common coarse people, who have no picturesque sentimental wretchedness! It is so needful we should remember their existence, else we may happen to leave them quite out of our religion and philosophy, and frame lofty theories which only fit a world of extremes. Therefore let Art always remind us of them; therefore let us always have men ready to give the loving pains of a life to the faithful representing of commonplace things—men who see beauty in these commonplace things, and delight in showing how kindly the light of heaven falls on them. There are few prophets in the world; few sublimely beautiful women; few heroes. I can't afford to give all my love and reverence to such rarities: I want a great deal of those feelings for my everyday fellow men, especially for the few in the foreground of the great multitude, whose faces I know, whose hands I touch, for whom I have to make way with kindly courtesy. Neither are picturesque lazzaroni or romantic criminals half so frequent as your common labourer, who gets his own bread, and eats it vulgarly but creditably with his own pocketknife. It is more needful that I should have a fibre of sympathy connecting me with that vulgar citizen who weighs out my sugar in a vilely assorted cravat and waistcoat, than with the handsomest rascal in red scarf and green feathers;—more needful that my heart should swell with loving admiration at some trait of gentle goodness in the faulty people who sit at the same hearth with me, or in the clergyman of my own parish, who is perhaps rather too corpulent, and in other respects is not an Oberlin or a Tillotson, than at the deeds of heroes whom I shall never know except by hearsay, or at the sublimest abstract of all clerical graces that was ever conceived by an able novelist. . . .

* * *

Adam, you perceive, was a warm admirer, perhaps a partial judge, of Mr. Irwine, as, happily, some of us still are of the people we have known familiarly. Doubtless it will be despised as a weakness by that lofty order of minds who pant after the ideal, and are oppressed by a general sense that their emotions are of too exquisite a character to find fit objects among their everyday fellow men. I have often been favoured with the confidence of these select natures, and find them to concur in the experience that great men are over-estimated and small men are insupportable; that if you would love a woman without ever looking back on your love as a folly, she must die while you are courting her; and if you would maintain the slightest belief in human heroism, you must never make a pilgrimage to see the hero. I confess I have often meanly shrunk from confessing to these accomplished and acute gentlemen what my own experience has been. I am afraid I have often smiled with hypocritical assent, and gratified them with an epigram on the fleeting nature of our illusions, which anyone moderately acquainted with French literature can command at a moment's notice. Human converse, I think some wise man has remarked, is not rigidly sincere. But I herewith discharge my conscience, and declare, that I have had quite enthusiastic movements of admiration towards old gentlemen who spoke the worst English, who were occasionally fretful in their temper, and who had never moved in a higher sphere of influence than that of parish overseer; and that the way in which I have come to the conclusion that human nature is lovable—the way I have learnt something of its deep pathos, its sublime mysteries—has been by living a great deal among people more or less commonplace and vulgar, of whom you would perhaps hear nothing very surprising if you were to inquire about them in the neighbourhoods where they dwelt. Ten to one most of the small shopkeepers in their vicinity saw nothing at all in them. For I have observed this remarkable coincidence, that the select natures who pant after the ideal, and find nothing in pantaloons or petticoats great enough to command their reverence and love, are curiously in unison with the narrowest and pettiest. For example, I have often heard Mr. Gedge, the landlord of the Royal Oak, who used to turn a bloodshot eye on his neighbours in the village of Shepperton, sum up his opinion of the people in his own parish—and they were all the people he knew—in these emphatic words: "Ay, sir, I've said it often, and I'll say it again, they're a poor lot i' this parish—a poor lot, sir, big and little." I think he had a dim idea that if he could migrate to a distant parish, he might find neighbours worthy of him; and indeed he did subsequently transfer himself to the Saracen's Head, which was doing a thriving business in the back street of a neighbouring market-town. But, oddly enough, he has found the people up that back street of precisely the same stamp as the inhabitants of Shepperton—"a poor lot, sir, big and little, and them as comes for a go o' gin are no better than them as comes for a pint o' twopenny—a poor lot."

The Decay of Lying
(selection)

Oscar Wilde

A Dialogue

Persons: Cyril and Vivian.

Scene: The library of a country house in Nottinghamshire.

Cyril *(coming in through the open window from the terrace):* My dear Vivian, don't coop yourself up all day in the library. It is a perfectly lovely afternoon. The air is exquisite. There is a mist upon the woods, like the purple bloom upon a plum. Let us go and lie on the grass and smoke cigarettes and enjoy Nature.

Vivian: Enjoy Nature! I am glad to say that I have entirely lost that faculty. People tell us that Art makes us love Nature more than we loved her before; that it reveals her secrets to us; and that after a careful study of Corot and Constable we see things in her that had escaped our observation. My own experience is that the more we study Art, the less we care for Nature. What Art really reveals to us is Nature's lack of design, her curious crudities, her extraordinary monotony, her absolutely unfinished condition. Nature has good intentions, of course, but, as Aristotle once said, she cannot carry them out. When I look at a landscape I cannot help seeing all its defects. It is fortunate for us, however, that Nature is so imperfect, as otherwise we should have no art at all. Art is our spirited protest, our gallant attempt to teach Nature her proper place. As for the infinite variety of Nature, that is a pure myth. It is not to be found in Nature herself. It resides in the imagination, or fancy, or cultivated blindness of the man who looks at her.

Cyril: Well, you need not look at the landscape. You can lie on the grass and smoke and talk.

Vivian: But Nature is so uncomfortable. Grass is hard and lumpy and damp, and full of dreadful black insects. Why, even Morris's poorest workman could make you a more comfortable seat than the whole of Nature can. Nature pales before the furniture of "the street which from Oxford has borrowed its name," as the poet you love so much once vilely phrased it. I don't complain. If Nature had been comfortable, mankind would never have invented architecture, and I prefer houses to the open air. In a house we all feel of the proper proportions. Everything is subordinated to us, fashioned for our use and our pleasure. Egotism itself, which is so necessary to a proper sense of human dignity, is entirely the result of indoor life. Out of doors one becomes abstract and impersonal. One's individuality absolutely leaves one. And then Nature is so indifferent, so unappreciative. Whenever I am walking in the park here, I always feel that I am no more to her than the cattle that browse on the slope, or the burdock that blooms in the ditch. Nothing is more evident than that Nature hates Mind. Thinking is the most unhealthy thing in the world, and people die of it just as they die of any other disease. Fortunately, in England at any rate, thought is not catching. Our splendid physique as a people is entirely due to our national stupidity. I only hope we shall be able to keep this great historic bulwark of our happiness for many years to come; but I am afraid that we are beginning to be over-educated; at least everybody who is incapable of learning has taken to teaching—that is really what our enthusiasm for education has come to. In the meantime, you had better go back to your wearisome uncomfortable Nature, and leave me to correct my proofs.

Cyril: Writing an article! That is not very consistent after what you have just said.

Vivian: Who wants to be consistent? The dullard and the doctrinaire, the tedious people who carry out their principles to the bitter end of action, to the *reductio ad absurdum* of practice. Not I. Like

Emerson, I write over the door of my library the word "Whim." Besides, my article is really a most salutary and valuable warning. If it is attended to, there may be a new Renaissance of Art.

Cyril: What is the subject?

Vivian: I intend to call it "The Decay of Lying: A Protest."

Cyril: Lying! I should have thought that our politicians kept up that habit.

Vivian: I assure you that they do not. They never rise beyond the level of misrepresentation, and actually condescend to prove, to discuss, to argue. How different from the temper of the true liar, with his frank, fearless statements, his superb irresponsibility, his healthy, natural disdain of proof of any kind! After all, what is a fine lie? Simply that which is its own evidence. If a man is sufficiently unimaginative to produce evidence in support of a lie, he might just as well speak the truth at once. No, the politicians won't do. Something may, perhaps, be urged on behalf of the Bar. The mantle of the Sophist has fallen on its members. Their feigned ardours and unreal rhetoric are delightful. They can make the worse appear the better cause, as though they were fresh from Leontine schools, and have been known to wrest from reluctant juries triumphant verdicts of acquittal for their clients, even when those clients, as often happens, were clearly and unmistakably innocent. But they are briefed by the prosaic, and are not ashamed to appeal to precedent. In spite of their endeavours, the truth will out. Newspapers, even, have degenerated. They may now be absolutely relied upon. One feels it as one wades through their columns. It is always the unreadable that occurs. I am afraid that there is not much to be said in favour of either the lawyer or the journalist. Besides, what I am pleading for is Lying in art. Shall I read you what I have written? It might do you a great deal of good.

Cyril: Certainly, if you give me a cigarette. Thanks. By the way, what magazine do you intend it for?

Vivian: For the *Retrospective Review.* I think I told you that the elect had revived it.

Cyril: Whom do you mean by "the elect"?

Vivian: Oh, The Tired Hedonists, of course. It is a club to which I belong. We are supposed to wear faded roses in our buttonholes when we meet, and to have a sort of cult for Domitian. I am afraid you are not eligible. You are too fond of simple pleasures.

Cyril: I should be blackballed on the ground of animal spirits, I suppose?

Vivian: Probably. Besides, you are a little too old. We don't admit anybody who is of the usual age.

Cyril: Well, I should fancy you are all a good deal bored with each other.

Vivian: We are. That is one of the objects of the club. Now, if you promise not to interrupt too often, I will read you my article.

Cyril: You will find me all attention.

Vivian (reading in a very clear, musical voice): "THE DECAY OF LYING: A PROTEST.—One of the chief causes that can be assigned for the curiously commonplace character of most of the literature of our age is undoubtedly the decay of Lying as an art, a science, and a social pleasure. The ancient historians gave us delightful fiction in the form of fact; the modern novelist presents us with dull facts under the guise of fiction. The blue book is rapidly becoming his ideal both for method and manner. He has his tedious *document humain*, his miserable little *coin de la création*, into which he peers with his microscope. He is to be found at the Librairie Nationale, or at the British Museum, shamelessly reading up his subject. He has not even the courage of other people's ideas, but insists on going directly to life for everything, and ultimately, between encyclopaedias and personal experience, he comes to the ground, having drawn his types from the family circle or from the weekly washerwoman, and having acquired an amount of useful information from which never, even in his most meditative moments, can he thoroughly free himself.

"The loss that results to literature in general from this false ideal of our time can hardly be overestimated. People have a careless way of talking about a 'born liar,' just as they talk about a 'born poet.' But in both cases they are wrong. Lying and poetry are arts—arts, as Plato saw, not unconnected with each other—and they require the most careful study, the most disinterested devotion. Indeed, they have their technique, just as the more material arts of painting and sculpture have, their subtle secrets of form and colour, their craft mysteries, their deliberate artistic methods. As one knows the poet by his fine music, so one can recognise the liar by his rich rhythmic utterance, and in neither case will the casual inspiration of the moment suffice. Here, as elsewhere, practice must precede perfection. But in modern days while the fashion of writing poetry has become far too common, and should, if possible, be discouraged, the fashion of lying has almost fallen into disrepute. Many a young man starts in life with a natural gift for exaggeration which, if nurtured in congenial and sympathetic surroundings, or by the imitation of the best models, might grow into something really great and wonderful. But, as a rule, he comes to nothing. He either falls into careless habits of accuracy—" *Cyril:* My dear fellow!

Vivian: Please don't interrupt in the middle of a sentence. "He either falls into careless habits of accuracy, or takes to frequenting the society of the aged and the well-informed. Both things are equally fatal to his imagination, as indeed they would be fatal to the imagination of anybody, and in a short time he develops a morbid and unhealthy faculty of truth-telling, begins to verify all statements made in his presence, has no hesitation in contradicting people who are much younger than himself, and often ends by writing novels which are so lifelike that no one can possibly believe in their probability. This is no isolated instance that we are giving. It is simply one example out of many; and if something cannot be done to check, or at least to modify, our monstrous worship of facts, Art will become sterile, and beauty will pass away from the land.

*　*　*

Cyril: Do you object to modernity of form, then?

Vivian: Yes. It is a huge price to pay for a very poor result. Pure modernity of form is always somewhat vulgarizing. It cannot help being so. The public imagine that, because they are interested in their immediate surroundings, Art should be interested in them also, and should take them as her subject matter. But the mere fact that they are interested in these things makes them unsuitable subjects for Art. The only beautiful things, as somebody once said, are the things that do not concern us. As long as a thing is useful or necessary to us, or affects us in any way, either for pain or for pleasure, or appeals strongly to our sympathies, or is a vital part of the environment in which we live, it is outside the proper sphere of art. To art's subject matter we should be more or less indifferent. We should, at any rate, have no preferences, no prejudices, no partisan feeling of any kind. It is exactly because Hecuba is nothing to us that her sorrows are such an admirable motive for a tragedy. I do not know anything in the whole history of literature sadder than the artistic career of Charles Reade. He wrote one beautiful book, *The Cloister and the Hearth*, a book as much above *Romola* as *Romola* is above *Daniel Deronda*, and wasted the rest of his life in a foolish attempt to be modern, to draw public attention to the state of our convict prisons, and the management of our private lunatic asylums. Charles Dickens was depressing enough in all conscience when he tried to arouse our sympathy for the victims of the poor law administration; but Charles Reade, an artist, a scholar, a man with a true sense of beauty, raging and roaring over the abuses of contemporary life like a common pamphleteer or a sensational journalist, is really a sight for the angels to weep over. Believe me, my dear Cyril, modernity of form and modernity of subject matter are entirely and absolutely wrong. We have mistaken the common livery of the age for the vesture of the Muses, and spend our days in the sordid streets and hideous suburbs of our vile cities when we should be out on the hillside with Apollo. Certainly we are a degraded race, and have sold our birthright for a mess of facts.

Cyril: There is something in what you say, and there is no doubt that whatever amusement we may find in reading a purely modern novel, we have rarely any artistic pleasure in rereading it. And this is perhaps the best rough test of what is literature and what is not. If one cannot enjoy reading a book over and over again, there is no use reading it at all. But what do you say about the return to Life and Nature? This is the panacea that is always being recommended to us.

Vivian: I will read you what I say on that subject. The passage comes later on in the article, but I may as well give it to you now:

"The popular cry of our time is 'Let us return to Life and Nature; they will recreate Art for us, and send the red blood coursing through her veins; they will shoe her feet with swiftness and make her hand strong.' But, alas! we are mistaken in our amiable and well-meaning efforts. Nature is always behind the age. And as for Life, she is the solvent that breaks up Art, the enemy that lays waste her house."

Cyril: What do you mean by saying that Nature is always behind the age?

Vivian: Well, perhaps that is rather cryptic. What I mean is this. If we take Nature to mean natural simple instinct as opposed to self-conscious culture, the work produced under this influence is always old-fashioned, antiquated, and out of date. One touch of Nature may make the whole world kin, but two touches of Nature will destroy any work of Art. If, on the other hand, we regard Nature as the collection of phenomena external to man, people only discover in her what they bring to her. She has no suggestions of her own. Wordsworth went to the lakes, but he was never a lake poet. He found in stones the sermons he had already hidden there. He went moralizing about the district, but his good work was produced when he returned, not to Nature but to poetry. Poetry gave him "Laodamia," and the fine sonnets, and the great Ode, such as it is. Nature gave him "Martha Ray" and "Peter Bell," and the address to Mr. Wilkinson's spade.

Cyril: I think that view might be questioned. I am rather inclined to believe in "the impulse from a vernal wood," though of course the artistic value of such an impulse depends entirely on the kind of temperament that receives it, so that the return to Nature would come to mean simply the advance to a great personality. You would agree with that, I fancy. However, proceed with your article.

Vivian (reading): "Art begins with abstract decoration, with purely imaginative and pleasurable work dealing with what is unreal and nonexistent. This is the first stage. Then Life becomes fascinated with this new wonder, and asks to be admitted into the charmed circle. Art takes life as part of her rough material, recreates it, and refashions it in fresh forms, is absolutely indifferent to fact, invents, imagines, dreams, and keeps between herself and reality the impenetrable barrier of beautiful style, of decorative or ideal treatment. The third stage is when Life gets the upper hand, and drives Art out into the wilderness. This is the true decadence, and it is from this that we are now suffering.

* * *

155

Vivian (still reading): "Now, everything is changed. Facts are not merely finding a footing-place in history, but they are usurping the domain of Fancy, and have invaded the kingdom of Romance. Their chilling touch is over everything. They are vulgarizing mankind. The crude commercialism of America, its materialising spirit, its indifference to the poetical side of things, and its lack of imagination and of high unattainable ideals, are entirely due to that country having adopted for its national hero a man who, according to his own confession, was incapable of telling a lie, and it is not too much to say that the story of George Washington and the cherry tree has done more harm, and in a shorter space of time, than any other moral tale in the whole of literature."

Cyril: My dear boy!

Vivian: I assure you it is the case, and the amusing part of the whole thing is that the story of the cherry tree is an absolute myth. However, you must not think that I am too despondent about the artistic future either of America or of our own country. Listen to this:

"That some change will take place before this century has drawn to its close we have no doubt whatsoever. Bored by the tedious and improving conversation of those who have neither the wit to exaggerate nor the genius to romance, tired of the intelligent person whose reminiscences are always based upon memory, whose statements are invariably limited by probability, and who is at any time liable to be corroborated by the merest Philistine who happens to be present, Society sooner or later must return to its lost leader, the cultured and fascinating liar. Who he was who first, without ever having gone out to the rude chase, told the wandering cavemen at sunset how he had dragged the Megatherium from the purple darkness of its jasper cave, or slain the Mammoth in single combat and brought back its gilded tusks, we cannot tell, and not one of our modern anthropologists, for all their much-boasted science, has had the ordinary courage to tell us. Whatever was his name or race, he certainly was the true founder of social intercourse. For the aim of the liar is simply to charm, to delight, to give pleasure. He is the very basis of civilized society, and without him a dinner party, even at the mansions of the great, is as dull as a lecture at the Royal Society, or a debate at the Incorporated Authors, or one of Mr. Burnand's farcical comedies.

"Nor will he be welcomed by society alone. Art, breaking from the prisonhouse of realism, will run to greet him, and will kiss his false, beautiful lips, knowing that he alone is in possession of the great secret of all her manifestations, the secret that Truth is entirely and absolutely a matter of style; while Life—poor, probable, uninteresting human life—tired of repeating herself for the benefit of Mr. Herbert Spencer, scientific historians, and the compilers of statistics in general, will follow meekly after him, and try to reproduce, in her own simple and untutored way, some of the marvels of which he talks.

"No doubt there will always be critics who, like a certain writer in the *Saturday Review,* will gravely censure the teller of fairy tales for his defective knowledge of natural history, who will measure imaginative work by their own lack of any imaginative faculty, and will hold up their ink-stained hands in horror if some honest gentleman, who has never been farther than the yew trees of his own garden, pens a fascinating book of travels like Sir John Mandeville, or, like great Raleigh, writes a whole history of the world, without knowing anything whatsoever about the past. To excuse themselves they will try and shelter under the shield of him who made Prospero the magician, and gave him Caliban and Ariel as his servants, who heard the Tritons blowing their horns round the coral reefs of the Enchanted Isle, and the fairies singing to each other in a wood near Athens, who led the phantom kings in dim procession across the misty Scottish heath, and hid Hecate in a cave with the weird sisters. They will call upon Shakespeare—they always do—and will quote that hackneyed passage forgetting that this unfortunate aphorism about Art holding the mirror up to Nature, is deliberately said by Hamlet in order to convince the bystanders of his absolute insanity in all art matters."

Cyril: Ahem! Another cigarette, please.

Vivian: My dear fellow, whatever you may say, it is merely a dramatic utterance, and no more represents Shakespeare's real views upon art than the speeches of Iago represent his real views upon morals. But let me get to the end of the passage:

"Art finds her own perfection within, and not outside of, herself. She is not to be judged by any external standard of resemblance. She is a veil, rather than a mirror. She has flowers that no forests know of, birds that no woodland possesses. She makes and unmakes many worlds, and can draw the moon from heaven with a scarlet thread. Hers are the 'forms more real than living man,' and hers the great archetypes of which things that have existence are but unfinished copies. Nature has, in her eyes, no laws, no uniformity. She can work miracles at her will, and when she calls monsters from the deep they come. She can bid the almond tree blossom in winter, and send the snow upon the ripe cornfield. At her word the frost lays its silver finger on the burning mouth of June, and the winged lions creep out from the hollows of the Lydian hills. The dryads peer from the thicket as she passes by, and the brown fauns smile strangely at her when she comes near them. She has hawk-faced gods that worship her, and the centaurs gallop at her side."

Cyril: I like that. I can see it. Is that the end?

Vivian: No. There is one more passage, but it is purely practical. It simply suggests some methods by which we could revive this lost art of Lying.

Cyril: Well, before you read it to me, I should like to ask you a question. What do you mean by saying that life, "poor, probable, uninteresting human life," will try to reproduce the marvels of art? I can quite understand your objection to art being treated as a mirror. You think it would reduce genius to the position of a cracked looking glass. But you don't mean to say that you seriously believe that Life imitates Art, that Life in fact is the mirror, and Art the reality?

Vivian: Certainly I do. Paradox though it may seem—and paradoxes are always dangerous things—it is none the less true that Life imitates art far more than Art imitates life. We have all seen in our own day in England how a certain curious and fascinating type of beauty, invented and emphasized by two imaginative painters, has so influenced Life that whenever one goes to a private view or to an artistic salon one sees, here the mystic eyes of Rossetti's dream, the long ivory throat, the strange square-cut jaw, the loosened shadowy hair that he so ardently loved, there the sweet maidenhood of "The Golden Stair," the blossom-like mouth and weary loveliness of the "Laus Amoris," the passion-pale face of Andromeda, the thin hands and lithe beauty of the Vivian in "Merlin's Dream." And it has always been so. A great artist invents a type, and Life tries to copy it, to reproduce it in a popular form, like an enterprising publisher. Neither Holbein nor Vandyck found in England what they have given us. They brought their types with them, and Life with her keen imitative faculty set herself to supply the master with models. The Greeks, with their quick artistic instinct, understood this, and set in the bride's chamber the statue of Hermes or of Apollo, that she might bear children as lovely as the works of art that she looked at in her rapture or her pain. They knew that Life gains from art not merely spirituality, depth of thought and feeling, soul-turmoil or soul-peace, but that she can form herself on the very lines and colours of art, and can reproduce the dignity of Pheidias as well as the grace of Praxiteles. Hence came their objection to realism. They disliked it on purely social grounds. They felt that it inevitably makes people ugly, and they were perfectly right. We try to improve the conditions of the race by means of good air, free sunlight, wholesome water, and hideous bare buildings for the better housing of the lower orders. But these things merely produce health, they do not produce beauty. For this, Art is required, and the true disciples of the great artist are not his studio-imitators, but those who become like his works of art, be they plastic as in Greek days, or pictorial as in modern times; in a word, Life is Art's best, Art's only pupil.

* * *

Vivian (still speaking): All that I desire to point out is the general principle that Life imitates Art far more than Art imitates Life, and I feel sure that if you think seriously about it you will find that it is true. Life holds the mirror up to Art, and either reproduces some strange type imagined by painter or sculptor, or realizes in fact what has been dreamed in fiction. Scientifically speaking, the basis of life—the energy of life, as Aristotle would call it—is simply the desire for expression, and Art is always presenting various forms through which the expression can be attained. Life seizes on them and uses them, even if they be to her own hurt. Young men have committed suicide because Rolla did so, have died by their own hand because by his own hand Werther died. Think of what we owe to the imitation of Christ, of what we owe to the imitation of Caesar.

Cyril: The theory is certainly a very curious one, but to make it complete you must show that Nature, no less than Life, is an imitation of Art. Are you prepared to prove that?

Vivian: My dear fellow, I am prepared to prove anything.

Cyril: Nature follows the landscape painter, then, and takes her effects from him?

Vivian: Certainly. Where, if not from the Impressionists, do we get those wonderful brown fogs that come creeping down our streets, blurring the gas lamps and changing the houses into monstrous shadows? To whom, if not to them and their master, do we owe the lovely silver mists that brood over our river, and turn to faint forms of fading grace curved bridge and swaying barge? The extraordinary change that has taken place in the climate of London during the last ten years is entirely due to a particular school of Art. You smile. Consider the matter from a scientific or a metaphysical point of view, and you will find that I am right. For what is Nature? Nature is no great mother who has borne us. She is our creation. It is in our brain that she quickens to life. Things are because we see them, and what we see, and how we see it, depends on the Arts that have influenced us. To look at a thing is very different from seeing a thing. One does not see anything until one sees its beauty. Then, and then only, does it come into existence. At present, people see fogs, not because there are fogs, but because poets and painters have taught them the mysterious loveliness of such effects. There may have been fogs for centuries in London. I dare say there were. But no one saw them, and so we do not know anything about them. They did not exist till Art had invented them. Now, it must be admitted, fogs are carried to excess. They have become the mere mannerism of a clique, and the exaggerated realism of their method gives dull people bronchitis. Where the cultured catch an effect, the uncultured catch cold. And so, let us be humane, and invite Art to turn her wonderful eyes elsewhere. She has done so already, indeed. That white quivering sunlight that one sees now in France, with its strange blotches of mauve, and its restless violet shadows, is her latest fancy, and, on the whole, Nature reproduces it quite admirably. Where she used to give us Corots and Daubignys, she gives us now exquisite Monets and entrancing Pissaros. Indeed there are moments, rare, it is true, but still to be observed from time to time, when Nature becomes absolutely modern. Of course she is not always to be relied upon. The fact is that she is in this unfortunate position. Art creates an incomparable and unique effect, and, having done so, passes on to other things. Nature, upon the other hand, forgetting that imitation can be made the sincerest form of insult, keeps on repeating this effect until we all become absolutely wearied of it. Nobody of any real culture, for instance, ever talks nowadays about the beauty of a sunset. Sunsets are quite old-fashioned. They belong to the time when Turner was the last note in art. To admire them is a distinct sign of provincialism of temperament. Upon the other hand they go on. Yesterday evening Mrs. Arundel insisted on my going to the window, and looking at the glorious sky, as she called it. Of course I had to look at it. She is one of those absurdly pretty Philistines to whom one can deny nothing. And what was it? It was simply a very second-rate Turner, a Turner of a bad period, with all the painter's worst faults exaggerated and overemphasized. Of course, I am quite ready to admit that Life very often commits the same error. She produces her false Renés and her sham Vautrins, just as Nature gives us, on one day a doubtful Cuyp, and on another a more than questionable Rousseau. Still, Nature irritates one more when she does things of that kind. It seems so stupid, so obvious, so unnecessary. A false Vautrin might be delightful. A doubtful Cuyp is unbearable. However, I don't want to be too hard on Nature. I wish the Channel, especially at Hastings, did not look quite so often like a Henry Moore, grey pearl with yellow lights, but then, when Art is more varied, Nature will, no doubt, be more varied also. That she imitates Art, I don't think even her worst enemy would deny now. It is the one thing that keeps her in touch with civilized man. But have I proved my theory to your satisfaction?

Cyril: You have proved it to my dissatisfaction, which is better. But even admitting this strange imitative instinct in Life and Nature, surely you would acknowledge that Art expresses the temper of its age, the spirit of its time, the moral and social conditions that surround it, and under whose influence it is produced.

Vivian: Certainly not! Art never expresses anything but itself. This is the principle of my new aesthetics; and it is this, more than that vital connexion between form and substance, on which Mr. Pater dwells, that makes music the type of all the arts. Of course, nations and individuals, with that healthy natural vanity which is the secret of existence, are always under the impression that it is of them that the Muses are talking, always trying to find in the calm dignity of imaginative art some mirror of their own turbid passions, always forgetting that the singer of life is not Apollo but Marsyas. Remote from reality, and with her eyes turned away from the shadows of the cave, Art reveals her own perfection, and the wondering crowd that watches the opening of the marvellous, many-petalled rose fancies that it is its own history that is being told to it, its own spirit that is finding expression in a new form. But it is not so. The highest art rejects the burden of the human spirit, and gains more from a new medium or a fresh material than she does from any enthusiasm for art, or from any lofty passion, or from any great awakening of the human consciousness. She develops purely on her own lines. She is not symbolic of any age. It is the ages that are her symbols.

Even those who hold that Art is representative of time and place and people cannot help admitting that the more imitative an art is, the less it represents to us the spirit of its age. The evil faces of the Roman emperors look out at us from the foul porphyry and spotted jasper in which the realistic artists of the day delighted to work, and we fancy that in those cruel lips and heavy sensual jaws we can find the secret of the ruin of the Empire. But it was not so. The vices of Tiberius could not destroy that supreme civilization, any more than the virtues of the Antonines could save it. It fell for other, for less interesting reasons. The sibyls and prophets of the Sistine may indeed serve to interpret for some that new birth of the emancipated spirit that we call the Renaissance; but what do the drunken boors and bawling peasants of Dutch art tell us about the great soul of Holland? The more abstract, the more ideal an art is, the more it reveals to us the temper of its age. If we wish to understand a nation by means of its art, let us look at its architecture or its music.

Cyril: I quite agree with you there. The spirit of an age may be best expressed in the abstract ideal arts, for the spirit itself is abstract and ideal. Upon the other hand, for the visible aspect of an age, for its looks, as the phrase goes, we must of course go to the arts of imitation.

Vivian: I don't think so. After all, what the imitative arts really give us are merely the various styles of particular artists, or of certain schools of artists. Surely you don't imagine that the people of the Middle Ages bore any resemblance at all to the figures on mediaeval stained glass, or in mediaeval stone and wood carving, or on mediaeval metal work, or tapestries, or illuminated MSS. They were probably very ordinary-looking people, with nothing grotesque, or remarkable, or fantastic in their appearance. The Middle Ages, as we know them in art, are simply a definite form of style, and there is no reason at all why an artist with this style should not be produced in the nineteenth century. No great artist ever sees things as they really are. If he did, he would cease to be an artist.

* * *

Vivian: Art never expresses anything but itself. It has an independent life, just as Thought has, and develops purely on its own lines. It is not necessarily realistic in an age of realism, nor spiritual in an age of faith. So far from being the creation of its time, it is usually in direct opposition to it, and the only history that it preserves for us is the history of its own progress. Sometimes it returns upon its footsteps, and revives some antique form, as happened in the archaistic movement of late Greek Art, and in the pre-Raphaelite movement of our own day. At other times it entirely anticipates its age, and produces in one century work that it takes another century to understand, to appreciate, and to enjoy. In no case does it reproduce its age. To pass from the art of a time to the time itself is the great mistake that all historians commit.

The second doctrine is this. All bad art comes from returning to Life and Nature, and elevating them into ideals. Life and Nature may sometimes be used as part of Art's rough material, but before they are of any real service to art they must be translated into artistic conventions. The moment Art surrenders its imaginative medium it surrenders everything. As a method Realism is a complete failure, and the two things that every artist should avoid are modernity of form and modernity of subject matter. To us, who live in the nineteenth century, any century is a suitable subject for art except our own. The only beautiful things are the things that do not concern us. It is, to have the pleasure of quoting myself, exactly because Hecuba is nothing to us that her sorrows are so suitable a motive for a tragedy. Besides, it is only the modern that ever becomes old-fashioned. M. Zola sits down to give us a picture of the Second Empire. Who cares for the Second Empire now? It is out of date. Life goes faster than Realism, but Romanticism is always in front of Life.

The third doctrine is that Life imitates Art far more than Art imitates Life. This results not merely from Life's imitative instinct, but from the fact that the self-conscious aim of Life is to find expression, and that Art offers it certain beautiful forms through which it may realize that energy. It is a theory that has never been put forward before, but it is extremely fruitful, and throws an entirely new light upon the history of Art.

It follows, as a corollary from this, that external Nature also imitates Art. The only effects that she can show us are effects that we have already seen through poetry, or in paintings. This is the secret of Nature's charm, as well as the explanation of Nature's weakness.

The final revelation is that Lying, the telling of beautiful untrue things, is the proper aim of Art. But of this I think I have spoken at sufficient length. And now let us go out on the terrace, where "droops the milk-white peacock like a ghost," while the evening star "washes the dusk with silver." At twilight nature becomes a wonderfully suggestive effect, and is not without loveliness, though perhaps its chief use is to illustrate quotations from the poets. Come! We have talked long enough.

QUESTIONS FOR DISCUSSION

According to Eliot, why is "the faithful representing of commonplace things" in art morally necessary? (146)

1. Why does Eliot compare writing a novel to "narrating my experience on oath"? (143)

2. Why does Eliot say she "would not, even if I had the choice," be a clever novelist creating a world better than the real one? (144)

3. Why does Eliot think that reading novels with unrealistically perfect characters could lead readers "to turn a harder, colder eye" on "real breathing men and women"? (144)

4. Why does Eliot believe that fostering "deep human sympathy" is the highest purpose of art? (146)

Why does Vivian say, "The highest art rejects the burden of the human spirit"? (162)

1. What does Vivian mean when he says that Life is "the solvent that breaks up Art, the enemy that lays waste her house"? (155)

2. Why does Vivian accuse facts of "usurping the domain of Fancy" and "vulgarizing mankind"? (156)

3. According to Vivian, why is art "a veil, rather than a mirror"? (158)

4. Why does Vivian say, "The only beautiful things . . . are the things that do not concern us"? (164)

FOR FURTHER REFLECTION

1. Do you think art should represent everyday reality or reject it and create an alternative?

2. Do artists have moral obligations concerning their creations?

3. Does Eliot make a convincing case that the purpose of art is to develop sympathy for others?

4. Do you agree with Vivian that what we see "depends on the Arts that have influenced us"?

SCIENCE

Many of the ethical concerns that arise from scientific discovery are focused on the consequences of those discoveries. As modern scientific technology has come to dominate our world, those consequences are often so far-reaching and complex that it is difficult to discern what they are and how they operate. There is, however, another area of science that also mandates ethical consideration: experimental research. Research, especially in all branches of biological science including medicine, must often make use of living subjects in order to test hypotheses and establish firmly grounded knowledge. Often this research results in a certain degree of pain and suffering for the subjects and sometimes irremediable damage, if not death. Ethical debates on this issue are fundamentally about the broader question of what means are legitimate to achieve a beneficial end. The following selections are not only concerned with the boundaries of permissible scientific research but also with who should have the authority to determine those boundaries.

The story "Rappaccini's Daughter," by American author **Nathaniel Hawthorne** (1804–1864), chronicles the romance of a young student with the daughter of a famous doctor and scientist, Giacomo Rappaccini. As the story unfolds, it becomes apparent that Rappaccini is experimenting not only on the plants in his garden but also on a human subject, his own daughter. Although Rappaccini's experimentation is called into question, the complexity of his motives captures the ethical issues involved.

French physiologist **Claude Bernard** (1813–1878) was instrumental in establishing the practice of using living subjects in medical research. In his book *An Introduction to the Study of Experimental Medicine*, he addresses the ethical issues that this kind of experimentation raises. The portion on vivisection focuses on these issues and raises questions about the extent to which nonscientists should be able to determine what practices are ethical in the scientific realm.

Rappaccini's Daughter

Nathaniel Hawthorne

A **young man, named Giovanni Guasconti, came, very long** ago, from the more southern region of Italy, to pursue his studies at the University of Padua. Giovanni, who had but a scanty supply of gold ducats in his pocket, took lodgings in a high and gloomy chamber of an old edifice, which looked not unworthy to have been the palace of a Paduan noble, and which, in fact, exhibited over its entrance the armorial bearings of a family long since extinct. The young stranger, who was not unstudied in the great poem of his country, recollected that one of the ancestors of this family, and perhaps an occupant of this very mansion, had been pictured by Dante as a partaker of the immortal agonies of his Inferno. These reminiscences and associations, together with the tendency to heartbreak natural to a young man for the first time out of his native sphere, caused Giovanni to sigh heavily, as he looked around the desolate and ill-furnished apartment.

"Holy Virgin, Signor," cried old dame Lisabetta, who, won by the youth's remarkable beauty of person, was kindly endeavoring to give the chamber a habitable air, "what a sigh was that to come out of a young man's heart! Do you find this old mansion gloomy? For the love of heaven, then, put your head out of the window, and you will see as bright sunshine as you have left in Naples."

Guasconti mechanically did as the old woman advised, but could not quite agree with her that the Paduan sunshine was as cheerful as that of southern Italy. Such as it was, however, it fell upon a garden beneath the window, and expended its fostering influences on a variety of plants, which seemed to have been cultivated with exceeding care.

"Does this garden belong to the house?" asked Giovanni.

"Heaven forbid, Signor!—unless it were fruitful of better pot-herbs than any that grow there now," answered old Lisabetta. "No; that garden is cultivated by the own hands of Signor Giacomo Rappaccini, the famous doctor, who, I warrant him, has been heard of as far as Naples. It is said that he distils these plants into medicines that are as potent as a charm. Oftentimes you may see the Signor Doctor at work, and perchance the Signora his daughter, too, gathering the strange flowers that grow in the garden."

The old woman had now done what she could for the aspect of the chamber, and, commending the young man to the protection of the saints, took her departure.

Giovanni still found no better occupation than to look down into the garden beneath his window. From its appearance, he judged it to be one of those botanic gardens, which were of earlier date in Padua than elsewhere in Italy, or in the world. Or, not improbably, it might once have been the pleasure place of an opulent family; for there was the ruin of a marble fountain in the center, sculptured with rare art, but so woefully shattered that it was impossible to trace the original design from the chaos of remaining fragments. The water, however, continued to gush and sparkle into the sunbeams as cheerfully as ever. A little gurgling sound ascended to the young man's window, and made him feel as if the fountain were an immortal spirit, that sung its song unceasingly, and without heeding the vicissitudes around it; while one century embodied it in marble, and another scattered the perishable garniture on the soil. All about the pool into which the water subsided, grew various plants, that seemed to require a plentiful supply of moisture for the nourishment of gigantic leaves, and, in some instances, flowers gorgeously magnificent. There was one shrub in particular, set in a marble vase in the midst of the pool, that bore a profusion of purple blossoms, each of which had the luster and richness of a gem; and the whole together made a show so resplendent that it seemed enough to illuminate the garden, even had there been no sunshine. Every portion of the soil was peopled with plants and herbs, which, if less beautiful, still bore tokens of assiduous care; as if all had their individual virtues, known to the scientific mind that fostered them. Some were placed in urns, rich with old carving, and others in common garden pots; some crept serpentlike along the ground, or climbed on high, using whatever means of ascent was offered them. One plant had wreathed itself round a statue of Vertumnus, which was thus quite veiled and shrouded in a drapery of hanging foliage, so happily arranged that it might have served a sculptor for a study.

While Giovanni stood at the window, he heard a rustling behind a screen of leaves, and became aware that a person was at work in the garden. His figure soon emerged into view, and showed itself to be that of no common laborer, but a tall, emaciated, sallow, and sickly looking man, dressed in a scholar's garb of black. He was beyond the middle term of life, with gray hair, a thin gray beard, and a face singularly marked with intellect and cultivation, but which could never, even in his more youthful days, have expressed much warmth of heart.

Nothing could exceed the intentness with which this scientific gardener examined every shrub which grew in his path; it seemed as if he was looking into their inmost nature, making observations in regard to their creative essence, and discovering why one leaf grew in this shape, and another in that, and wherefore such and such flowers differed among themselves in hue and perfume. Nevertheless, in spite of this deep intelligence on his part, there was no approach to intimacy between himself and these vegetable existences. On the contrary, he avoided their actual touch, or the direct inhaling of their odors, with a caution that impressed Giovanni most disagreeably; for the man's demeanor was that of one walking among malignant influences, such as savage beasts, or deadly snakes, or evil spirits, which, should he allow them one moment of license, would wreak upon him some terrible fatality. It was strangely frightful to the young man's imagination, to see this air of insecurity in a person cultivating a garden, that most simple and innocent of human toils, and which had been alike the joy and labor of the unfallen parents of the race. Was this garden, then, the Eden of the present world?— and this man, with such a perception of harm in what his own hands caused to grow, was he the Adam?

The distrustful gardener, while plucking away the dead leaves or pruning the too luxuriant growth of the shrubs, defended his hands with a pair of thick gloves. Nor were these his only armor. When, in his walk through the garden, he came to the magnificent plant that hung its purple gems beside the marble fountain, he placed a kind of mask over his mouth and nostrils, as if all this beauty did but conceal a deadlier malice. But finding his task still too dangerous, he drew back, removed the mask, and called loudly, but in the infirm voice of a person affected with inward disease:

"Beatrice!—Beatrice!"

"Here am I, my father! What would you?" cried a rich and youthful voice from the window of the opposite house; a voice as rich as a tropical sunset, and which made Giovanni, though he knew not why, think of deep hues of purple or crimson, and of perfumes heavily delectable.—"Are you in the garden?"

"Yes, Beatrice," answered the gardener, "and I need your help."

Soon there emerged from under a sculptured portal the figure of a young girl, arrayed with as much richness of taste as the most splendid of the flowers, beautiful as the day, and with a bloom so deep and vivid that one shade more would have been too much. She looked redundant with life, health, and energy; all of which attributes were bound down and compressed, as it were, and girdled tensely, in their luxuriance, by her virgin zone. Yet Giovanni's fancy must have grown morbid, while he looked down into the garden; for the impression which the fair stranger made upon him was as if here were another flower, the human sister of those vegetable ones, as beautiful as they—more beautiful than the richest of them—but still to be touched only with a glove, nor to be approached without a mask. As Beatrice came down the garden path, it was observable that she handled and inhaled the odor of several of the plants, which her father had most sedulously avoided.

"Here, Beatrice," said the latter—"see how many needful offices require to be done to our chief treasure. Yet, shattered as I am, my life might pay the penalty of approaching it so closely as circumstances demand. Henceforth, I fear, this plant must be consigned to your sole charge."

"And gladly will I undertake it," cried again the rich tones of the young lady, as she bent toward the magnificent plant, and opened her arms as if to embrace it. "Yes, my sister, my splendor, it shall be Beatrice's task to nurse and serve thee; and thou shalt reward her with thy kisses and perfumed breath, which to her is as the breath of life!"

Then, with all the tenderness in her manner that was so strikingly expressed in her words, she busied herself with such attentions as the plant seemed to require; and Giovanni, at his lofty window, rubbed his eyes, and almost doubted whether it were a girl tending her favorite flower, or one sister performing the duties of affection to another. The scene soon terminated. Whether Doctor Rappaccini had finished his labors in the garden, or that his watchful eye had caught the stranger's face, he now took his daughter's arm and retired. Night was already closing in; oppressive exhalations seemed to proceed from the plants, and steal upward past the open window; and Giovanni, closing the lattice, went to his couch, and dreamed of a rich flower and beautiful girl. Flower and maiden were different and yet the same, and fraught with some strange peril in either shape.

But there is an influence in the light of the morning that tends to rectify whatever errors of fancy, or even of judgment, we may have incurred during the sun's decline, or among the shadows of the night, or in the less wholesome glow of moonshine. Giovanni's first movement on starting from sleep, was to throw open the window, and gaze down into the garden which his dreams had made so fertile of mysteries. He was surprised, and a little ashamed, to find how real and matter-of-fact an affair it proved to be, and in the first rays of the sun, which gilded the dew-drops that hung upon leaf and blossom, and, while giving a brighter beauty to each rare flower, brought everything within the limits of ordinary experience. The young man rejoiced, that, in the heart of the barren city, he had the privilege of overlooking this spot of lovely and luxuriant vegetation. It would serve, he said to himself, as a symbolic language, to keep him in communion with nature. Neither the sickly and thought-worn Doctor Giacomo Rappaccini, it is true, nor his brilliant daughter, were now visible; so that Giovanni could not determine how much of the singularity which he attributed to both, was due to their own qualities, and how much to his wonder-working fancy. But he was inclined to take a most rational view of the whole matter.

In the course of the day, he paid his respects to Signor Pietro Baglioni, professor of medicine in the university, a physician of eminent repute, to whom Giovanni had brought a letter of introduction. The professor was an elderly personage, apparently of genial nature, and habits that might almost be called jovial; he kept the young man to dinner, and made himself very agreeable by the freedom and liveliness of his conversation, especially when warmed by a flask or two of Tuscan wine. Giovanni, conceiving that men of science, inhabitants of the same city, must needs be on familiar terms with one another, took an opportunity to mention the name of Doctor Rappaccini. But the professor did not respond with so much cordiality as he had anticipated.

"Ill would it become a teacher of the divine art of medicine," said Professor Pietro Baglioni, in answer to a question of Giovanni, "to withhold due and well-considered praise of a physician so eminently skilled as Rappaccini. But, on the other hand, I should answer it but scantily to my conscience, were I to permit a worthy youth like yourself, Signor Giovanni, the son of an ancient friend, to imbibe erroneous ideas respecting a man who might hereafter chance to hold your life and death in his hands. The truth is, our worshipful Doctor Rappaccini has as much science as any member of the faculty—with perhaps one single exception—in Padua, or all Italy. But there are certain grave objections to his professional character."

"And what are they?" asked the young man.

"Has my friend Giovanni any disease of body or heart, that he is so inquisitive about physicians?" said the professor, with a smile. "But as for Rappaccini, it is said of him—and I, who know the man well, can answer for its truth—that he cares infinitely more for science than for mankind. His patients are interesting to him only as subjects for some new experiment. He would sacrifice human life, his own among the rest, or whatever else was dearest to him, for the sake of adding so much as a grain of mustard seed to the great heap of his accumulated knowledge."

"Methinks he is an awful man, indeed," remarked Guasconti, mentally recalling the cold and purely intellectual aspect of Rappaccini. "And yet, worshipful professor, is it not a noble spirit? Are there many men capable of so spiritual a love of science?"

"God forbid," answered the professor, somewhat testily—"at least, unless they take sounder views of the healing art than those adopted by Rappaccini. It is his theory, that all medicinal virtues are comprised within those substances which we term vegetable poisons. These he cultivates with his own hands, and is said even to have produced new varieties of poison, more horribly deleterious than nature, without the assistance of this learned person, would ever have plagued the world withal. That the Signor Doctor does less mischief than might be expected, with such dangerous substances, is undeniable. Now and then, it must be owned, he has effected— or seemed to effect—a marvelous cure. But, to tell you my private mind, Signor Giovanni, he should receive little credit for such instances of success—they being probably the work of chance—but should be held strictly accountable for his failures, which may justly be considered his own work."

The youth might have taken Baglioni's opinions with many grains of allowance, had he known that there was a professional warfare of long continuance between him and Doctor Rappaccini, in which the latter was generally thought to have gained the advantage. If the reader be inclined to judge for himself, we refer him to certain black-letter tracts on both sides, preserved in the medical department of the University of Padua.

"I know not, most learned professor," returned Giovanni, after musing on what had been said of Rappaccini's exclusive zeal for science—"I know not how dearly this physician may love his art; but surely there is one object more dear to him. He has a daughter."

"Aha!" cried the professor with a laugh. "So now our friend Giovanni's secret is out. You have heard of this daughter, whom all the young men in Padua are wild about, though not half a dozen have ever had the good hap to see her face. I know little of the Signora Beatrice, save that Rappaccini is said to have instructed her deeply in his science, and that, young and beautiful as fame reports her, she is already qualified to fill a professor's chair. Perchance her father destines her for mine! Other absurd rumors there be, not worth talking about, or listening to. So now, Signor Giovanni, drink off your glass of Lacryma."

Guasconti returned to his lodgings somewhat heated with the wine he had quaffed, and which caused his brain to swim with strange fantasies in reference to Doctor Rappaccini and the beautiful Beatrice. On his way, happening to pass by a florist's, he bought a fresh bouquet of flowers.

Ascending to his chamber, he seated himself near the window, but within the shadow thrown by the depth of the wall, so that he could look down into the garden with little risk of being discovered. All beneath his eye was a solitude. The strange plants were basking in the sunshine, and now and then nodding gently to one another, as if in acknowledgment of sympathy and kindred. In the midst, by the shattered fountain, grew the magnificent shrub, with its purple gems clustering all over it; they glowed in the air, and gleamed back again out of the depths of the pool, which thus seemed to overflow with colored radiance from the rich reflection that was steeped in it. At first, as we have said, the garden was a solitude. Soon, however—as Giovanni had half hoped, half feared, would be the case—a figure appeared beneath the antique sculptured portal, and came down between the rows of plants, inhaling their various perfumes, as if she were one of those beings of old classic fable, that lived upon sweet odors. On again beholding Beatrice, the young man was even startled to perceive how much her beauty exceeded his recollection of it; so brilliant, so vivid in its character, that she glowed amid the sunlight, and, as Giovanni whispered to himself, positively illuminated the more shadowy intervals of the garden path. Her face being now more revealed than on the former occasion, he was struck by its expression of simplicity and sweetness; qualities that had not entered into his idea of her character, and which made him ask anew, what manner of mortal she might be. Nor did he fail again to observe, or imagine, an analogy between the beautiful girl and the gorgeous shrub that hung its gem-like flowers over the fountain; a resemblance which Beatrice seemed to have indulged a fantastic humor in heightening, both by the arrangement of her dress and the selection of its hues.

Approaching the shrub, she threw open her arms, as with a passionate ardor, and drew its branches into an intimate embrace; so intimate, that her features were hidden in its leafy bosom, and her glistening ringlets all intermingled with the flowers.

"Give me thy breath, my sister," exclaimed Beatrice; "for I am faint with common air! And give me this flower of thine, which I separate with gentlest fingers from the stem, and place it close beside my heart."

With these words, the beautiful daughter of Rappaccini plucked one of the richest blossoms of the shrub, and was about to fasten it in her bosom. But now, unless Giovanni's draughts of wine had bewildered his senses, a singular incident occurred. A small orange-colored reptile, of the lizard or chameleon species, chanced to be creeping along the path, just at the feet of Beatrice. It appeared to Giovanni—but, at the distance from which he gazed, he could scarcely have seen anything so minute—it appeared to him, however, that a drop or two of moisture from the broken stem of the flower descended upon the lizard's head. For an instant, the reptile contorted itself violently, and then lay motionless in the sunshine. Beatrice observed this remarkable phenomenon, and crossed herself, sadly, but without surprise; nor did she therefore hesitate to arrange the fatal flower in her bosom. There it blushed, and almost glimmered with the dazzling effect of a precious stone, adding to her dress and aspect the one appropriate charm, which nothing else in the world could have supplied. But Giovanni, out of the shadow of his window, bent forward and shrank back, and murmured and trembled.

"Am I awake? Have I my senses?" said he to himself. "What is this being?—beautiful, shall I call her?—or inexpressibly terrible?"

Beatrice now strayed carelessly through the garden, approaching closer beneath Giovanni's window, so that he was compelled to thrust his head quite out of its concealment, in order to gratify the intense and painful curiosity which she excited. At this moment, there came a beautiful insect over the garden wall; it had perhaps wandered through the city and found no flowers nor verdure among those antique haunts of men, until the heavy perfumes of Doctor Rappaccini's shrubs had lured it from afar. Without alighting on the flowers, this winged brightness seemed to be attracted by Beatrice, and lingered in the air and fluttered about her head. Now here it could not be but that Giovanni Guasconti's eyes deceived him. Be that as it might, he fancied that while Beatrice was gazing at the insect with childish delight, it grew faint and fell at her feet—its bright wings shivered; it was dead—from no cause that he could discern, unless it were the atmosphere of her breath. Again Beatrice crossed herself and sighed heavily, as she bent over the dead insect.

An impulsive movement of Giovanni drew her eyes to the window. There she beheld the beautiful head of the young man—rather a Grecian than an Italian head, with fair, regular features, and a glistening of gold among his ringlets—gazing down upon her like a being that hovered in midair. Scarcely knowing what he did, Giovanni threw down the bouquet which he had hitherto held in his hand.

"Signora," said he, "there are pure and healthful flowers. Wear them for the sake of Giovanni Guasconti!"

"Thanks, Signor," replied Beatrice, with her rich voice that came forth as it were like a gush of music; and with a mirthful expression half childish and half womanlike. "I accept your gift, and would fain recompense it with this precious purple flower; but if I toss it into the air, it will not reach you. So Signor Guasconti must even content himself with my thanks."

She lifted the bouquet from the ground, and then as if inwardly ashamed at having stepped aside from her maidenly reserve to respond to a stranger's greeting, passed swiftly homeward through the garden. But, few as the moments were, it seemed to Giovanni when she was on the point of vanishing beneath the sculptured portal, that his beautiful bouquet was already beginning to wither in her grasp. It was an idle thought; there could be no possibility of distinguishing a faded flower from a fresh one, at so great a distance.

For many days after this incident, the young man avoided the window that looked into Doctor Rappaccini's garden, as if something ugly and monstrous would have blasted his eyesight, had he been betrayed into a glance. He felt conscious of having put himself, to a certain extent, within the influence of an unintelligible power, by the communication which he had opened with Beatrice. The wisest course would have been, if his heart were in any real danger, to quit his lodgings and Padua itself, at once; the next wiser, to have accustomed himself, as far as possible, to the familiar and daylight view of Beatrice; thus bringing her rigidly and systematically within the limits of ordinary experience. Least of all, while avoiding her sight, should Giovanni have remained so near this extraordinary being, that the proximity and possibility even of intercourse, should give a kind of substance and reality to the wild vagaries which his imagination ran riot continually in producing. Guasconti had not a deep heart—or at all events, its depths were not sounded now—but he had a quick fancy, and an ardent southern temperament, which rose every instant to a higher fever-pitch. Whether or no Beatrice possessed those terrible attributes—that fatal breath—the affinity with those so beautiful and deadly flowers—which were indicated by what Giovanni had witnessed, she had at least instilled a fierce and subtle poison into his system. It was not love, although her rich beauty was a madness to him; nor horror, even while he fancied her spirit to be imbued with the same baneful essence that seemed to pervade her physical frame; but a wild offspring of both love and horror that had each parent in it, and burned like one and shivered like the other. Giovanni knew not what to dread; still less did he know what to hope; yet hope and dread kept a continual warfare in his breast, alternately vanquishing one another and starting up afresh to renew the contest. Blessed are all simple emotions, be they dark or bright! It is the lurid intermixture of the two that produces the illuminating blaze of the infernal regions.

Sometimes he endeavored to assuage the fever of his spirit by a rapid walk through the streets of Padua, or beyond its gates; his footsteps kept time with the throbbings of his brain, so that the walk was apt to accelerate itself to a race. One day, he found himself arrested; his arm was seized by a portly personage who had turned back on recognizing the young man, and expended much breath in overtaking him.

"Signor Giovanni!—stay, my young friend!"—cried he. "Have you forgotten me? That might well be the case, if I were as much altered as yourself."

It was Baglioni, whom Giovanni had avoided, ever since their first meeting, from a doubt that the professor's sagacity would look too deeply into his secrets. Endeavoring to recover himself, he stared forth wildly from his inner world into the outer one, and spoke like a man in a dream.

"Yes; I am Giovanni Guasconti. You are Professor Pietro Baglioni. Now let me pass!"

"Not yet—not yet, Signor Giovanni Guasconti," said the professor, smiling, but at the same time scrutinizing the youth with an earnest glance. "What; did I grow up side by side with your father, and shall his son pass me like a stranger, in these old streets of Padua? Stand still, Signor Giovanni; for we must have a word or two before we part."

"Speedily, then, most worshipful professor, speedily!" said Giovanni, with feverish impatience. "Does not your worship see that I am in haste?"

Now, while he was speaking, there came a man in black along the street, stooping and moving feebly, like a person in inferior health. His face was all overspread with a most sickly and sallow hue, but yet so pervaded with an expression of piercing and active intellect, that an observer might easily have overlooked the merely physical attributes, and have seen only this wonderful energy. As he passed, this person exchanged a cold and distant salutation with Baglioni, but fixed his eyes upon Giovanni with an intentness that seemed to bring out whatever was within him worthy of notice. Nevertheless, there was a peculiar quietness in the look, as if taking merely a speculative, not a human interest, in the young man.

"It is Doctor Rappaccini!" whispered the professor, when the stranger had passed.—"Has he ever seen your face before?"

"Not that I know," answered Giovanni, starting at the name.

"He *has* seen you!—he must have seen you!" said Baglioni, hastily. "For some purpose or other, this man of science is making a study of you. I know that look of his! It is the same that coldly illuminates his face, as he bends over a bird, a mouse, or a butterfly, which, in pursuance of some experiment, he has killed by the perfume of a flower—a look as deep as nature itself, but without nature's warmth of love. Signor Giovanni, I will stake my life upon it, you are the subject of one of Rappaccini's experiments!"

"Will you make a fool of me?" cried Giovanni, passionately. "*That*, Signor Professor, were an untoward experiment."

"Patience, patience!" replied the imperturbable professor. "I tell thee, my poor Giovanni, that Rappaccini has a scientific interest in thee. Thou hast fallen into fearful hands! And the Signora Beatrice? What part does she act in this mystery?"

But Guasconti, finding Baglioni's pertinacity intolerable, here broke away, and was gone before the professor could again seize his arm. He looked after the young man intently, and shook his head.

"This must not be," said Baglioni to himself. "The youth is the son of my old friend, and shall not come to any harm from which the arcana of medical science can preserve him. Besides, it is too insufferable an impertinence in Rappaccini, thus to snatch the lad out of my own hands, as I may say, and make use of him for his infernal experiments. This daughter of his! It shall be looked to. Perchance, most learned Rappaccini, I may foil you where you little dream of it!"

Meanwhile, Giovanni had pursued a circuitous route, and at length found himself at the door of his lodgings. As he crossed the threshold, he was met by old Lisabetta, who smirked and smiled, and was evidently desirous to attract his attention; vainly, however, as the ebullition of his feelings had momentarily subsided into a cold and dull vacuity. He turned his eyes full upon the withered face that was puckering itself into a smile, but seemed to behold it not. The old dame, therefore, laid her grasp upon his cloak.

"Signor!—Signor!" whispered she, still with a smile over the whole breadth of her visage, so that it looked not unlike a grotesque carving in wood, darkened by centuries—"Listen, Signor! There is a private entrance into the garden!"

"What do you say?" exclaimed Giovanni, turning quickly about, as if an inanimate thing should start into feverish life.—"A private entrance into Doctor Rappaccini's garden!"

"Hush! hush!—not so loud!" whispered Lisabetta, putting her hand over his mouth. "Yes; into the worshipful doctor's garden, where you may see all his fine shrubbery. Many a young man in Padua would give gold to be admitted among those flowers."

Giovanni put a piece of gold into her hand.

"Show me the way," said he.

A surmise, probably excited by his conversation with Baglioni, crossed his mind, that this interposition of old Lisabetta might perchance be connected with the intrigue, whatever were its nature, in which the Professor seemed to suppose that Doctor Rappaccini was involving him. But such a suspicion, though it disturbed Giovanni, was inadequate to restrain him. The instant he was aware of the possibility of approaching Beatrice, it seemed an absolute necessity of his existence to do so. It mattered not whether she were angel or demon; he was irrevocably within her sphere, and must obey the law that whirled him onward, in ever lessening circles, toward a result which he did not attempt to foreshadow. And yet, strange to say, there came across him a sudden doubt, whether this intense interest on his part were not delusory—whether it were really of so deep and positive a nature as to justify him in now thrusting himself into an incalculable position—whether it were not merely the fantasy of a young man's brain, only slightly, or not at all, connected with his heart!

He paused—hesitated—turned half about—but again went on. His withered guide led him along several obscure passages, and finally undid a door, through which, as it was opened, there came the sight and sound of rustling leaves, with the broken sunshine glimmering among them. Giovanni stepped forth, and forcing himself through the entanglement of a shrub that wreathed its tendrils over the hidden entrance, he stood beneath his own window, in the open area of Doctor Rappaccini's garden.

How often is it the case, that, when impossibilities have come to pass, and dreams have condensed their misty substance into tangible realities, we find ourselves calm, and even coldly self-possessed, amid circumstances which it would have been a delirium of joy or agony to anticipate! Fate delights to thwart us thus. Passion will choose his own time to rush upon the scene, and lingers sluggishly behind, when an appropriate adjustment of events would seem to summon his appearance. So was it now with Giovanni. Day after day, his pulses had throbbed with feverish blood, at the improbable idea of an interview with Beatrice, and of standing with her, face to face, in this very garden, basking in the oriental sunshine of her beauty, and snatching from her full gaze the mystery which he deemed the riddle of his own existence. But now there was a singular and untimely equanimity within his breast. He threw a glance around the garden to discover if Beatrice or her father were present, and perceiving that he was alone, began a critical observation of the plants.

The aspect of one and all of them dissatisfied him; their gorgeousness seemed fierce, passionate, and even unnatural. There was hardly an individual shrub which a wanderer, straying by himself through a forest, would not have been startled to find growing wild, as if an unearthly face had glared at him out of the thicket. Several, also, would have shocked a delicate instinct by an appearance of artificialness, indicating that there had been such commixture, and, as it were, adultery of various vegetable species, that the production was no longer of God's making, but the monstrous offspring of man's depraved fancy, glowing with only an evil mockery of beauty. They were probably the result of experiment, which, in one or two cases, had succeeded in mingling plants individually lovely into a compound possessing the questionable and ominous character that distinguished the whole growth of the garden. In fine, Giovanni recognized but two or three plants in the collection, and those of a kind that he well knew to be poisonous. While busy with these contemplations, he heard the rustling of a silken garment, and turning, beheld Beatrice emerging from beneath the sculptured portal.

Giovanni had not considered with himself what should be his deportment; whether he should apologize for his intrusion into the garden, or assume that he was there with the privity, at least, if not by the desire, of Doctor Rappaccini or his daughter. But Beatrice's manner placed him at his ease, though leaving him still in doubt by what agency he had gained admittance. She came lightly along the path, and met him near the broken fountain. There was surprise in her face, but brightened by a simple and kind expression of pleasure.

"You are a connoisseur in flowers, Signor," said Beatrice with a smile, alluding to the bouquet which he had flung her from the window. "It is no marvel, therefore, if the sight of my father's rare collection has tempted you to take a nearer view. If he were here, he could tell you many strange and interesting facts as to the nature and habits of these shrubs, for he has spent a lifetime in such studies, and this garden is his world."

"And yourself, lady"—observed Giovanni—"if fame says true—you, likewise, are deeply skilled in the virtues indicated by these rich blossoms, and these spicy perfumes. Would you deign to be my instructress, I should prove an apter scholar than under Signor Rappaccini himself."

"Are there such idle rumors?" asked Beatrice, with the music of a pleasant laugh. "Do people say that I am skilled in my father's science of plants? What a jest is there! No; though I have grown up among these flowers, I know no more of them than their hues and perfume; and sometimes, methinks I would fain rid myself of even that small knowledge. There are many flowers here, and those not the least brilliant, that shock and offend me, when they meet my eye. But, pray, Signor, do not believe these stories about my science. Believe nothing of me save what you see with your own eyes."

"And must I believe all that I have seen with my own eyes?" asked Giovanni pointedly, while the recollection of former scenes made him shrink. "No, Signora, you demand too little of me. Bid me believe nothing, save what comes from your own lips."

It would appear that Beatrice understood him. There came a deep flush to her cheek; but she looked full into Giovanni's eyes, and responded to his gaze of uneasy suspicion with a queenlike haughtiness.

"I do so bid you, Signor!" she replied. "Forget whatever you may have fancied in regard to me. If true to the outward senses, still it may be false in its essence. But the words of Beatrice Rappaccini's lips are true from the heart outward. Those you may believe!"

A fervor glowed in her whole aspect, and beamed upon Giovanni's consciousness like the light of truth itself. But while she spoke, there was a fragrance in the atmosphere around her, rich and delightful, though evanescent, yet which the young man, from an indefinable reluctance, scarcely dared to draw into his lungs. It might be the odor of the flowers. Could it be Beatrice's breath, which thus embalmed her words with a strange richness, as if by steeping them in her heart? A faintness passed like a shadow over Giovanni, and flitted away; he seemed to gaze through the beautiful girl's eyes into her transparent soul, and felt no more doubt or fear.

The tinge of passion that had colored Beatrice's manner vanished; she became gay, and appeared to derive a pure delight from her communion with the youth, not unlike what the maiden of a lonely island might have felt, conversing with a voyager from the civilized world. Evidently her experience of life had been confined within the limits of that garden. She talked now about matters as simple as the daylight or summer clouds, and now asked questions in reference to the city, or Giovanni's distant home, his friends, his mother, and his sisters; questions indicating such seclusion, and such lack of familiarity with modes and forms, that Giovanni responded as if to an infant. Her spirit gushed out before him like a fresh rill, that was just catching its first glimpse of the sunlight, and wondering, at the reflections of earth and sky which were flung into its bosom. There came thoughts, too, from a deep source, and fantasies of a gemlike brilliancy, as if diamonds and rubies sparkled upward among the bubbles of the fountain. Ever and anon, there gleamed across the young man's mind a sense of wonder, that he should be walking side by side with the being who had so wrought upon his imagination—whom he had idealized in such hues of terror—in whom he had positively witnessed such manifestations of dreadful attributes—that he should be conversing with Beatrice like a brother, and should find her so human and so maiden-like. But such reflections were only momentary; the effect of her character was too real, not to make itself familiar at once.

In this free intercourse, they had strayed through the garden, and now, after many turns among its avenues, were come to the shattered fountain, beside which grew the magnificent shrub with its treasury of glowing blossoms. A fragrance was diffused from it, which Giovanni recognized as identical with that which he had attributed to Beatrice's breath, but incomparably more powerful. As her eyes fell upon it, Giovanni beheld her press her hand to her bosom, as if her heart were throbbing suddenly and painfully.

"For the first time in my life," murmured she, addressing the shrub, "I had forgotten thee!"

"I remember, Signora," said Giovanni, "that you once promised to reward me with one of these living gems for the bouquet, which I had the happy boldness to fling to your feet. Permit me now to pluck it as a memorial of this interview."

He made a step toward the shrub, with extended hand. But Beatrice darted forward, uttering a shriek that went through his heart like a dagger. She caught his hand, and drew it back with the whole force of her slender figure. Giovanni felt her touch thrilling through his fibers.

"Touch it not!" exclaimed she, in a voice of agony. "Not for thy life! It is fatal!"

Then, hiding her face, she fled from him, and vanished beneath the sculptured portal. As Giovanni followed her with his eyes, he beheld the emaciated figure and pale intelligence of Doctor Rappaccini, who had been watching the scene, he knew not how long, within the shadow of the entrance.

No sooner was Guasconti alone in his chamber, than the image of Beatrice came back to his passionate musings, invested with all the witchery that had been gathering around it ever since his first glimpse of her, and now likewise imbued with a tender warmth of girlish womanhood. She was human: her nature was endowed with all gentle and feminine qualities; she was worthiest to be worshipped; she was capable, surely, on her part, of the height and heroism of love. Those tokens, which he had hitherto considered as proofs of a frightful peculiarity in her physical and moral system, were now either forgotten, or, by the subtle sophistry of passion, transmuted into a golden crown of enchantment, rendering Beatrice the more admirable, by so much as she was the more unique. Whatever had looked ugly, was now beautiful; or, if incapable of such a change, it stole away and hid itself among those shapeless half-ideas, which throng the dim region beyond the daylight of our perfect consciousness. Thus did Giovanni spend the night, nor fell asleep, until the dawn had begun to awake the slumbering flowers in Doctor Rappaccini's garden, whither his dreams doubtless led him. Up rose the sun in his due season, and flinging his beams upon the young man's eyelids, awoke him to a sense of pain. When thoroughly aroused, he became sensible of a burning and tingling agony in his hand—in his right hand—the very hand which Beatrice had grasped in her own, when he was on the point of plucking one of the gemlike flowers. On the back of that hand there was now a purple print, like that of four small fingers, and the likeness of a slender thumb upon his wrist.

Oh, how stubbornly does love—or even that cunning semblance of love which flourishes in the imagination, but strikes no depth of root into the heart—how stubbornly does it hold its faith, until the moment come, when it is doomed to vanish into thin mist! Giovanni wrapt a handkerchief about his hand, and wondered what evil thing had stung him, and soon forgot his pain in a reverie of Beatrice.

After the first interview, a second was in the inevitable course of what we call fate. A third; a fourth; and a meeting with Beatrice in the garden was no longer an incident in Giovanni's daily life, but the whole space in which he might be said to live; for the anticipation and memory of that ecstatic hour made up the remainder. Nor was it otherwise with the daughter of Rappaccini. She watched for the youth's appearance, and flew to his side with confidence as unreserved as if they had been playmates from early infancy—as if they were such playmates still. If, by any unwonted chance, he failed to come at the appointed moment, she stood beneath the window, and sent up the rich sweetness of her tones to float around him in his chamber, and echo and reverberate throughout his heart—"Giovanni! Giovanni! Why tarriest thou? Come down!" And down he hastened into that Eden of poisonous flowers.

But, with all this intimate familiarity, there was still a reserve in Beatrice's demeanor, so rigidly and invariably sustained, that the idea of infringing it scarcely occurred to his imagination. By all appreciable signs, they loved; they had looked love, with eyes that conveyed the holy secret from the depths of one soul into the depths of the other, as if it were too sacred to be whispered by the way; they had even spoken love, in those gushes of passion when their spirits darted forth in articulated breath, like tongues of long-hidden flame; and yet there had been no seal of lips, no clasp of hands, nor any slightest caress, such as love claims and hallows. He had never touched one of the gleaming ringlets of her hair; her garment—so marked was the physical barrier between them—had never been waved against him by a breeze. On the few occasions when Giovanni had seemed tempted to overstep the limit, Beatrice grew so sad, so stern, and withal wore such a look of desolate separation, shuddering at itself, that not a spoken word was requisite to repel him. At such times, he was startled at the horrible suspicions that rose, monsterlike, out of the caverns of his heart, and stared him in the face; his love grew thin and faint as the morning mist; his doubts alone had substance. But when Beatrice's face brightened again, after the momentary shadow, she was transformed at once from the mysterious, questionable being, whom he had watched with so much awe and horror; she was now the beautiful and unsophisticated girl, whom he felt that his spirit knew with a certainty beyond all other knowledge.

A considerable time had now passed since Giovanni's last meeting with Baglioni. One morning, however, he was disagreeably surprised by a visit from the professor, whom he had scarcely thought of for whole weeks, and would willingly have forgotten still longer. Given up, as he had long been, to a pervading excitement, he could tolerate no companions, except upon condition of their perfect sympathy with his present state of feeling. Such sympathy was not to be expected from Professor Baglioni.

The visitor chatted carelessly, for a few moments, about the gossip of the city and the university, and then took up another topic.

"I have been reading an old classic author lately," said he, "and met with a story that strangely interested me. Possibly you may remember it. It is of an Indian prince, who sent a beautiful woman as a present to Alexander the Great. She was as lovely as the dawn, and gorgeous as the sunset; but what especially distinguished her was a certain rich perfume in her breath—richer than a garden of Persian roses. Alexander, as was natural to a youthful conqueror, fell in love at first sight with this magnificent stranger. But a certain sage physician, happening to be present, discovered a terrible secret in regard to her."

"And what was that?" asked Giovanni, turning his eyes downward to avoid those of the professor.

"That this lovely woman," continued Baglioni, with emphasis, "had been nourished with poisons from her birth upward, until her whole nature was so imbued with them, that she herself had become the deadliest poison in existence. Poison was her element of life. With that rich perfume of her breath, she blasted the very air. Her love would have been poison!—her embrace death! Is not this a marvellous tale?"

"A childish fable," answered Giovanni, nervously starting from his chair. "I marvel how your worship finds time to read such nonsense, among your graver studies."

"By the bye," said the professor, looking uneasily about him, "what singular fragrance is this in your apartment? Is it the perfume of your gloves? It is faint, but delicious, and yet, after all, by no means agreeable. Were I to breathe it long, methinks it would make me ill. It is like the breath of a flower—but I see no flowers in the chamber."

"Nor are there any," replied Giovanni, who had turned pale as the professor spoke; "nor, I think, is there any fragrance, except in your worship's imagination. Odors, being a sort of element combined of the sensual and the spiritual, are apt to deceive us in this manner. The recollection of a perfume—the bare idea of it—may easily be mistaken for a present reality."

"Aye; but my sober imagination does not often play such tricks," said Baglioni; "and were I to fancy any kind of odor, it would be that of some vile apothecary drug, wherewith my fingers are likely enough to be imbued. Our worshipful friend Rappaccini, as I have heard, tinctures his medicaments with odors richer than those of Araby. Doubtless, likewise, the fair and learned Signora Beatrice would minister to her patients with draughts as sweet as a maiden's breath. But woe to him that sips them!"

Giovanni's face evinced many contending emotions. The tone in which the professor alluded to the pure and lovely daughter of Rappaccini was a torture to his soul; and yet, the intimation of a view of her character, opposite to his own, gave instantaneous distinctness to a thousand dim suspicions, which now grinned at him like so many demons. But he strove hard to quell them, and to respond to Baglioni with a true lover's perfect faith.

"Signor Professor," said he, "you were my father's friend—perchance, too, it is your purpose to act a friendly part toward his son. I would fain feel nothing toward you save respect and deference. But I pray you to observe, Signor, that there is one subject on which we must not speak. You know not the Signora Beatrice. You cannot, therefore, estimate the wrong—the blasphemy, I may even say—that is offered to her character by a light or injurious word."

"Giovanni!—my poor Giovanni!" answered the professor, with a calm expression of pity, "I know this wretched girl far better than yourself. You shall hear the truth in respect to the poisoner

Rappaccini, and his poisonous daughter. Yes; poisonous as she is beautiful! Listen; for even should you do violence to my gray hairs, it shall not silence me. That old fable of the Indian woman has become a truth, by the deep and deadly science of Rappaccini, and in the person of the lovely Beatrice!"

Giovanni groaned and hid his face.

"Her father," continued Baglioni, "was not restrained by natural affection from offering up his child, in this horrible manner, as the victim of his insane zeal for science. For—let us do him justice—he is as true a man of science as ever distilled his own heart in an alembic. What, then, will be your fate? Beyond a doubt, you are selected as the material of some new experiment. Perhaps the result is to be death—perhaps a fate more awful still! Rappaccini, with what he calls the interest of science before his eyes, will hesitate at nothing."

"It is a dream!" muttered Giovanni to himself, "surely it is a dream!"

"But," resumed the Professor, "be of good cheer, son of my friend! It is not yet too late for the rescue. Possibly, we may even succeed in bringing back this miserable child within the limits of ordinary nature, from which her father's madness has estranged her. Behold this little silver vase! It was wrought by the hands of the renowned Benvenuto Cellini, and is well worthy to be a love gift to the fairest dame in Italy. But its contents are invaluable. One little sip of this antidote would have rendered the most virulent poisons of the Borgias innocuous. Doubt not that it will be as efficacious against those of Rappaccini. Bestow the vase, and the precious liquid within it, on your Beatrice, and hopefully await the result."

Baglioni laid a small, exquisitely wrought silver phial on the table, and withdrew, leaving what he had said to produce its effect upon the young man's mind.

"We will thwart Rappaccini yet!" thought he, chuckling to himself, as he descended the stairs. "But, let us confess the truth of him, he is a wonderful man!—a wonderful man indeed! A vile empiric, however, in his practice, and therefore not to be tolerated by those who respect the good old rules of the medical profession!"

Throughout Giovanni's whole acquaintance with Beatrice, he had occasionally, as we have said, been haunted by dark surmises as to her character. Yet, so thoroughly had she made herself felt by him as a simple, natural, most affectionate and guileless creature, that the image now held up by Professor Baglioni, looked as strange and incredible, as if it were not in accordance with his own original conception. True, there were ugly recollections connected with his first glimpses of the beautiful girl; he could not quite forget the bouquet that withered in her grasp, and the insect that perished amid the sunny air, by no ostensible agency save the fragrance of her breath. These incidents, however, dissolving in the pure light of her character, had no longer the efficacy of facts, but were acknowledged as mistaken fantasies, by whatever testimony of the senses they might appear to be substantiated. There is something truer and more real, than what we can see with the eyes, and touch with the finger. On such better evidence, had Giovanni founded his confidence in Beatrice, though rather by the necessary force of her high attributes, than by any deep and generous faith on his part. But, now, his spirit was incapable of sustaining itself at the height to which the early enthusiasm of passion had exalted it; he fell down, groveling among earthly doubts, and defiled therewith the pure whiteness of Beatrice's image. Not that he gave her up; he did but distrust. He resolved to institute some decisive test that should satisfy him, once for all, whether there were those dreadful peculiarities in her physical nature, which could not be supposed to exist without some corresponding monstrosity of soul. His eyes, gazing down afar, might have deceived him as to the lizard, the insect, and the flowers. But if he could witness, at the distance of a few paces, the sudden blight of one fresh and healthful flower in Beatrice's hand, there would be room for no further question. With this idea, he hastened to the florist's, and purchased a bouquet that was still gemmed with the morning dewdrops.

It was now the customary hour of his daily interview with Beatrice. Before descending into the garden, Giovanni failed not to look at his figure in the mirror; a vanity to be expected in a beautiful young man, yet, as displaying itself at that troubled and feverish moment, the token of a certain shallowness of feeling and insincerity of character. He did gaze, however, and said to himself, that his features had never before possessed so rich a grace, nor his eyes such vivacity, nor his cheeks so warm a hue of superabundant life.

"At least," thought he, "her poison has not yet insinuated itself into my system. I am no flower to perish in her grasp!"

With that thought, he turned his eyes on the bouquet, which he had never once laid aside from his hand. A thrill of indefinable horror shot through his frame, on perceiving that those dewy flowers were already beginning to droop; they wore the aspect of things that had been fresh and lovely, yesterday. Giovanni grew white as marble, and stood motionless before the mirror, staring at his own reflection there, as at the likeness of something frightful. He remembered Baglioni's remark about the fragrance that seemed to pervade the chamber. It must have been the poison in his breath! Then he shuddered—shuddered at himself! Recovering from his stupor, he began to watch, with curious eye, a spider that was busily at work, hanging its web from the antique cornice of the apartment, crossing and re-crossing the artful system of interwoven lines, as vigorous and active a spider as ever dangled from an old ceiling. Giovanni bent toward the insect, and emitted a deep, long breath. The spider suddenly ceased its toil; the web vibrated with a tremor originating in the body of the small artizan. Again Giovanni sent forth a breath, deeper, longer, and imbued with a venomous feeling out of his heart; he knew not whether he were wicked or only desperate. The spider made a convulsive gripe with his limbs, and hung dead across the window.

"Accursed! Accursed!" muttered Giovanni, addressing himself. "Hast thou grown so poisonous, that this deadly insect perishes by thy breath?"

At that moment, a rich, sweet voice came floating up from the garden: "Giovanni! Giovanni! It is past the hour! Why tarriest thou! Come down!"

"Yes," muttered Giovanni again. "She is the only being whom my breath may not slay! Would that it might!"

He rushed down, and in an instant, was standing before the bright and loving eyes of Beatrice. A moment ago, his wrath and despair had been so fierce that he could have desired nothing so much as to wither her by a glance. But, with her actual presence, there came influences which had too real an existence to be at once shaken off; recollections of the delicate and benign power of her feminine nature, which had so often enveloped him in a religious calm; recollections of many a holy and passionate outgush of her heart, when the pure fountain had been unsealed from its depths, and made visible in its transparency to his mental eye; recollections which, had Giovanni known how to estimate them, would have assured him that all this ugly mystery was but an earthly illusion, and that, whatever mist of evil might seem to have gathered over her, the real Beatrice was a heavenly angel. Incapable as he was of such high faith, still her presence had not utterly lost its magic. Giovanni's rage was quelled into an aspect of sullen insensibility. Beatrice, with a quick spiritual sense, immediately felt that there was a gulf of blackness between them, which neither he nor she could pass. They walked on together, sad and silent, and came thus to the marble fountain, and to its pool of water on the ground, in the midst of which grew the shrub that bore gemlike blossoms. Giovanni was affrighted at the eager enjoyment—the appetite, as it were—with which he found himself inhaling the fragrance of the flowers.

"Beatrice," asked he abruptly, "whence came this shrub!"

"My father created it," answered she, with simplicity.

"Created it! created it!" repeated Giovanni. "What mean you, Beatrice?"

"He is a man fearfully acquainted with the secrets of nature," replied Beatrice; "and, at the hour when I first drew breath, this plant sprang from the soil, the offspring of his science, of his intellect, while I was but his earthly child. Approach it not!" continued she, observing with terror that Giovanni was drawing nearer to the shrub. "It has qualities that you little dream of. But I, dearest Giovanni—I grew up and blossomed with the plant, and was nourished with its breath. It was my sister, and I loved it with a human affection: for—alas! hast thou not suspected it? there was an awful doom."

Here Giovanni frowned so darkly upon her that Beatrice paused and trembled. But her faith in his tenderness reassured her, and made her blush that she had doubted for an instant.

"There was an awful doom," she continued—"the effect of my father's fatal love of science—which estranged me from all society of my kind. Until heaven sent thee, dearest Giovanni, Oh! how lonely was thy poor Beatrice!"

"Was it a hard doom?" asked Giovanni, fixing his eyes upon her.

"Only of late have I known how hard it was," answered she tenderly. "Oh, yes; but my heart was torpid, and therefore quiet."

Giovanni's rage broke forth from his sullen gloom like a lightning flash out of a dark cloud.

"Accursed one!" cried he, with venomous scorn and anger. "And finding thy solitude wearisome, thou hast severed me, likewise, from all the warmth of life, and enticed me into thy region of unspeakable horror!"

"Giovanni!" exclaimed Beatrice, turning her large bright eyes upon his face. The force of his words had not found its way into her mind; she was merely thunderstruck.

"Yes, poisonous thing!" repeated Giovanni, beside himself with passion. "Thou hast done it! Thou hast blasted me! Thou hast filled my veins with poison! Thou hast made me as hateful, as ugly, as loathsome and deadly a creature as thyself—a world's wonder of hideous monstrosity! Now—if our breath be happily as fatal to ourselves as to all others—let us join our lips in one kiss of unutterable hatred, and so die!"

"What has befallen me?" murmured Beatrice, with a low moan out of her heart. "Holy Virgin pity me, a poor heartbroken child!"

"Thou! Dost thou pray?" cried Giovanni, still with the same fiendish scorn. "Thy very prayers, as they come from thy lips, taint the atmosphere with death. Yes, yes; let us pray! Let us to church, and dip our fingers in the holy water at the portal! They that come after us will perish as by a pestilence. Let us sign crosses in the air! It will be scattering curses abroad in the likeness of holy symbols!"

"Giovanni," said Beatrice calmly, for her grief was beyond passion, "Why dost thou join thyself with me thus in those terrible words? I, it is true, am the horrible thing thou namest me. But thou!—what hast thou to do, save with one other shudder at my hideous misery, to go forth out of the garden and mingle with thy race, and forget that there ever crawled on earth such a monster as poor Beatrice?"

"Dost thou pretend ignorance?" asked Giovanni, scowling upon her. "Behold! This power have I gained from the pure daughter of Rappaccini!"

There was a swarm of summer insects flitting through the air, in search of the food promised by the flower odors of the fatal garden. They circled round Giovanni's head, and were evidently attracted toward him by the same influence which had drawn them, for an instant, within the sphere of several of the shrubs. He sent forth a breath among them, and smiled bitterly at Beatrice, as at least a score of the insects fell dead upon the ground.

"I see it! I see it!" shrieked Beatrice. "It is my father's fatal science? No, no, Giovanni; it was not I! Never, never! I dreamed only to love thee, and be with thee a little time, and so to let thee pass away, leaving but thine image in mine heart. For, Giovanni—believe it—though my body be nourished with poison, my spirit is God's creature, and craves love as its daily food. But my father!—he has united us in this fearful sympathy. Yes; spurn me!—tread upon me!—kill me! Oh, what is death, after such words as thine? But it was not I! Not for a world of bliss would I have done it!"

Giovanni's passion had exhausted itself in its outburst from his lips. There now came across him a sense, mournful, and not without tenderness, of the intimate and peculiar relationship between Beatrice and himself. They stood, as it were, in an utter solitude, which would be made none the less solitary by the densest throng of human life. Ought not, then, the desert of humanity around them to press this insulated pair closer together? If they should be cruel to one another, who was there to be kind to them? Besides, thought Giovanni, might there not still be a hope of his returning within the limits of ordinary nature, and leading Beatrice—the redeemed Beatrice—by the hand? Oh, weak, and selfish, and unworthy spirit, that could dream of an earthly union and earthly happiness as possible, after such deep love had been so bitterly wronged as was Beatrice's love by Giovanni's blighting words! No, no; there could be no such hope. She must pass heavily, with that broken heart, across the borders of time—she must bathe her hurts in some fount of paradise, and forget her grief in the light of immortality—and *there* be well!

But Giovanni did not know it.

"Dear Beatrice," said he, approaching her, while she shrank away, as always at his approach, but now with a different impulse— "dearest Beatrice, our fate is not yet so desperate. Behold! There is a medicine, potent, as a wise physician has assured me, and almost divine in its efficacy. It is composed of ingredients the most opposite to those by which thy awful father has brought this calamity upon thee and me. It is distilled of blessed herbs. Shall we not quaff it together, and thus be purified from evil?"

"Give it me!" said Beatrice, extending her hand to receive the little silver phial which Giovanni took from his bosom. She added, with a peculiar emphasis: "I will drink—but do thou await the result."

She put Baglioni's antidote to her lips; and, at the same moment, the figure of Rappaccini emerged from the portal, and came slowly toward the marble fountain. As he drew near, the pale man of science seemed to gaze with a triumphant expression at the beautiful youth and maiden, as might an artist who should spend his life in achieving a picture or a group of statuary, and finally be satisfied with his success. He paused—his bent form grew erect with conscious power, he spread out his hands over them, in the attitude of a father imploring a blessing upon his children. But those were the same hands that had thrown poison into the stream of their lives! Giovanni trembled. Beatrice shuddered very nervously, and pressed her hand upon her heart.

"My daughter," said Rappaccini, "thou art no longer lonely in the world! Pluck one of those precious gems from thy sister shrub, and bid thy bridegroom wear it in his bosom. It will not harm him now! My science, and the sympathy between thee and him, have so wrought within his system, that he now stands apart from common men, as thou dost, daughter of my pride and triumph, from ordinary women. Pass on, then, through the world, most dear to one another, and dreadful to all besides!"

"My father," said Beatrice, feebly—and still, as she spoke, she kept her hand upon her heart—"wherefore didst thou inflict this miserable doom upon thy child?"

"Miserable!" exclaimed Rappaccini. "What mean you, foolish girl? Dost thou deem it misery to be endowed with marvelous gifts, against which no power nor strength could avail an enemy? Misery, to be able to quell the mightiest with a breath? Misery, to be as terrible as thou art beautiful? Wouldst thou, then, have preferred the condition of a weak woman, exposed to all evil, and capable of none?"

"I would fain have been loved, not feared," murmured Beatrice, sinking down upon the ground.—"But now it matters not; I am going, father, where the evil, which thou hast striven to mingle with my being, will pass away like a dream—like the fragrance of these poisonous flowers, which will no longer taint my breath among the flowers of Eden. Farewell, Giovanni! Thy words of hatred are like lead within my heart—but they, too, will fall away as I ascend. Oh, was there not, from the first, more poison in thy nature than in mine?"

To Beatrice—so radically had her earthly part been wrought upon by Rappaccini's skill—as poison had been life, so the powerful antidote was death. And thus the poor victim of man's ingenuity and of thwarted nature, and of the fatality that attends all such efforts of perverted wisdom, perished there, at the feet of her father and Giovanni. Just at that moment, Professor Pietro Baglioni looked forth from the window, and called loudly, in a tone of triumph mixed with horror, to the thunderstricken man of science:

"Rappaccini! Rappaccini! And is *this* the upshot of your experiment?"

Vivisection

Claude Bernard

We have succeeded in discovering the laws of inorganic matter only by penetrating into inanimate bodies and machines; similarly we shall succeed in learning the laws and properties of living matter only by displacing living organs in order to get into their inner environment. After dissecting cadavers, then, we must necessarily dissect living beings, to uncover the inner or hidden parts of the organisms and see them work; to this sort of operation we give the name of vivisection, and without this mode of investigation, neither physiology nor scientific medicine is possible; to learn how man and animals live, we cannot avoid seeing great numbers of them die, because the mechanisms of life can be unveiled and proved only by knowledge of the mechanisms of death.

Men have felt this truth in all ages; and in medicine, from the earliest times, men have performed not only therapeutic experiments but even vivisection. We are told that the kings of Persia delivered men condemned to death to their physicians, so that they might perform on them vivisections useful to science. According to Galen, Attalus III (Philometor), who reigned at Pergamum, one hundred thirty-seven years before Jesus Christ, experimented with poisons and antidotes on criminals condemned to death. Celsus recalls and approves the vivisection which Herophilus and Erasistratus performed on criminals with the Ptolemies' consent. It is not cruel, he says, to inflict on a few criminals, sufferings which may benefit multitudes of innocent people throughout all centuries. The Grand Duke of Tuscany had a criminal given over to the professor of anatomy,

Fallopius, at Pisa, with permission to kill or dissect him at pleasure. As the criminal had a quartan fever, Fallopius wished to investigate the effects of opium on the paroxysms. He administered two drams of opium during an intermission; death occurred after the second experiment. Similar instances have occasionally recurred, and the story is well known of the archer of Meudon who was pardoned because a nephrotomy was successfully performed on him. Vivisection of animal also goes very far back. Galen may be considered its founder. He performed his experiments especially on monkeys and on young pigs and described the instruments and methods used in experimenting. Galen performed almost no other kind of experiment than that which we call disturbing experiments, which consist in wounding, destroying, or removing a part, so as to judge its function by the disturbance caused by its removal. He summarized earlier experiments and studied for himself the effects of destroying the spinal cord at different heights, of perforating the chest on one side or both sides at once; the effects of section of the nerves leading to the intercostal muscles and of section of the recurrent nerve. He tied arteries and performed experiments on the mechanism of deglutition. Since Galen, at long intervals in the midst of medical systems, eminent vivisectors have always appeared. As such, the names of Graaf, Harvey, Aselli, Pecquet, Haller, etc., have been handed down to us. In our time, and especially under the influence of Magendie, vivisection has entered physiology and medicine once for all, as an habitual or indispensable method of study.

The prejudices clinging to respect for corpses long halted the progress of anatomy. In the same way, vivisection in all ages has met with prejudices and detractors. We cannot aspire to destroy all the prejudice in the world; neither shall we allow ourselves here to answer the arguments of detractors of vivisection; since they thereby deny experimental medicine, i.e., scientific medicine. However, we shall consider a few general questions, and then we shall set up the scientific goal which vivisection has in view.

First, have we a right to perform experiments and vivisections on man? Physicians make therapeutic experiments daily on their patients, and surgeons perform vivisections daily on their subjects. Experiments, then, may be performed on man, but within what limits? It is our duty and our right to perform an experiment on man whenever it can save his life, cure him or gain him some personal benefit. The principle of medical and surgical morality, therefore, consists in never performing on man an experiment which might be harmful to him to any extent, even though the result might be highly advantageous to science, i.e., to the health of others. But performing experiments and operations exclusively from the point of view of the patient's own advantage does not prevent their turning out profitably to science. It cannot indeed be otherwise; an old physician who has often administered drugs and treated many patients is more experienced, that is, he will experiment better on new patients, because he has learned from experiments made on others. A surgeon who has performed operations on different kinds of patients learns and perfects himself experimentally. Instruction comes only through experience; and that fits perfectly into the definitions given at the beginning of this introduction.

May we make experiments on men condemned to death or vivisect them? Instances have been cited, analogous to the one recalled above, in which men have permitted themselves to perform dangerous operations on condemned criminals, granting them pardon in exchange. Modern ideas of morals condemn such actions; I completely agree with these ideas; I consider it wholly permissible, however, and useful to science, to make investigations on the properties of tissues immediately after the decapitations of criminals. A helminthologist had a condemned woman without her knowledge swallow larvae of intestinal worms, so as to see whether the worms developed in the intestines after her death. Others have made analogous experiments on patients with phthisis doomed to an early death; some men have made experiments on themselves. As experiments of this kind are of great interest to science and can be conclusive only on man, they seem to be wholly permissible when they involve no suffering or harm to the subject of the experiment. For we must not deceive ourselves, morals do not forbid making experiments on one's neighbor or on one's self; in everyday life men do nothing but experiment on one another. Christian morals forbid only one thing, doing ill to one's neighbor. So, among the experiments that may be tried on man, those that can only harm are forbidden, those that are innocent are permissible, and those that may do good are obligatory.

Another question presents itself. Have we the right to make experiments on animals and vivisect them? As for me, I think we have this right, wholly and absolutely. It would be strange indeed if we recognized man's right to make use of animals in every walk of life, for domestic service, for food, and then forbade him to make use of them for his own instruction in one of the sciences most useful to humanity. No hesitation is possible; the science of life can be established only through experiment, and we can save living beings from death only after sacrificing others. Experiments must be made either on man or on animals. Now I think that physicians already make too many dangerous experiments on man, before carefully studying them on animals. I do not admit that it is moral to try more or less dangerous or active remedies on patients in hospitals, without first experimenting with them on dogs; for I shall prove, further on, that results obtained on animals may all be conclusive for man when we know how to experiment properly. If it is immoral, then, to make an experiment on man when it is dangerous to him, even though the result may be useful to others, it is essentially moral to make experiments on an animal, even though painful and dangerous to him, if they may be useful to man.

After all this, should we let ourselves be moved by the sensitive cries of people of fashion or by the objections of men unfamiliar with scientific ideas? All feelings deserve respect, and I shall be very careful never to offend anyone's. I easily explain them to myself, and that is why they cannot stop me. I understand perfectly how physicians under the influence of false ideas, and lacking the scientific sense, fail to appreciate the necessity of experiment and vivisection in establishing biological science. I also understand perfectly how people of fashion, moved by ideas wholly different from those that animate physiologists, judge vivisection quite differently. It cannot be otherwise. Somewhere in this introduction we said that, in science, ideas are what give facts their value and meaning. It is the same in morals, it is everywhere the same. Facts materially alike may have opposite scientific meanings, according to the ideas with which they are connected. A cowardly assassin, a hero, and a warrior each plunges a dagger into the breast of his fellow. What differentiates them, unless it be the ideas which guide their hands? A surgeon, a physiologist, and Nero give themselves up alike to mutilation of living beings. What differentiates them also, if not ideas? I therefore shall not follow the example of LeGallois, in trying to justify physiologists in the eyes of strangers to science who reproach them with cruelty; the difference in ideas explains everything. A physiologist is not a man of fashion, he is a man of science, absorbed by the scientific idea which he pursues: he no longer hears the cry of animals, he no longer sees the blood that flows, he sees only his idea and perceives only organisms concealing problems which he intends to solve. Similarly, no surgeon is stopped by the most moving cries and sobs, because he sees only his idea and the purpose of his operation. Similarly again, no anatomist feels himself in a horrible slaughterhouse; under the influence of a scientific idea, he delightedly follows a nervous filament through stinking livid flesh, which to any other man would be an object of disgust and horror. After what has gone before we shall deem all discussion of vivisection futile or absurd. It is impossible for men, judging facts by such different ideas, ever to agree; and as it is impossible to satisfy everybody, a man of science should attend only to the opinion of men of science who understand him, and should derive rules of conduct only from his own conscience.

The scientific principle of vivisection is easy, moreover, to grasp. It is always a question of separating or altering certain parts of the living machine, so as to study them and thus to decide how they function and for what. Vivisection, considered as an analytic method of investigation of the living, includes many successive steps, for we may need to act either on organic apparatus, or on organs, or on tissue, or on the histological units themselves. In extemporized and other vivisections, we produce mutilations whose results we study by preserving the animals. At other times, vivisection is only an autopsy on the living, or a study of properties of tissues immediately after death. The various processes of analytic study of the mechanisms of life in living animals are indispensable, as we shall see, to physiology, to pathology, and to therapeutics. However, it would not do to believe that vivisection in itself can constitute the whole experimental method as applied to the study of vital phenomena.

Vivisection is only anatomical dissection of the living; it is necessarily combined with all the other physico-chemical means of
investigation which must be carried into the organism. Reduced to
itself, vivisection would have only a limited range and in certain
cases must even mislead us as to the actual role of organs. By these
reservations I do not deny the usefulness or even the necessity of
vivisection in the study of vital phenomena. I merely declare it insufficient. Our instruments for vivisection are indeed so coarse and our
senses so imperfect that we can reach only the coarse and complex
parts of an organism. Vivisection under the microscope would make
much finer analysis possible, but it presents much greater difficulties
and is applicable only to very small animals.

But when we reach the limits of vivisection we have other means
of going deeper and dealing with the elementary parts of organisms where the elementary properties of vital phenomena have their
seat. We may introduce poisons into the circulation, which carry
their specific action to one or another histological unit. Localized
poisonings, as Fontana and J. Müller have already used them, are
valuable means of physiological analysis. Poisons are veritable
reagents of life, extremely delicate instruments which dissect vital
units. I believe myself the first to consider the study of poisons from
this point of view, for I am of the opinion that studious attention to
agents which alter histological units should form the common foundation of general physiology, pathology, and therapeutics. We must
always, indeed, go back to the organs to find the simplest explana-
tions of life.

To sum up, dissection is a displacing of a living organism by
means of instruments and methods capable of isolating its different
parts. It is easy to understand that such dissection of the living presupposes dissection of the dead.

QUESTIONS FOR DISCUSSION

Why does Beatrice die as "the poor victim of man's ingenuity and of thwarted nature"? (199)

1. Why does Giovanni wonder if Rappaccini's garden is "the Eden of the present world"? (173)

2. Why does Baglioni say that Rappaccini would sacrifice any life to add "a grain of mustard seed" to human knowledge? (176)

3. Why are Giovanni's feelings for Beatrice "a wild offspring of both love and horror"? (181)

4. After Beatrice dies, why does Baglioni call to Rappaccini "in a tone of triumph mixed with horror"? (199)

According to Bernard, why does "scientific medicine" require the dissection of living beings? (201)

1. What does Bernard mean when he says "in everyday life men do nothing but experiment on one another"? (203)

2. Why does Bernard believe that people have the right "wholly and absolutely" to conduct experiments on animals? (204)

3. Why does Bernard insist that "we can save living beings from death only after sacrificing others"? (204)

4. Why does Bernard declare that "all discussion of vivisection" with nonscientists is "futile or absurd"? (205)

FOR FURTHER REFLECTION

1. What limits should be placed on experimentation with human subjects?

2. Should scientists listen to the opinions of nonscientists about the ethics of particular experiments?

3. Do "efforts of perverted wisdom" like Rappaccini's always result in fatality?

4. Is medical experimentation compatible with deep empathy for others ?

GENDER
GENDER

209

Debates over the kind of education appropriate to different sectors of society have often focused on how those sectors and their populations represent differences in capacity and social structures. One of the most acute forms that this debate has taken through the centuries has been with regard to gender differences: Are men and women so fundamentally distinct, or are their roles in society so determined, that the education of each should be different? In many parts of the world, attitudes toward women over the last century have shifted in favor of equal opportunity in not only education but also employment. However, even in these arenas, old and ingrained habits of thought still persist. The following selections represent the terms of this gender divide in sharply pointed contrast.

"Lilies," from *Sesame and Lilies* (1865) by the British art critic and social reformer **John Ruskin** (1819–1900), was originally delivered as a lecture. In this selection, Ruskin sees the nature of women as fundamentally different from that of men. Although he argues that women should be educated, he also asserts that their education should be appropriate to their own unique interests and capabilities. By treating the education of women differently from that of men, he maintains that we will allow women to follow their own natural instincts and in that way attain fulfilling lives.

In the seventh chapter of her book *The Feminine Mystique* (1963), American author and feminist **Betty Friedan** (1921–2006) criticizes the emphasis on gender difference in education in the United States. She claims that education for women is often directed only toward biological and social expectations, rather than toward the interests and passions of the women concerned. Friedan both rejects the idea of a distinct feminine character and criticizes those with Ruskin's viewpoint for propagating the myth.

Lilies

(selection)

John Ruskin

Of Queens' Gardens

Believing that all literature and all education are only useful so far as they tend to confirm this calm, beneficent, and *therefore* kingly, power—first, over ourselves, and, through ourselves, over all around us, I am now going to ask you to consider with me farther, what special portion or kind of this royal authority, arising out of noble education, may rightly be possessed by women; and how far they also are called to a true queenly power. Not in their households merely, but over all within their sphere. And in what sense, if they rightly understood and exercised this royal or gracious influence, the order and beauty induced by such benignant power would justify us in speaking of the territories over which each of them reigned, as "Queens' Gardens."

And here, in the very outset, we are met by a far deeper question, which—strange though this may seem—remains among many of us yet quite undecided, in spite of its infinite importance.

We cannot determine what the queenly power of women should be, until we are agreed what their ordinary power should be. We cannot consider how education may fit them for any widely extending duty, until we are agreed what is their true constant duty. And there never was a time when wilder words were spoken, or more vain imagination permitted, respecting this question—quite vital to all social happiness. The relations of the womanly to the manly nature, their different capacities of intellect or of virtue, seem never to have been yet measured with entire consent. We hear of the mission and of the rights of Woman, as if these could ever be separate from the mission and the rights of Man;—as if she and her lord were creatures of independent kind and of irreconcileable claim. This, at least, is wrong. And not less wrong—perhaps even more foolishly wrong (for I will anticipate thus far what I hope to prove)—is the idea that woman is only the shadow and attendant image of her lord, owing him a thoughtless and servile obedience, and supported altogether in her weakness by the pre-eminence of his fortitude.

This, I say, is the most foolish of all errors respecting her who was made to be the helpmate of man. As if he could be helped effectively by a shadow, or worthily by a slave!

Let us try, then, whether we cannot get at some clear and harmonious idea (it must be harmonious if it is true) of what womanly mind and virtue are in power and office, with respect to man's; and how their relations, rightly accepted, aid, and increase, the vigour, and honour, and authority of both. . . .

But how, you will ask, is the idea of this guiding function of the woman reconcileable with a true wifely subjection? Simply in that it is a *guiding*, not a determining, function. Let me try to show you briefly how these powers seem to be rightly distinguishable.

We are foolish, and without excuse foolish, in speaking of the "superiority" of one sex to the other, as if they could be compared in similar things. Each has what the other has not: each completes the other, and is completed by the other: they are in nothing alike, and the happiness and perfection of both depends on each asking and receiving from the other what the other only can give.

Now their separate characters are briefly these. The man's power is active, progressive, defensive. He is eminently the doer, the creator, the discoverer, the defender. His intellect is for speculation and invention; his energy for adventure, for war, and for conquest, wherever war is just, wherever conquest necessary. But the woman's power is for rule, not for battle,—and her intellect is not for invention or creation, but for sweet ordering, arrangement, and decision. She sees the qualities of things, their claims, and their places. Her great function is Praise: she enters into no contest, but infallibly adjudges the crown of contest. By her office, and place, she is protected from all danger and temptation. The man, in his rough work in open world, must encounter all peril and trial:—to him, therefore, the failure, the offence, the inevitable error: often he must be wounded, or subdued, often misled, and *always* hardened. But he guards the woman from all this; within his house, as ruled by her, unless she herself has sought it, need enter no danger, no temptation, no cause of error or offence. This is the true nature of home—it is the place of Peace; the shelter, not only from all injury, but from all terror, doubt, and division. In so far as it is not this, it is not home; so far as the anxieties of the outer life penetrate into it, and the inconsistently-minded, unknown, unloved, or hostile society of the outer world is allowed by either husband or wife to cross the threshold, it ceases to be home; it is then only a part of that outer world which you have roofed over, and lighted fire in. But so far as it is a sacred place, a vestal temple, a temple of the hearth watched over by Household Gods, before whose faces none may come but those whom they can receive with love,—so far as it is this, and roof and fire are types only of a nobler shade and light,—shade as of the rock in a weary land, and light as of the Pharos in the stormy sea;—so far it vindicates the name, and fulfils the praise, of Home.

And wherever a true wife comes, this home is always round her. The stars only may be over her head; the glowworm in the night-cold grass may be the only fire at her foot: but home is yet wherever she is; and for a noble woman it stretches far round her, better than ceiled with cedar, or painted with vermilion, shedding its quiet light far, for those who else were homeless.

This, then, I believe to be,—will you not admit it to be,—the woman's true place and power? But do not you see that, to fulfil this, she must—as far as one can use such terms of a human creature—be incapable of error? So far as she rules, all must be right, or nothing is. She must be enduringly, incorruptibly good; instinctively, infallibly wise—wise, not for self-development, but for self-renunciation: wise, not that she may set herself above her husband, but that she may never fail from his side: wise, not with the narrowness of insolent and loveless pride, but with the passionate gentleness of an infinitely variable, because infinitely applicable, modesty of service—the true changefulness of woman. In that great sense—"La donna e mobile," not "Qual piùm' al vento;" no, nor yet "Variable as the shade, by the light quivering aspen made;" but variable as the *light*, manifold in fair and serene division, that it may take the colour of all that it falls upon, and exalt it.

* * *

I have been trying, thus far, to show you what should be the place, and what the power of woman. Now, secondly, we ask, What kind of education is to fit her for these?

And if you indeed think this a true conception of her office and dignity, it will not be difficult to trace the course of education which would fit her for the one, and raise her to the other. . . .

All such knowledge should be given her as may enable her to understand, and even to aid, the work of men: and yet it should be given, not as knowledge,—not as if it were, or could be, for her an object to know; but only to feel, and to judge. It is of no moment, as a matter of pride or perfectness in herself, whether she knows many languages or one; but it is of the utmost, that she should be able to show kindness to a stranger, and to understand the sweetness of a stranger's tongue. It is of no moment to her own worth or dignity that she should be acquainted with this science or that; but it is of the highest that she should be trained in habits of accurate thought; that she should understand the meaning, the inevitableness, and the loveliness of natural laws, and follow at least some one path of scientific attainment, as far as to the threshold of that bitter Valley of Humiliation, into which only the wisest and bravest of men can descend, owning themselves for ever children, gathering pebbles on a boundless shore. It is of little consequence how many positions of cities she knows, or how many dates of events, or how many names of celebrated persons—it is not the object of education to turn a woman into a dictionary; but it is deeply necessary that she should be taught to enter with her whole personality into the history she reads; to picture the passages of it vitally in her own bright imagination; to apprehend, with her fine instincts, the pathetic circumstances and dramatic relations, which the historian too often only eclipses by his reasoning, and disconnects by his arrangement; it is for her to trace the hidden equities of divine reward, and catch sight, through the darkness, of the fateful threads of woven fire that connect error with its retribution. But, chiefly of all, she is to be taught to extend the limits of her sympathy with respect to that history which is being for ever determined, as the moments pass in which she draws her peaceful breath; and to the contemporary calamity which, were it but rightly mourned by her, would recur no more hereafter. She is to exercise herself in imagining what would be the effects upon her mind and conduct, if she were daily brought into the presence of the suffering which is not the less real because shut from her sight. She is to be taught somewhat to understand the nothingness of the proportion which that little world in which she lives and loves, bears to the world in which God lives and loves;—and solemnly she is to be taught to strive that her thoughts of piety may not be feeble in proportion to the number they embrace, nor her prayer more languid than it is for the momentary relief from pain of her husband or her child, when it is uttered for the multitudes of those who have none to love them,—and is "for all who are desolate and oppressed. . . ."

I believe, then, with this exception, that a girl's education should be nearly, in its course and material of study, the same as a boy's; but quite differently directed. A woman, in any rank of life, ought to know whatever her husband is likely to know, but to know it in a different way. His command of it should be foundational and progressive, hers, general and accomplished for daily and helpful use. Not but that it would often be wiser in men to learn things in a womanly sort of way, for present use, and to seek for the discipline and training of their mental powers in such branches of study as will be afterwards fittest for social service; but, speaking broadly, a man ought to know any language or science he learns, thoroughly, while a woman ought to know the same language, or science, only so far as may enable her to sympathise in her husband's pleasures, and in those of his best friends.

Yet, observe, with exquisite accuracy as far as she reaches. There is a wide difference between elementary knowledge and superficial knowledge—between a firm beginning, and a feeble smattering. A woman may always help her husband by what she knows, however little; by what she half-knows, or mis-knows, she will only tease him.

* * *

Thus far, then, of the nature, thus far of the teaching, of woman, and thus of her household office, and queenliness. We come now to our last, our widest question,—What is her queenly office with respect to the state?

Generally, we are under an impression that a man's duties are public, and a woman's private. But this is not altogether so. A man has a personal work or duty, relating to his own home, and a public work or duty, which is the expansion of the other, relating to the state. So a woman has a personal work or duty, relating to her own home, and a public work and duty, which is also the expansion of that.

Now the man's work for his own home is, as has been said, to secure its maintenance, progress, and defence; the woman's to secure its order, comfort, and loveliness.

Expand both these functions. The man's duty, as a member of a commonwealth, is to assist in the maintenance, in the advance, in the defence of the state. The woman's duty, as a member of the commonwealth, is to assist in the ordering, in the comforting, and in the beautiful adornment of the state.

What the man is at his own gate, defending it, if need be, against insult and spoil, that also, not in a less, but in a more devoted measure, he is to be at the gate of his country, leaving his home, if need be, even to the spoiler, to do his more incumbent work there.

And, in like manner, what the woman is to be within her gates, at the centre of order, the balm of distress, and the mirror of beauty; that she is also to be without her gates, where order is more difficult, distress more imminent, loveliness more rare.

And as within the human heart there is always set an instinct for all its real duties,—an instinct which you cannot quench, but only warp and corrupt if you withdraw it from its true purpose;—as there is the intense instinct of love, which, rightly disciplined, maintains all the sanctities of life, and, misdirected, undermines them;

and *must* do either the one or the other;—so there is in the human heart an inextinguishable instinct, the love of power, which, rightly directed, maintains all the majesty of law and life, and misdirected, wrecks them.

Deep rooted in the innermost life of the heart of man, and of the heart of woman, God set it there, and God keeps it there. Vainly, as falsely, you blame or rebuke the desire of power!—For Heaven's sake, and for Man's sake, desire it all you can. But *what* power? That is all the question. Power to destroy? the lion's limb, and the dragon's breath? Not so. Power to heal, to redeem, to guide, and to guard. Power of the sceptre and shield; the power of the royal hand that heals in touching,—that binds the fiend, and looses the captive; the throne that is founded on the rock of Justice, and descended from only by steps of mercy. Will you not covet such power as this, and seek such throne as this, and be no more housewives, but queens?

The Feminine Mystique

(selection)

Betty Friedan

The mystery to me is not that these girls defend themselves against an involvement with the life of the mind, but that educators should be mystified by their defense, or blame it on the "student culture," as certain educators do. The one lesson a girl could hardly avoid learning, if she went to college between 1945 and 1960, was *not* to get interested, seriously interested, in anything besides getting married and having children, if she wanted to be normal, happy, adjusted, feminine, have a successful husband, successful children, and a normal, feminine, adjusted, successful sex life. She might have learned some of this lesson at home, and some of it from the other girls in college, but she also learned it, incontrovertibly, from those entrusted with developing her critical, creative intelligence: her college professors.

A subtle and almost unnoticed change had taken place in the academic culture for American women in the last fifteen years: the new sex-direction of their educators. Under the influence of the feminine mystique, some college presidents and professors charged with the education of women had become more concerned with their students' future capacity for sexual orgasm than with their future use of trained intelligence. In fact, some leading educators of women began to concern themselves, conscientiously, with protecting students from the temptation to use their critical, creative intelligence—by the ingenious method of educating it *not* to be critical or creative. Thus higher education added its weight to the process by which American women during this period were shaped increasingly to

221

their biological function, decreasingly to the fulfillment of their individual abilities. Girls who went to college could hardly escape those bits and pieces of Freud and Margaret Mead, or avoid a course in "Marriage and Family Life" with its functional indoctrination on "how to play the role of woman."

The new sex-direction of women's education was not, however, confined to any specific course or academic department. It was implicit in all the social sciences; but more than that, it became a part of education itself, not only because the English professor, or the guidance counselor, or the college president read Freud and Mead, but because education was the prime target of the new mystique—the education of American girls with, or like, boys. If the Freudians and the functionalists were right, educators were guilty of defeminizing American women, of dooming them to frustration as housewives and mothers, or to celibate careers, to life without orgasm. It was a damning indictment; many college presidents and educational theorists confessed their guilt without a murmur and fell into the sex-directed line. There were a few cries of outrage, of course, from the old-fashioned educators who still believed the mind was more important than the marriage bed, but they were often near retirement and soon to be replaced by younger, more thoroughly sex-indoctrinated teachers, or they were so wrapped up in their special subjects that they had little say in over-all school policies.

The general educational climate was ripe for the new sex-directed line, with its emphasis on adjustment. The old aim of education, the development of intelligence through vigorous mastery of the major intellectual disciplines, was already in disfavor among the child-centered educators. Teachers College at Columbia was the natural breeding ground for educational functionalism. As psychology and anthropology and sociology permeated the total scholarly atmosphere, education for femininity also spread from Mills, Stephens, and the finishing schools (where its basis was more traditional than theoretical) to the proudest bastions of the women's Ivy League, the colleges which pioneered higher education for women in America, and were noted for their uncompromising intellectual standards.

Instead of opening new horizons and wider worlds to able women, the sex-directed educator moved in to teach them adjustment within the world of home and children. Instead of teaching truths to counter the popular prejudices of the past, or critical ways of thinking against which prejudice cannot survive, the sex-directed educator handed girls a sophisticated soup of uncritical prescriptions and presentiments, far more binding on the mind and prejudicial to the future than all the traditional do's and don'ts. Most of it was done consciously and for the best of helpful reasons by educators who really believed the mystique as the social scientists handed it to them. If a male professor or college president did not find this mystique a positive comfort, a confirmation of his own prejudices, he still had no reason *not* to believe it.

The few college presidents and professors who were women either fell into line or had their authority—as teachers and as women—questioned. If they were spinsters, if they had not had babies, they were forbidden by the mystique to speak as women. (*Modern Woman: The Lost Sex* would forbid them even to teach.) The brilliant scholar, who did not marry but inspired many generations of college women to the pursuit of truth, was sullied as an educator of women. She was not named president of the women's college whose intellectual tradition she carried to its highest point; the girls' education was put in the hands of a handsome, husbandly man, more suitable to indoctrinating girls for their proper feminine role. The scholar often left the woman's college to head a department in a great university, where the potential PhD's were safely men, for whom the lure of scholarship, the pursuit of truth, was not deemed a deterrent to sexual fulfillment.

In terms of the new mystique, the woman scholar was suspect, simply by virtue of being one. She was not just working to support her home; she must have been guilty of an unfeminine commitment, to have kept working in her field all those hard, grinding, ill-paid years to the PhD. In self-defense she sometimes adopted frilly blouses or another innocuous version of the feminine protest. (At psychoanalytic conventions, an observer once noticed, the lady analysts camouflage themselves with pretty, flowery, smartly feminine hats that would make the casual suburban housewife look positively masculine.) MD or PhD, those hats and frilly blouses say, *let nobody question our femininity*. But the fact is, their femininity was questioned. One famous women's college adopted in defense the slogan, "We are not educating women to be scholars; we are educating them to be wives and mothers." (The girls themselves finally got so tired of repeating this slogan in full that they abbreviated it to "WAM.")

In building the sex-directed curriculum, not everyone went as far as Lynn White, former president of Mills College, but if you started with the premise that women should no longer be educated like men, but for their role as women, you almost had to end with his curriculum—which amounted to replacing college chemistry with a course in advanced cooking.

The sex-directed educator begins by accepting education's responsibility for the frustration, general and sexual, of American women.

> On my desk lies a letter from a young mother, a few years out of college:
>
> "I have come to realize that I was educated to be a successful man and must now learn by myself to be a successful woman." The basic irrelevance of much of what passes as women's education in America could not be more compactly phrased. . . . The failure of our educational system to take into account these simple and basic differences between the life patterns of average men and women is at least in part responsible for the deep discontent and restlessness which affects millions of women. . . .
>
> It would seem that if women are to restore their self-respect they must reverse the tactics of the older feminism which indignantly denied inherent differences in the intellectual and emotional tendencies of men and women. Only by recognizing and insisting upon the importance of such differences can women save themselves, in their own eyes, of conviction as inferiors.[1]

The sex-directed educator equates as masculine our "vastly overrated cultural creativity," "our uncritical acceptance of 'progress' as good in itself," "egotistic individualism," "innovation," "abstract construction," "quantitative thinking"—of which, of course, the dread symbol is either communism or the atom bomb. Against these, equated as feminine, are "the sense of persons, of the immediate, of intangible qualitative relationships, an aversion for statistics and quantities," "the intuitive," "the emotional," and all the forces that "cherish" and "conserve" what is "good, true, beautiful, useful, and holy."

A feminized higher education might include sociology, anthropology, psychology. ("These are studies little concerned with the laurel-crowned genius of the strong man," praises the educational protector of femininity. "They are devoted to exploring the quiet and unspectacular forces of society and of the mind. . . . They embrace the feminine preoccupation with conserving and cherishing.") It would hardly include either pure science (since abstract theory and quantitative thinking are unfeminine) or fine art, which is masculine, "flamboyant and abstract." The applied or minor arts, however, are feminine: ceramics, textiles, work shaped more by the hand than the brain. "Women love beauty as much as men do but they want a beauty connected with the processes of living . . . the hand is as remarkable and as worthy of respect as the brain."

The sex-directed educator cites approvingly Cardinal Tisserant's saying, "Women should be educated so that they can argue with their husbands." Let us stop altogether professional training for women, he insists: all women must be educated to be housewives. Even home economics and domestic science, as they are now taught at college, are masculine because "they have been pitched at the level of professional training."[2]

Here is a truly feminine education:

> One may prophesy with confidence that as women begin to make their distinctive wishes felt in curricular terms, not merely will every women's college and coeducational institution offer a firm nuclear course in the Family, but from it will radiate curricular series dealing with food and nutrition, textiles and clothing, health and nursing, house planning and interior decoration, garden design and applied botany, and child-development. . . . Would it be impossible to present a

beginning course in foods as exciting and as difficult to work up after college, as a course in post-Kantian philosophy would be? . . . Let's abandon talk of proteins, carbohydrates and the like, save inadvertently, as for example, when we point out that a British hyper-boiled Brussel sprout is not merely inferior in flavor and texture, but in vitamin content. Why not study the theory and preparation of a Basque paella, of a well-marinated shish kebob, lamb kidneys sauteed in sherry, an authoritative curry, the use of herbs, even such simple sophistications as serving cold artichokes with fresh milk.[3]

The sex-directed educator is hardly impressed by the argument that a college curriculum should not be contaminated or diluted with subjects like cooking or manual training, which can be taught successfully at the high school level. Teach them to the girls in high school, and "with greater intensity and imagination" again in college. Boys, also, should get some "family-minded" education, but not in their valuable college time; early high school manual training is enough to "enable them, in future years to work happily at a bench in the garage or in the garden, surrounded by an admiring circle of children . . . or at the barbecue."[4]

This kind of education, in the name of life-adjustment, became a fact on many campuses, high school as well as college. It was not dreamed up to turn back the growth of women, but it surely helped. When American educators finally began to investigate the waste of our national resources of creative intelligence, they found that the lost Einsteins, Schweitzers, Roosevelts, Edisons, Fords, Fermis, Frosts were feminine. Of the brightest forty percent of U.S. high school graduates, only half went on to college; of the half who stopped, *two out of three were girls.*[5] When Dr. James B. Conant went across the nation to find out what was wrong with the American high school, he discovered too many students were taking easy how-to courses which didn't really stretch their minds. Again, most of those who should have been studying physics, advanced algebra, analytic geometry, four years of language—and were not— were girls. They had the intelligence, the special gift which was not sex-directed, but they also had the sex-directed attitude that such studies were "unfeminine."

Sometimes a girl wanted to take a hard subject, but was advised by a guidance counselor or teacher that it was a waste of time—as, for instance, the girl in a good eastern high school who wanted to be an architect. Her counselor strongly advised her against applying for admission anywhere in architecture, on the grounds that women are rare in that profession, and she would never get in anyhow. She stubbornly applied to two universities who give degrees in architecture; both, to her amazement, accepted her. Then her counselor told her that even though she had been accepted, there was really no future for women in architecture; she would spend her life in a drafting room. She was advised to go to a junior college where the work would be much easier than in architecture and where she would learn all she needed to know when she married.[6]

The influence of sex-directed education was perhaps even more insidious on the high school level than it was in the colleges, for many girls who were subjected to it never got to college. I picked up a lesson plan for one of these life-adjustment courses now taught in junior high in the suburban county where I live. Entitled "The Slick Chick," it gives functional "do's and don'ts for dating" to girls of eleven, twelve, thirteen—a kind of early or forced recognition of their sexual function. Though many have nothing yet with which to fill a brassiere, they are told archly not to wear a sweater without one, and to be sure to wear slips so boys can't see through their skirts. It is hardly surprising that by the sophomore year, many bright girls in this high school are more than conscious of their sexual function, bored with all the subjects in school, and have no ambition other than to marry and have babies. One cannot help wondering (especially when some of these girls get pregnant as high school sophomores and marry at fifteen or sixteen) if they have not been educated for their sexual function too soon, while their other abilities go unrecognized.

This stunting of able girls from nonsexual growth is nationwide. Of the top ten percent of graduates of Indiana high schools in 1955, only fifteen percent of the boys did not continue their education: thirty-six percent of the girls did not go on.[7] In the very years in which higher education has become a necessity for almost everyone who wants a real function in our exploding society, *the proportion of women among college students has declined, year by year.* In the fifties, women also dropped out of college at a faster rate than the men: only thirty-seven percent of the women graduated, in contrast to fifty-five percent of the men.[8] By the sixties, an equal proportion of boys was dropping out of college.[9] But, in this era of keen competition for college seats, the one girl who enters college for every two boys is "more highly selected," and less likely to be dropped from college for academic failure. Women drop out, as David Riesman says, either to marry or because they fear too much education is a "marriage bar." The average age of first marriage, in the last fifteen years, has dropped to the youngest in the history of this country, the youngest in any of the countries of the Western world, almost as young as it used to be in the so-called underdeveloped countries. In the new nations of Asia and Africa, with the advent of science and education, the marriage age of women is now rising. Today, thanks in part to the functional sex-direction of women's education, the annual rate of population increase in the United States is among the highest in the world—nearly three times that of the western European nations, nearly double Japan's, and close on the heels of Africa and India.[10]

The sex-directed educators have played a dual role in this trend: by actively educating girls to their sexual function (which perhaps they would fulfill without such education, in a way less likely to prevent their growth in other directions); and by abdicating their responsibility for the education of women, in the strict intellectual sense. With or without education, women are likely to fulfill their biological role, and experience sexual love and motherhood. But without education, women or men are not likely to develop deep interests that go beyond biology.

Education should, and can, make a person "broad in outlook, and open to new experience, independent and disciplined in his thinking, deeply committed to some productive activity, possessed of convictions based on understanding of the world and on his own integration of personality."[11] The main barrier to such growth in girls is their own rigid preconception of woman's role, which sex-directed educators reinforce, either explicitly or by not facing their own ability, and responsibility, to break through it. . . .

One might ask: if an education geared to the growth of the human mind weakens femininity, will an education geared to femininity weaken the growth of the mind? What is femininity, if it can be destroyed by an education which makes the mind grow, or induced by not letting the mind grow?

One might even ask a question in Freudian terms: what happens when sex becomes not only id for women, but ego and superego as well; when education, instead of developing the self, is concentrated on developing the sexual functions? What happens when education gives new authority to the feminine "shoulds"—which already have the authority of tradition, convention, prejudice, popular opinion—instead of giving women the power of critical thought, the independence and autonomy to question blind authority, new or old? At Pembroke, the women's college at Brown University in Providence, R.I., a guest psychoanalyst was recently invited to lead a buzz session on "what it means to be a woman." The students seemed disconcerted when the guest analyst, Dr. Margaret Lawrence, said, in simple, un-Freudian English, that it was rather silly to tell women today that their main place is in the home, when most of the work women used to do is now done outside the home, and everyone else in the family spends most of his time outside the house. Hadn't they better be educated to join the rest of the family, out there in the world?

This, somehow, was not what the girls expected to hear from a lady psychoanalyst. Unlike the usual functional, sex-directed lesson, it upset a conventional feminine "should." It also implied that they should begin to make certain decisions of their own, about their education and their future.

The functional lesson is much more soothing to the unsure sophomore who has not yet quite made the break from childhood. It does not defy the comfortable, safe conventions; it gives her sophisticated words for accepting her parents' view, the popular view, without having to figure out views of her own. It also reassures her that she doesn't have to work in college; that she can be lazy, follow impulse. She doesn't have to postpone present pleasure for future goals; she doesn't have to read eight books for a history paper, take the tough physics course. It might give her a masculinity complex. After all, didn't the book say:

> Woman's intellectuality is to a large extent paid for by the loss of valuable feminine qualities. . . . All observations point to the fact that the intellectual woman is masculinized; in her warm, intuitive knowledge has yielded to cold unproductive thinking.[12]

A girl doesn't have to be very lazy, very unsure, to take the hint. Thinking, after all, is hard work. In fact, she would have to do some very cold hard thinking about her own warm, intuitive knowledge to challenge this authoritative statement.

It is no wonder that several generations of American college girls of fine mind and fiery spirit took the message of the sex-directed educators, and fled college and career to marry and have babies before they became so "intellectual" that, heaven forbid, they wouldn't be able to enjoy sex "in a feminine way."

Even without the help of sex-directed educators, the girl growing up with brains and spirit in America learns soon enough to watch her step, "to be like all the others," not to be herself. She learns not to work too hard, think too often, ask too many questions. In high schools, in coeducational colleges, girls are reluctant to speak out in class for fear of being typed as "brains." This phenomenon has been borne out by many studies;[13] any bright girl or woman can document it from personal experience. Bryn Mawr girls have a special term for the way they talk when boys are around, compared to the real talk they can permit themselves when they are not afraid to let their intelligence show. In the coeducational colleges, girls are regarded by others—and think of themselves—primarily in terms of their sexual function as dates, future wives. They "seek my security in him" instead of finding themselves, and each act of self-betrayal tips the scale further away from identity to passive self-contempt. . . .

It takes a very daring educator today to attack the sex-directed line, for he must challenge, in essence, the conventional image of femininity. The image says that women are passive, dependent, conformist, incapable of critical thought or original contribution to society; and in the best traditions of the self-fulfilling prophecy, sex-directed education continues to make them so, as in an earlier era, lack of education made them so. No one asks whether a passively feminine, uncomplicated, dependent woman—in a primitive village or in a suburb—actually enjoys greater happiness, greater sexual fulfillment than a woman who commits herself in college to serious interests beyond the home. No one, until very recently when Russians orbited moons and men in space, asked whether adjustment should be education's aim. In fact, the sex-directed educators, so bent on women's feminine adjustment, could gaily cite the most ominous facts about American housewives—their emptiness, idleness, boredom, alcoholism, drug addiction, disintegration to fat, disease, and despair after forty, when their sexual function has been filled—without deviating a bit from their crusade to educate all women to this sole end.

So the sex-directed educator disposes of the thirty years women are likely to live after forty with three blithe proposals:

> 1. A course in "Law and Order for the Housewife" to enable her to deal, as a widow, with insurances, taxes, wills, investments.
>
> 2. Men might retire earlier to help keep their wives company.
>
> 3. A brief fling in "volunteer community services, politics, the arts or the like"—though, since the woman will be untrained the main value will be personal therapy. "To choose only one example, a woman who wants some really novel experience may start a campaign to rid her city or country of that nauseous eczema of our modern world, the billboard.
>
> "The billboards will remain and multiply like bacteria infesting the landscape, but at least she will have had a vigorous adult education course in local politics. Then she can relax and devote herself to the alumnae activities of the institution from which she graduated. Many a woman approaching middle years has found new vigor and

enthusiasm in identifying herself with the on-going life of
her college and in expanding her maternal instincts, now
that her own children are grown, to encompass the new
generations of students which inhabit its campus."[14]

She could also take a part-time job, he said, but she shouldn't take
work away from men who must feed their families, and, in fact, she
won't have the skills or experience for a very "exciting" job.

. . . there is great demand for experienced and reliable
women who can relieve younger women of family responsibilities on regular days or afternoons, so that they may either
develop community interests or hold part-time jobs of their
own. . . . There is no reason why women of culture and breeding, who in any case for years have probably done most of their
own housework, should recoil from such arrangements.[15]

If the feminine mystique has not destroyed her sense of humor,
a woman might laugh at such a candid description of the life her
expensive sex-directed education fits her for: an occasional alumnae
reunion and someone else's housework. The sad fact is, in the era
of Freud and functionalism and the feminine mystique, few educators escaped such a sex-distortion of their own values. Max Lerner,[16]
even Riesman in *The Lonely Crowd*, suggested that women need
not seek their own autonomy through productive contribution to
society—they might better help their husbands hold on to theirs,
through play. And so sex-directed education segregated recent generations of able American women as surely as separate-but-equal
education segregated able American Negroes from the opportunity
to realize their full abilities in the mainstream of American life.

It does not explain anything to say that in this era of conformity
colleges did not really educate anybody. The Jacob report,[17] which
leveled this indictment against American colleges generally, and
even the more sophisticated indictment by Sanford and his group,
does not recognize that the colleges' failure to educate women for an
identity beyond their sexual role was undoubtedly a crucial factor in
perpetuating, if not creating, that conformity which educators now
so fashionably rail against. For it is impossible to educate women to

devote themselves so early and completely to their sexual role—women who, as Freud said, can be very active indeed in achieving a passive end—without pulling men into the same comfortable trap. In effect, sex-directed education led to a lack of identity in women most easily solved by early marriage. And a premature commitment to any role—marriage or vocation—closes off the experiences, the testing, the failures and successes in various spheres of activity that are necessary for a person to achieve full maturity, individual identity.

The danger of stunting of boys' growth by early domesticity was recognized by the sex-directed educators. As Margaret Mead put it recently:

> Early domesticity has always been characteristic of most savages, of most peasants, and of the urban poor. . . . If there are babies, it means, you know, the father's term paper gets all mixed up with the babies' bottle. . . . Early student marriage is domesticating boys so early they don't have a chance for full intellectual development. They don't have a chance to give their entire time, not necessarily to study in the sense of staying in the library—but in the sense that the married students don't have time to experience, to think, to sit up all night in bull sessions, to develop as individuals. This is not only important for the intellectuals, but also the boys who are going to be the future statesmen of the country and lawyers and doctors and all sorts of professional men.[18]

But what of the girls who will never even write the term papers because of the baby's bottle? Because of the feminine mystique, few have seen it as a tragedy that they thereby trap themselves in that one passion, one occupation, one role for life. Advanced educators in the early 1960s have their own cheerful fantasies about postponing women's education until after they have had their babies; they thereby acknowledge that they have resigned themselves almost unanimously to the early marriages, which continue unabated.

But by choosing femininity over the painful growth to full identity, by never achieving the hard core of self that comes not from fantasy but from mastering reality, these girls are doomed to suffer ultimately that bored, diffuse feeling of purposelessness, nonexistence, noninvolvement with the world that can be called *anomie*, or lack of identity, or merely felt as the problem that has no name.

Still, it is too easy to make education the scapegoat. Whatever the mistakes of the sex-directed educators, other educators have fought a futile, frustrating rear-guard battle trying to make able women "envision new goals and grow by reaching for them." In the last analysis, millions of able women in this free land chose, themselves, not to use the door education could have opened for them. The choice—and the responsibility—for the race back home was finally their own.

Notes

1. Lynn White, *Educating our Daughters*, New York, 1950, pp. 18–48.
2. *Ibid.*, p. 76.
3. *Ibid.*, pp. 77 ff.
4. *Ibid.*, p. 79.
5. See Dael Wolfle, *America's Resources of Specialized Talent*, New York, 1954.
6. Cited in an address by Judge Mary H. Donlon in proceedings of "Conference on the Present Status and Prospective Trends of Research on the Education of Women," 1957, American Council on Education, Washington, D.C.
7. See "The Bright Girl: A Major Source of Untapped Talent," *Guidance Newsletter*, Science Research Associates Inc., Chicago, Ill., May, 1959.
8. See Dael Wolfle, *op. cit.*
9. John Summerskill, "Dropouts from College," in *The American College*, p. 631.
10. Joseph M. Jones, "Does Overpopulation Mean Poverty?" Center for International Economic Growth, Washington, 1962. See also *United Nations Demographic Yearbook*, New York, 1960, pp. 580 ff. By 1958, in the United States, more girls were marrying from 15–19 years of age than from any other age group. In all of the other advanced nations, and many of the emerging underdeveloped nations, most girls married from 20–24 or after 25. The U.S. pattern of teenage marriage could only be found in countries like Paraguay, Venezuela, Honduras, Guatemala, Mexico, Egypt, Iraq, and the Fiji Islands.
11. Nevitt Sanford, "Higher Education as a Social Problem" in *The American College*, p. 23.
12. Helene Deutsch, *op. cit.*, Vol. I, p. 290.
13. Mirra Komarovsky, *op. cit.*, p. 70. Research studies indicate that 40 percent of college girls "play dumb" with men. Since the ones who do not include those not excessively overburdened with intelligence, the great majority of American girls who are gifted with high intelligence evidently learn to hide it.
14. Lynn White, *op. cit.*, p. 117.
15. *Ibid.*, pp. 119 f.

16. Max Lerner, *America As a Civilization*, New York, 1957, pp. 608–611:

> The crux of it lies neither in the biological nor economic disabilities of women but in their sense of being caught between a man's world which they have no real will to achieve and a world of their own in which they find it hard to be fulfilled.... When Walt Whitman exhorted women "to give up toys and fictions and launch forth, as men do, amid real, independent, stormy life," he was thinking— as were many of his contemporaries—of the wrong kind of equalitarianism.... If she is to discover her identity, she must start by basing her belief in herself on her womanliness rather than on the movement for feminism. Margaret Mead has pointed out that the biological life cycle of the woman has certain well-marked phases from menarche through the birth of her children to her menopause; that in these stages of her life cycle, as in her basic bodily rhythms, she can feel secure in her womanhood and does not have to assert her potency as the male does. Similarly, while the multiple roles that she must play in life are bewildering, she can fulfill them without distraction if she knows that her central role is that of a woman.... Her central function, however, remains that of creating a lifestyle for herself and for the home in which she is life creator and life sustainer.

17. See Philip E. Jacob, *Changing Values in College*, New York, 1957.
18. Margaret Mead, "New Look at Early Marriages," interview in *U.S. News and World Report*, June 6, 1960.

QUESTIONS FOR DISCUSSION

Why does Ruskin believe that women must be "wise, not for self-development, but for self-renunciation"? (215)

1. According to Ruskin, why have the "relations of the womanly to the manly nature" never been agreed upon? (213)

2. How does Ruskin differentiate between man's "determining" function and woman's "guiding" function? (214)

3. Why does a "true wife" create a home "wherever she is"? (215)

4. Why does Ruskin believe women should be taught in a way that leads them "only to feel, and to judge" a subject, but not to know it? (216)

According to Friedan, why did many college women in the 1950s "defend themselves against an involvement with the life of the mind"? (221)

1. Why did many educators and professors in the 1950s believe that education was "defeminizing American women"? (222)

2. Why does Friedan believe that the "sophisticated soup of uncritical prescriptions and presentiments" is more binding on young women than "the traditional do's and don'ts"? (223)

3. According to Friedan, why would a male professor have "no reason *not* to believe" the feminine mystique? (223)

4. Why does Friedan end the chapter by saying the primary responsibility for women's choice "not to use the door education could have opened for them" is "finally their own"? (234)

FOR FURTHER REFLECTION

1. Which description of the way women should live and learn do you find more appealing, Ruskin's or Friedan's?

2. Do you believe it is possible or useful to attempt to define a role for women?

3. To what extent do you think education today is, in Friedan's sense, "sex-directed"? To what degree do you think it should be?

4. Does limiting the role of women necessarily lead to limiting the role of men as well?

WAR

War and poetry are inseparably linked in all times and places. The power of poetry to stir strong emotions has been used again and again to rally entire nations to war. It has provided memorable words and images to elevate the grinding work of war-making above the grim realities of pain and loss that are the inevitable consequences, giving voice to the impulse of patriotism. At the same time, poets responding to war often strive to jolt their audiences into a heightened awareness of the toll that war takes on everyone touched by it, military and civilian alike. The following poems are intimately linked. The World War I poet Wilfred Owen picks up a Latin phrase in Horace's work and makes it the title and culmination of his own poem, a scathing critique of the sentiments of Horace, who used his words to valorize war.

The Roman poet **Horace** (65–8 BCE) wrote during the reign of the Emperor Augustus in the early years of the Roman Empire. The poem included here is taken from the third book of his *Odes* and contains the line "Dulce et decorum est pro patria mori" ("It's sweet and fitting to die for one's country"), a line that has been used repeatedly in literature and public life to both reinforce and ironically subvert unthinking patriotism.

British poet and soldier **Wilfred Owen** (1893–1918) experienced the full impact of modern warfare in the trenches in France during World War I, including the horrors of gas warfare that he describes so vividly. Virtually all of his poetry was a direct response to his combat experiences and began to take shape during his hospital stay in 1917 when he was recovering from being wounded. He returned to active duty and was killed in 1918, one week before the war ended.

Ode 3.2

Horace

Let the boy toughen by military service
learn how to make bitterest hardship his friend,
and as a horseman, with fearful lance,
go to vex the insolent Parthians,

spending his life in the open, in the heart
of dangerous action. And seeing him, from
the enemy's walls, let the warring
tyrant's wife, and her grown-up daughter, sigh:

"Ah, don't let the inexperienced lover
provoke the lion that's dangerous to touch,
whom a desire for blood sends raging
so swiftly through the core of destruction."

It's sweet and fitting to die for one's country.
Yet death chases after the soldier who runs,
and it won't spare the cowardly back
or the limbs, of peace-loving young men.

Virtue, that's ignorant of sordid defeat,
shines out with its honor unstained, and never
takes up the axes or puts them down
at the request of a changeable mob.

Virtue, that opens the heavens for those who
did not deserve to die, takes a road denied
to others, and scorns the vulgar crowd
and the bloodied earth, on ascending wings.

And there's a true reward for loyal silence:
I forbid the man who divulged those secret
rites of Ceres, to exist beneath
the same roof as I, or untie with me

the fragile boat: often careless Jupiter
included the innocent with the guilty,
but lame-footed Punishment rarely
forgets the wicked man, despite his start.

Dulce et Decorum Est

Wilfred Owen

Bent double, like old beggars under sacks,
Knock-kneed, coughing like hags, we cursed through sludge,
Till on the haunting flares we turned our backs
And towards our distant rest began to trudge.
Men marched asleep. Many had lost their boots
But limped on, blood-shod. All went lame; all blind;
Drunk with fatigue; deaf even to the hoots
Of tired, outstripped Five-Nines that dropped behind.

Gas! GAS! Quick, boys!—An ecstasy of fumbling,
Fitting the clumsy helmets just in time;
But someone still was yelling out and stumbling,
And flound'ring like a man in fire or lime . . .
Dim, through the misty panes and thick green light,
As under a green sea, I saw him drowning.

In all my dreams, before my helpless sight,
He plunges at me, guttering, choking, drowning.

If in some smothering dreams you too could pace
Behind the wagon that we flung him in,
And watch the white eyes writhing in his face,
His hanging face, like a devil's sick of sin;
If you could hear, at every jolt, the blood
Come gargling from the froth-corrupted lungs,
Obscene as cancer, bitter as the cud

Of vile, incurable sores on innocent tongues,—
My friend, you would not tell with such high zest
To children ardent for some desperate glory,
The old Lie: Dulce et decorum est
Pro patria mori.

QUESTIONS FOR DISCUSSION

According to Horace, why is it "sweet and fitting to die for one's country"? (243)

1. Why does Horace describe the enemy's wife and daughter sighing over the "inexperienced lover"? (243)

2. Why does Horace contrast the valorous virtue of the hero with the "changeable mob" and the "vulgar crowd"? (243, 244)

3. Why does Horace say that death "won't spare the cowardly back . . ." of peace-loving young men"? (243)

4. Why does Horace personify virtue and say that it "takes a road denied / to others, and scorns the vulgar crowd"? (244)

Why does the speaker in Owen's poem declare that if the reader could see war's reality, he would not tell the "old Lie" that it is sweet and fitting to die for one's country? (246)

1. Why does the speaker describe the gas victim "As under a green sea . . . drowning"? (245)

2. Why does the speaker say that the scramble to put on gas masks is "An ecstasy of fumbling"? (245)

3. Why does the gas victim's face look to the speaker "like a devil's sick of sin"? (245)

4. Why does the speaker compare the gargling blood to "vile, incurable sores on innocent tongues"? (246)

FOR FURTHER REFLECTION

1. Is it "sweet and fitting" to die fighting for your country?

2. Under what circumstances is patriotism a virtue?

3. Why does Owen engage with Horace's ode, written almost two thousand years earlier?

4. Are young people today still joining the military "ardent for some desperate glory"?

LITERATURE

For centuries the role of the author has been celebrated and even venerated. But by the 1960s, the "death of the author" had become a popular concept among cultural circles. It was formulated most explicitly in a 1967 essay written by French critic Roland Barthes. He argued against reading texts with either the author's intention or biography in mind. For Barthes, the interpretation of a text lay in what was received by the reader, rather than what was directed by the author. The author no longer owned the story. This perspective was a radical break in attitude toward the author, tearing apart the humanist connection between writer and text that had stood for centuries.

English writer **Ben Jonson** (1572–1637) composed the poem "To the Memory of My Beloved, the Author Mr. William Shakespeare" (1623) as a paean to the man and his work. For Jonson, Shakespeare the man embodied the virtues of the works: the writer and his work were inseparable. This association of the two is so long-standing in the Western tradition that, even fifty years after Barthes declared the death of the author, public and critical opinion remains divided upon the issue, with many still supporting Jonson's Renaissance view of the author as the sole director of a text's meaning.

Barthes's essay stimulated great debate. One of his early respondents was the French philosopher **Michel Foucault** (1926–1984), whose essay "What Is an Author?" (1969) explored further the consequences of the author's death as a cultural figure. To switch from revering to not acknowledging the author requires an understanding of the origins of such a change, as well as recognition that the author has become a contested concept. Such a change in our appreciation of art might be far-reaching; without the author's presence and influence, each reading could herald a new act of interpretation.

To the Memory of My Beloved, the Author Mr. William Shakespeare

And What He Hath Left Us

Ben Jonson

To draw no envy, Shakespeare, on thy name,
Am I thus ample to thy book and fame,
While I confess thy writings to be such
As neither man nor Muse can praise too much.
'Tis true, and all men's suffrage. But these ways
Were not the paths I meant unto thy praise:
For silliest ignorance on these may light,
Which, when it sounds at best, but echoes right;
Or blind affection, which doth ne'er advance
The truth, but gropes, and urgeth all by chance;
Or crafty malice might pretend this praise,
And think to ruin where it seemed to raise.
These are as some infamous bawd or whore
Should praise a matron. What could hurt her more?
But thou art proof against them, and, indeed,
Above th' ill fortune of them, or the need.
I therefore will begin. Soul of the age!
The applause! delight! the wonder of our stage!
My Shakespeare, rise; I will not lodge thee by

Chaucer or Spenser, or bid Beaumont lie[1]
A little further to make thee a room:
Thou art a monument without a tomb,
And art alive still while thy book doth live,
And we have wits to read and praise to give.
That I not mix thee so, my brain excuses,
I mean with great, but disproportioned Muses;
For, if I thought my judgment were of years,
I should commit thee surely with thy peers,
And tell how far thou didst our Lyly outshine,
Or sporting Kyd, or Marlowe's mighty line.
And though thou hadst small Latin and less Greek,
From thence to honor thee I would not seek
For names, but call forth thund'ring Aeschylus,
Euripides, and Sophocles to us,
Pacuvius, Accius, him of Cordova dead,[2]
To life again, to hear thy buskin tread
And shake a stage; or, when thy socks were on,
Leave thee alone for the comparison
Of all that insolent Greece or haughty Rome
Sent forth, or since did from their ashes come.
Triumph, my Britain; thou hast one to show
To whom all scenes of Europe homage owe.
He was not of an age, but for all time!
And all the Muses still were in their prime
When like Apollo he came forth to warm
Our ears, or like a Mercury to charm.
Nature herself was proud of his designs,
And joyed to wear the dressing of his lines,

---

1. [All three authors—Geoffrey Chaucer (ca. 1340–1400), Edmund Spenser (ca. 1552–1599), Francis Beaumont (1584–1616)—are buried in Westminster Abbey, London. Shakespeare is buried in the Holy Trinity Church, Stratford-on-Avon (see "Avon," line 71).]
2. [I.e., Seneca, Roman tragedian of the first century C.E.; Marcus Pacuvius and Lucius Accius were Roman tragedians of the second century B.C.E. Aeschylus (525–456 B.C.E.), Euripides (ca. 484–406 B.C.E.), and Sophocles (ca. 496–406 B.C.E.) were all Greek dramatists.]

Which were so richly spun, and woven so fit,
As, since, she will vouchsafe no other wit:
The merry Greek, tart Aristophanes,
Neat Terence, witty Plautus now not please,
But antiquated and deserted lie,
As they were not of Nature's family.
Yet must I not give Nature all; thy Art,
My gentle Shakespeare, must enjoy a part.
For though the poet's matter Nature be,
His Art doth give the fashion; and that he
Who casts to write a living line must sweat
(Such as thine are) and strike the second heat
Upon the Muses' anvil; turn the same,
And himself with it, that he thinks to frame,
Or for the laurel he may gain a scorn;
For a good poet's made as well as born.
And such wert thou! Look how the father's face
Lives in his issue, even so the race
Of Shakespeare's mind and manners brightly shines
In his well-turnèd and true-filèd lines,
In each of which he seems to shake a lance,
As brandished at the eyes of ignorance.
Sweet swan of Avon, what a sight it were
To see thee in our waters yet appear,
And make those flights upon the banks of Thames
That so did take Eliza and our James!
But stay; I see thee in the hemisphere
Advanced and made a constellation there!
Shine forth, thou star of poets, and with rage
Or influence chide or cheer the drooping stage,
Which, since thy flight from hence, hath mourned like night,
And despairs day, but for thy volume's light.

What Is an Author?

Michel Foucault

The coming into being of the notion of "author" constitutes the privileged moment of *individualization* in the history of ideas, knowledge, literature, philosophy, and the sciences. Even today, when we reconstruct the history of a concept, literary genre, or school of philosophy, such categories seem relatively weak, secondary, and superimposed scansions in comparison with the solid and fundamental unit of the author and the work.

I shall not offer here a sociohistorical analysis of the author's persona. Certainly it would be worth examining how the author became individualized in a culture like ours, what status he has been given, at what moment studies of authenticity and attribution began, in what kind of system of valorization the author was involved, at what point we began to recount the lives of authors rather than of heroes, and how this fundamental category of "the-man-and-his-work criticism" began. For the moment, however, I want to deal solely with the relationship between text and author and with the manner in which the text points to this "figure" that, at least in appearance, is outside it and antecedes it.

Beckett nicely formulates the theme with which I would like to begin: " 'What does it matter who is speaking', someone said, 'what does it matter who is speaking.' " In this indifference appears one of the fundamental ethical principles of contemporary writing [*écriture*]. I say "ethical" because this indifference is not really a trait characterizing the manner in which one speaks and writes, but rather a kind of immanent rule, taken up over and over again, never fully applied, not designating writing as something completed, but dominating it as a practice. Since it is too familiar to require a lengthy analysis, this immanent rule can be adequately illustrated here by tracing two of its major themes.

First of all, we can say that today's writing has freed itself from the dimension of expression. Referring only to itself, but without being restricted to the confines of its interiority, writing is identified with its own unfolded exteriority. This means that it is an interplay of signs arranged less according to its signified content than according to the very nature of the signifier. Writing unfolds like a game [*jeu*] that invariably goes beyond its own rules and transgresses its limits. In writing, the point is not to manifest or exalt the act of writing, nor is it to pin a subject within language; it is rather a question of creating a space into which the writing subject constantly disappears.

The second theme, writing's relationship with death, is even more familiar. This link subverts an old tradition exemplified by the Greek epic, which was intended to perpetuate the immortality of the hero: if he was willing to die young, it was so that his life, consecrated and magnified by death, might pass into immortality; the narrative then redeemed this accepted death. In another way, the motivation, as well as the theme and the pretext of Arabian narratives—such as *The Thousand and One Nights*—was also the eluding of death: one spoke, telling stories into the early morning, in order to forestall death, to postpone the day of reckoning that would silence the narrator. Scheherazade's narrative is an effort, renewed each night, to keep death outside the circle of life.

Our culture has metamorphosed this idea of narrative, or writing, as something designed to ward off death. Writing has become linked to sacrifice, even to the sacrifice of life: it is now a voluntary effacement which does not need to be represented in books, since it is brought about in the writer's very existence. The work, which once had the duty of providing immortality, now possesses the right to kill, to be its author's murderer, as in the cases of Flaubert, Proust, and Kafka. That is not all, however: this relationship between writing and death is also manifested in the effacement of the writing subject's individual characteristics. Using all the contrivances that he sets up between himself and what he writes, the writing subject cancels out the signs of his particular individuality. As a result, the mark of the writer is reduced to nothing more than the singularity of his absence; he must assume the role of the dead man in the game of writing.

None of this is recent; criticism and philosophy took note of the disappearance—or death—of the author some time ago. But the consequences of their discovery of it have not been sufficiently examined, nor has its import been accurately measured. A certain number of notions that are intended to replace the privileged position of the author actually seem to preserve that privilege and suppress the real meaning of his disappearance. I shall examine two of these notions, both of great importance today.

The first is the idea of the work. It is a very familiar thesis that the task of criticism is not to bring out the work's relationships with the author, nor to reconstruct through the text a thought or experience, but rather, to analyze the work through its structure, its architecture, its intrinsic form, and the play of its internal relationships. At this point, however, a problem arises: "What is a work? What is this curious unity which we designate as a work? Of what elements is it composed? Is it not what an author has written?" Difficulties appear immediately. If an individual were not an author, could we say that what he wrote, said, left behind in his papers, or what has been collected of his remarks, could be called a "work"? When Sade was not considered an author, what was the status of his papers? Were they simply rolls of paper onto which he ceaselessly uncoiled his fantasies during his imprisonment?

Even when an individual has been accepted as an author, we must still ask whether everything that he wrote, said, or left behind is part of his work. The problem is both theoretical and technical. When undertaking the publication of Nietzsche's works, for example, where should one stop? Surely everything must be published, but what is "everything"? Everything that Nietzsche himself published, certainly. And what about the rough drafts for his works? Obviously. The plans for his aphorisms? Yes. The deleted passages and the notes at the bottom of the page? Yes. What if, within a workbook filled with aphorisms, one finds a reference, the notation of a meeting or of an address, or a laundry list: is it a work, or not? Why not? And so on, ad infinitum. How can one define a work amid the millions of traces left by someone after his death? A theory of the work does not exist, and the empirical task of those who naively undertake the editing of works often suffers in the absence of such a theory.

We could go even further: does *The Thousand and One Nights* constitute a work? What about Clement of Alexandria's *Miscellanies* or Diogenes Laertius' *Lives*?[1] A multitude of questions arises with regard to this notion of the work. Consequently, it is not enough to declare that we should do without the writer (the author) and study the work in itself. The word 'work' and the unity that it designates are probably as problematic as the status of the author's individuality.

Another notion which has hindered us from taking full measure of the author's disappearance, blurring and concealing the moment of this effacement and subtly preserving the author's existence, is the notion of writing [*ècriture*]. When rigorously applied, this notion should allow us not only to circumvent references to the author, but also to situate his recent absence. The notion of writing, as currently employed, is concerned with neither the act of writing nor the indication—be it symptom or sign—of a meaning which someone might have wanted to express. We try, with great effort, to imagine the general condition of each text, the condition of both the space in which it is dispersed and the time in which it unfolds.

In current usage, however, the notion of writing seems to transpose the empirical characteristics of the author into a transcendental anonymity. We are content to efface the more visible marks of the author's empiricity by playing off, one against the other, two ways of characterizing writing, namely, the critical and the religious approaches. Giving writing a primal status seems to be a way of retranslating, in transcendental terms, both the theological affirmation of its sacred character and the critical affirmation of its creative character. To admit that writing is, because of the very history that it made possible, subject to the test of oblivion and repression, seems

1. [Clement of Alexandria was a Christian theologian of the second century whose *Stromata* or *Miscellanies* was a commentary on the history of philosophy. Diogenes Laertius was a native of Cicilia who probably lived at about the same time. His *Lives of the Philosophers* ran to ten volumes.]

to represent, in transcendental terms, the religious principle of the hidden meaning (which requires interpretation) and the critical principle of implicit significations, silent determinations, and obscured contents (which gives rise to commentary). To imagine writing as absence seems to be a simple repetition, in transcendental terms, of both the religious principle of inalterable and yet never fulfilled tradition, and the aesthetic principle of the work's survival, its perpetuation beyond the author's death, and its enigmatic *excess* in relation to him.

This usage of the notion of writing runs the risk of maintaining the author's privileges under the protection of writing's a priori status: it keeps alive, in the grey light of neutralization, the interplay of those representations that formed a particular image of the author. The author's disappearance, which, since Mallarmé, has been a constantly recurring event, is subject to a series of transcendental barriers. There seems to be an important dividing line between those who believe that they can still locate today's discontinuities [*ruptures*] in the historico-transcendental tradition of the nineteenth century, and those who try to free themselves once and for all from that tradition.

It is not enough, however, to repeat the empty affirmation that the author has disappeared. For the same reason, it is not enough to keep repeating (after Nietzsche) that God and man have died a common death. Instead, we must locate the space left empty by the author's disappearance, follow the distribution of gaps and breaches, and watch for the openings that this disappearance uncovers.

First, we need to clarify briefly the problems arising from the use of the author's name. What is an author's name? How does it function? Far from offering a solution, I shall only indicate some of the difficulties that it presents.

The author's name is a proper name, and therefore it raises the problems common to all proper names. (Here I refer to Searle's analyses, among others.[2]) Obviously, one cannot turn a proper name into

2. [See John Searle, *Speech Acts: an Essay in the Philosophy of Language* (1969).]

a pure and simple reference. It has other than indicative functions: more than an indication, a gesture, a finger pointed at someone, it is the equivalent of a description. When one says "Aristotle," one employs a word that is the equivalent of one or a series of, definite descriptions, such as "the author of the *Analytics*," "the founder of ontology," and so forth. One cannot stop there, however, because a proper name does not have just one signification. When we discover that Rimbaud did not write *La Chasse spirituelle*[3] [*The Spiritual Pursuit*], we cannot pretend that the meaning of this proper name, or that of the author, has been altered. The proper name and the author's name are situated between the two poles of description and designation: they must have a certain link with what they name, but one that is neither entirely in the mode of designation nor in that of description; it must be a *specific* link. However—and it is here that the particular difficulties of the author's name arise—the links between the proper name and the individual named and between the author's name and what it names are not isomorphic and do not function in the same way. There are several differences.

If, for example, Pierre Dupont does not have blue eyes, or was not born in Paris, or is not a doctor, the name Pierre Dupont will still always refer to the same person; such things do not modify the link of designation. The problems raised by the author's name are much more complex, however. If I discover that Shakespeare was not born in the house that we visit today, this is a modification which, obviously, will not alter the functioning of the author's name. But if we proved that Shakespeare did not write those sonnets which pass for his, that would constitute a significant change and affect the manner in which the author's name functions. If we proved that Shakespeare wrote Bacon's *Organon* by showing that the same author wrote both the works of Bacon and those of Shakespeare, that would be a third type of change which would entirely modify the functioning of the author's name. The author's name is not, therefore, just a proper name like the rest.

---

3. [A supposedly lost poem by the French Symbolist poet Arthur Rimbaud (1854–91) which was published in the French newspaper *Combat* on 19 May 1949. It was eventually revealed to be a pastiche written by Akakia-Viala and Nicolas Bataille.]

Many other facts point out the paradoxical singularity of the author's name. To say that Pierre Dupont does not exist is not at all the same as saying that Homer or Hermes Trismegistus[4] did not exist. In the first case, it means that no one has the name Pierre Dupont; in the second, it means that several people were mixed together under one name, or that the true author had none of the traits traditionally ascribed to the personae of Homer or Hermes. To say that X's real name is actually Jacques Durand instead of Pierre Dupont is not the same as saying that Stendhal's name was Henri Beyle. One could also question the meaning and functioning of propositions like "Bourbaki is so-and-so, so-and-so, etc." and "Victor Eremita, Climacus, Anticlimacus, Frater Taciturnus, Constantine Constantius, all of these are Kierkegaard."

These differences may result from the fact that an author's name is not simply an element in a discourse (capable of being either subject or object, of being replaced by a pronoun, and the like); it performs a certain role with regard to narrative discourse, assuring a classificatory function. Such a name permits one to group together a certain number of texts, define them, differentiate them from and contrast them to others. In addition, it establishes a relationship among the texts. Hermes Trismegistus did not exist, nor did Hippocrates[5]—in the sense that Balzac existed—but the fact that several texts have been placed under the same name indicates that there has been established among them a relationship of homogeneity, filiation, authentification of some texts by the use of others, reciprocal explication, or concomitant utilization. The author's name serves to characterize a certain mode of being of discourse: the fact that the discourse has an author's name, that one can say "this was written by so-and-so" or "so-and-so is its author," shows that this discourse is not ordinary everyday speech that merely comes and goes, not something that is immediately consumable. On the contrary, it is a speech that must be received in a certain mode and that, in a given culture, must receive a certain status.

---

4. [Reputed author of ancient books of occult wisdom.]
5. [Greek physician of the 5th century BC. He is honored as the father of medicine, but the details of his life and work are obscure.]

It would seem that the author's name, unlike other proper names, does not pass from the interior of a discourse to the real and exterior individual who produced it; instead, the name seems always to be present, marking off the edges of the text, revealing, or at least characterizing, its mode of being. The author's name manifests the appearance of a certain discursive set and indicates the status of this discourse within a society and a culture. It has no legal status, nor is it located in the fiction of the work; rather, it is located in the break that founds a certain discursive construct and its very particular mode of being. As a result, we could say that in a civilization like our own there are a certain number of discourses that are endowed with the "author-function," while others are deprived of it. A private letter may well have a signer—it does not have an author; a contract may well have a guarantor—it does not have an author. An anonymous text posted on a wall probably has a writer—but not an author. The author-function is therefore characteristic of the mode of existence, circulation, and functioning of certain discourses within a society.

Let us analyze this "author-function" as we have just described it. In our culture, how does one characterize discourse containing the author-function? In what way is this discourse different from other discourses? If we limit our remarks to the author of a book or a text, we can isolate four different characteristics.

First of all, discourses are objects of appropriation. The form of ownership from which they spring is of a rather particular type, one that has been codified for many years. We should note that, historically, this type of ownership has always been subsequent to what one might call penal appropriation. Texts, books, and discourses really began to have authors (other than mythical, "sacralized," and "sacralizing" figures) to the extent that authors became subject to punishment, that is, to the extent that discourses could be transgressive. In our culture (and doubtless in many others), discourse was not originally a product, a thing, a kind of goods; it was essentially an act—an act placed in the bipolar field of the sacred and the profane, the licit and the illicit, the religious and the blasphemous. Historically, it was a gesture fraught with risks before becoming goods caught up in a circuit of ownership.

Once a system of ownership for texts came into being, once strict rules concerning author's rights, author-publisher relations, rights of reproduction, and related matters were enacted—at the end of the eighteenth and the beginning of the nineteenth century—the possibility of transgression attached to the act of writing took on, more and more, the form of an imperative peculiar to literature. It is as if the author, beginning with the moment at which he was placed in the system of property that characterizes our society, compensated for the status that he thus acquired by rediscovering the old bipolar field of discourse, systematically practicing transgression and thereby restoring danger to a writing which was now guaranteed the benefits of ownership.

The author-function does not affect all discourses in a universal and constant way, however. This is its second characteristic. In our civilization, it has not always been the same types of texts which have required attribution to an author. There was a time when the texts that we today call "literary" (narratives, stories, epics, tragedies, comedies) were accepted, put into circulation, and valorized without any question about the identity of their author; their anonymity caused no difficulties since their ancientness, whether real or imagined, was regarded as a sufficient guarantee of their status. On the other hand, those texts that we now would call scientific—those dealing with cosmology and the heavens, medicine and illnesses, natural sciences and geography—were accepted in the Middle Ages, and accepted as "true," only when marked with the name of their author. "Hippocrates said," "Pliny recounts,"[6] were not really formulas of an argument based on authority; they were the markers inserted in discourses that were supposed to be received as statements of demonstrated truth.

A reversal occurred in the seventeenth or eighteenth century. Scientific discourses began to be received for themselves, in the anonymity of an established or always redemonstrable truth; their membership in a systematic ensemble, and not the reference to the individual who produced them, stood as their guarantee. The

6. [Caius Plinius Secundus, Roman naturalist of the first century AD, author of the encyclopaedic *Natural History*.]

author-function faded away, and the inventor's name served only to christen a theorem, proposition, particular effect, property, body, group of elements, or pathological syndrome. By the same token, literary discourses came to be accepted only when endowed with the author-function. We now ask of each poetic or fictional text: from where does it come, who wrote it, when, under what circumstances, or beginning with what design? The meaning ascribed to it and the status or value accorded it depend upon the manner in which we answer these questions. And if a text should be discovered in a state of anonymity—whether as a consequence of an accident or the author's explicit wish—the game becomes one of rediscovering the author. Since literary anonymity is not tolerable, we can accept it only in the guise of an enigma. As a result, the author-function today plays an important role in our view of literary works. (These are obviously generalizations that would have to be refined insofar as recent critical practice is concerned.)

The third characteristic of this author-function is that it does not develop spontaneously as the attribution of a discourse to an individual. It is, rather, the result of a complex operation which constructs a certain rational being that we call "author." Critics doubtless try to give this intelligible being a realistic status, by discerning, in the individual, a "deep" motive, a "creative" power, or a "design," the milieu in which writing originates. Nevertheless, these aspects of an individual which we designate as making him an author are only a projection, in more or less psychologizing terms, of the operations that we force texts to undergo, the connections that we make, the traits that we establish as pertinent, the continuities that we recognize, or the exclusions that we practice. All these operations vary according to periods and types of discourse. We do not construct a "philosophical author" as we do a "poet," just as, in the eighteenth century, one did not construct a novelist as we do today. Still, we can find through the ages certain constants in the rules of author-construction.

It seems, for example, that the manner in which literary criticism once defined the author—or rather constructed the figure of the author beginning with existing texts and discourses—is directly derived from the manner in which Christian tradition authenticated (or rejected) the texts at its disposal. In order to "rediscover" an author in a work, modern criticism uses methods similar to those that Christian exegesis employed when trying to prove the value of a text by its author's saintliness. In *De viris illustribus* [*Concerning Illustrious Men*], Saint Jerome explains that homonymy is not sufficient to identify legitimately authors of more than one work: different individuals could have had the same name, or one man could have, illegitimately, borrowed another's patronymic. The name as an individual trademark is not enough when one works within a textual tradition.

How then can one attribute several discourses to one and the same author? How can one use the author-function to determine if one is dealing with one or several individuals? Saint Jerome proposes four criteria: (1) if among several books attributed to an author one is inferior to the others, it must be withdrawn from the list of the author's works (the author is therefore defined as a constant level of value); (2) the same should be done if certain texts contradict the doctrine expounded in the author's other works (the author is thus defined as a field of conceptual or theoretical coherence); (3) one must also exclude works that are written in a different style, containing words and expressions not ordinarily found in the writer's production (the author is here conceived as a stylistic unity); (4) finally, passages quoting statements that were made, or mentioning events that occurred after the author's death must be regarded as interpolated texts (the author is here seen as a historical figure at the crossroads of a certain number of events).

Modern literary criticism, even when—as is now customary—it is not concerned with questions of authentication, still defines the author the same way: the author provides the basis for explaining not only the presence of certain events in a work, but also their transformations, distortions, and diverse modifications (through his biography, the determination of his individual perspective, the analysis of his social position, and the revelation of his basic design). The author is also the principle of a certain unity of writing—all differences, having to be resolved, at least in part, by the principles of evolution, maturation, or influence. The author also serves to neutralize the contradictions that may emerge in a series of texts: there must be—at a certain level of his thought or desire, of his consciousness or unconscious—a point where contradictions are resolved, where incompatible elements are at last tied together or organized around a fundamental or originating contradiction. Finally, the author is a particular source of expression that, in more or less completed forms, is manifested equally well, and with similar validity, in works, sketches, letters, fragments, and so on. Clearly, Saint Jerome's four criteria of authenticity (criteria which seem totally insufficient for today's exegetes) do define the four modalities according to which modern criticism brings the author-function into play.

But the author-function is not a pure and simple reconstruction made secondhand from a text given as passive material. The text always contains a certain number of signs referring to the author. These signs, well known to grammarians, are personal pronouns, adverbs of time and place, and verb conjugation. Such elements do not play the same role in discourses provided with the author-function as in those lacking it. In the latter, such "shifters" refer to the real speaker and to the spatio-temporal coordinates of his discourse (although certain modifications can occur, as in the operation of relating discourses in the first person). In the former, however, their role is more complex and variable. Everyone knows that, in a novel narrated in the first person, neither the first person pronoun, nor the present indicative refer exactly either to the writer or to the moment in which he writes, but rather to an alter ego whose distance from the author varies, often changing in the course of the work. It would be just as wrong to equate the author with the real writer as to equate him with the fictitious speaker; the author-function is carried out and operates in the scission itself, in this division and this distance.

One might object that this is a characteristic peculiar to novelistic or poetic discourse, a "game" in which only "quasi-discourses" participate. In fact, however, all discourses endowed with the author-function do possess this plurality of self. The self that speaks in the preface to a treatise on mathematics—and that indicates the circumstances of the treatise's composition—is identical neither in its position nor in its functioning to the self that speaks in the course of a demonstration, and that appears in the form of "I conclude" or "I suppose." In the first case, the "I" refers to an individual without an equivalent who, in a determined place and time, completed a certain task; in the second, the "I" indicates an instance and a level of demonstration which any individual could perform provided that he accept the same system of symbols, play of axioms, and set of previous demonstrations. We could also, in the same treatise, locate a third self, one that speaks to tell the work's meaning, the obstacles encountered, the results obtained, and the remaining problems; this self is situated in the field of already existing or yet-to-appear mathematical discourses. The author-function is not assumed by the first of these selves at the expense of the other two, which would then be nothing more than a fictitious splitting in two of the first one. On the contrary, in these discourses the author-function operates so as to effect the dispersion of these three simultaneous selves.

No doubt analysis could discover still more characteristic traits of the author-function. I will limit myself to these four, however, because they seem both the most visible and the most important. They can be summarized as follows: (1) the author-function is linked to the juridical and institutional system that encompasses, determines, and articulates the universe of discourses; (2) it does not affect all discourses in the same way at all times and in all types of civilization; (3) it is not defined by the spontaneous attribution of a discourse to its producer, but rather by a series of specific and complex operations; (4) it does not refer purely and simply to a real individual, since it can give rise simultaneously to several selves, to several subjects—positions that can be occupied by different classes of individuals.

Up to this point I have unjustifiably limited my subject. Certainly the author-function in painting, music, and other arts should have been discussed, but even supposing that we remain within the world of discourse, as I want to do, I seem to have given the term "author" much too narrow a meaning. I have discussed the author only in the limited sense of a person to whom the production of a text, a book, or a work can be legitimately attributed. It is easy to see that in the sphere of discourse one can be the author of much more than a book—one can be the author of a theory, tradition, or discipline in which other books and authors will in their turn find a place. These authors are in a position which we shall call "transdiscursive." This is a recurring phenomenon—certainly as old as our civilization. Homer, Aristotle, and the Church Fathers, as well as the first mathematicians and the originators of the Hippocratic tradition, all played this role.

Furthermore, in the course of the nineteenth century, there appeared in Europe another, more uncommon, kind of author, whom one should confuse with neither the "great" literary authors, nor the authors of religious texts, nor the founders of science. In a somewhat arbitrary way we shall call those who belong in this last group "founders of discursivity." They are unique in that they are not just the authors of their own works. They have produced something else: the possibilities and the rules for the formation of other texts. In this sense, they are very different, for example, from a novelist, who is, in fact, nothing more than the author of his own text. Freud is not just the author of *The Interpretation of Dreams* or *Jokes and their Relation to the Unconscious*; Marx is not just the author of the *Communist Manifesto* or *Capital*: they both have established an endless possibility of discourse.

Obviously, it is easy to object. One might say that it is not true that the author of a novel is only the author of his own text; in a sense, he also, provided that he acquires some "importance," governs and commands more than that. To take a very simple example, one could say that Ann Radcliffe not only wrote *The Castles of Athlin and Dunbayne* and several other novels, but also made possible the appearance of the Gothic horror novel at the beginning of the nineteenth century; in that respect, her author-function exceeds her own work. But I think there is an answer to this objection. These founders of discursivity (I use Marx and Freud as examples, because I believe them to be both the first and the most important cases) make possible something altogether different from what a novelist makes possible. Ann Radcliffe's texts opened the way for a certain number of resemblances and analogies which have their model or principle in her work. The latter contains characteristic signs, figures, relationships, and structures which could be reused by others.

In other words, to say that Ann Radcliffe founded the Gothic horror novel means that in the nineteenth-century Gothic novel one will find, as in Ann Radcliffe's works, the theme of the heroine caught in the trap of her own innocence, the hidden castle, the character of the black cursed hero devoted to making the world expiate the evil done to him, and all the rest of it.

On the other hand, when I speak of Marx or Freud as founders of discursivity, I mean that they made possible not only a certain number of analogies, but also (and equally important) a certain number of differences. They have created a possibility for something other than their discourse, yet something belonging to what they founded. To say that Freud founded psychoanalysis does not (simply) mean that we find the concept of the libido or the technique of dream analysis in the works of Karl Abraham or Melanie Klein; it means that Freud made possible a certain number of divergences—with respect to his own texts, concepts, and hypotheses—that all arise from the psychoanalytical discourse itself.

This would seem to present a new difficulty, however: is the above not true, after all, of any founder of a science, or of any author who has introduced some important transformation into a science? After all, Galileo made possible not only those discourses that repeated the laws that he had formulated, but also statements very different from what he himself had said. If Cuvier is the founder of biology or Saussure the founder of linguistics, it is not because they were imitated, nor because people have since taken up again the concept of organism or sign; it is because Cuvier made possible, to a certain extent, a theory of evolution diametrically opposed to his own fixism; it is because Saussure made possible a generative grammar radically different from his structural analyses. Superficially, then, the initiation of discursive practices appears similar to the founding of any scientific endeavor.

Still, there is a difference, and a notable one. In the case of a science, the act that founds it is on an equal footing with its future transformations; this act becomes in some respects part of the set of modifications that it makes possible. Of course, this belonging can take several forms. In the future development of a science, the founding act may appear as little more than a particular instance of a more general phenomenon which unveils itself in the process. It can also turn out to be marred by intuition and empirical bias; one must then reformulate it, making it the object of a certain number of supplementary theoretical operations which establish it more rigorously, etc. Finally, it can seem to be a hasty generalization which must be limited, and whose restricted domain of validity must be retraced. In other words, the founding act of a science can always be reintroduced within the machinery of those transformations that derive from it.

In contrast, the initiation of a discursive practice is heterogeneous to its subsequent transformations. To expand a type of discursivity, such as psychoanalysis as founded by Freud, is not to give it a formal generality that it would not have permitted at the outset, but rather to open it up to a certain number of possible applications. To limit psychoanalysis as a type of discursivity is, in reality, to try to isolate in the founding act an eventually restricted number of propositions or statements to which, alone, one grants a founding value, and in relation to which certain concepts or theories accepted by Freud might be considered as derived, secondary, and accessory. In addition, one does not declare certain propositions in the work of these founders to be false: instead, when trying to seize the act of founding, one sets aside those statements that are not pertinent, either because they are deemed inessential, or because they are considered "prehistoric" and derived from another type of discursivity. In other words, unlike the founding of a science, the initiation of a discursive practice does not participate in its later transformations.

As a result, one defines a proposition's theoretical validity in relation to the work of the founders—while, in the case of Galileo and Newton, it is in relation to what physics or cosmology *is* (in its intrinsic structure and "normativity") that one affirms the validity of any proposition that those men may have put forth. To phrase it very schematically: the work of initiators of discursivity is not situated in the space that science defines; rather, it is the science or the discursivity which refers back to their work as primary coordinates.

In this way we can understand the inevitable necessity, within these fields of discursivity, for a "return to the origin." This return, which is part of the discursive field itself, never stops modifying it.

The return is not a historical supplement which would be added to the discursivity, or merely an ornament; on the contrary, it constitutes an effective and necessary task of transforming the discursive practice itself. Reexamination of Galileo's text may well change our knowledge of the history of mechanics, but it will never be able to change mechanics itself. On the other hand, reexamining Freud's texts, modifies psychoanalysis itself just as a reexamination of Marx's would modify Marxism.

What I have just outlined regarding the initiation of discursive practices is, of course, very schematic; this is true, in particular, of the opposition that I have tried to draw between discursive initiation and scientific founding. It is not always easy to distinguish between the two; moreover, nothing proves that they are two mutually exclusive procedures. I have attempted the distinction for only one reason: to show that the author-function, which is complex enough when one tries to situate it at the level of a book or a series of texts that carry a given signature, involves still more determining factors when one tries to analyze it in larger units, such as groups of works or entire disciplines.

To conclude, I would like to review the reasons why I attach a certain importance to what I have said.

First, there are theoretical reasons. On the one hand, an analysis in the direction that I have outlined might provide for an approach to a typology of discourse. It seems to me, at least at first glance, that such a typology cannot be constructed solely from the grammatical features, formal structures, and objects of discourse: more likely there exist properties or relationships peculiar to discourse (not reducible to the rules of grammar and logic), and one must use these to distinguish the major categories of discourse. The relationship (or nonrelationship) with an author, and the different forms this relationship takes, constitute—in a quite visible manner—one of these discursive properties.

On the other hand, I believe that one could find here an introduction to the historical analysis of discourse. Perhaps it is time to study discourses not only in terms of their expressive value or formal transformations, but according to their modes of existence. The modes of circulation, valorization, attribution, and appropriation of discourses vary with each culture and are modified within each. The manner in which they are articulated according to social relationships can be more readily understood, I believe, in the activity of the author-function and in its modifications, than in the themes or concepts that discourses set in motion.

It would seem that one could also, beginning with analyses of this type, reexamine the privileges of the subject. I realize that in undertaking the internal and architectonic analysis of a work (be it a literary text, philosophical system, or scientific work), in setting aside biographical and psychological references, one has already called back into question the absolute character and founding role of the subject. Still, perhaps one must return to this question, not in order to reestablish the theme of an originating subject, but to grasp the subject's points of insertion, modes of functioning, and system of dependencies. Doing so means overturning the traditional problem, no longer raising the questions "How can a free subject penetrate the substance of things and give it meaning? How can it activate the rules of a language from within and thus give rise to the designs which are properly its own?" Instead, these questions will be raised: "How, under what conditions, and in what forms can something like a subject appear in the order of discourse? What place can it occupy in each type of discourse, what functions can it assume, and by obeying what rules?" In short, it is a matter of depriving the subject (or its substitute) of its role as originator, and of analyzing the subject as a variable and complex function of discourse.

Second, there are reasons dealing with the "ideological" status of the author. The question then becomes: How can one reduce the great peril, the great danger with which fiction threatens our world? The answer is: One can reduce it with the author. The author allows a limitation of the cancerous and dangerous proliferation of significations within a world where one is thrifty not only with one's resources and riches, but also with one's discourses and their significations. The author is the principle of thrift in the proliferation of meaning. As a result, we must entirely reverse the traditional idea of the author. We are accustomed, as we have seen earlier, to saying that the author is the genial creator of a work in which he deposits,

with infinite wealth and generosity, an inexhaustible world of significations. We are used to thinking that the author is so different from
all other men, and so transcendent with regard to all languages that,
as soon as he speaks, meaning begins to proliferate, to proliferate
indefinitely.

The truth is quite the contrary: the author is not an indefinite
source of significations which fill a work; the author does not precede the works, he is a certain functional principle by which, in our
culture, one limits, excludes, and chooses; in short, by which one
impedes the free circulation, the free manipulation, the free composition, decomposition, and recomposition of fiction. In fact, if we
are accustomed to presenting the author as a genius, as a perpetual
surging of invention, it is because, in reality, we make him function in exactly the opposite fashion. One can say that the author is
an ideological product, since we represent him as the opposite of
his historically real function. (When a historically given function is
represented in a figure that inverts it, one has an ideological production.) The author is therefore the ideological figure by which one
marks the manner in which we fear the proliferation of meaning.

In saying this, I seem to call for a form of culture in which fiction would not be limited by the figure of the author. It would be
pure romanticism, however, to imagine a culture in which the fictive
would operate in an absolutely free state, in which fiction would be
put at the disposal of everyone and would develop without passing through something like a necessary or constraining figure.
Although, since the eighteenth century, the author has played the
role of the regulator of the fictive, a role quite characteristic of our
era of industrial and bourgeois society, of individualism and private property, still, given the historical modifications that are taking
place, it does not seem necessary that the author-function remain
constant in form, complexity, and even in existence. I think that,
as our society changes, at the very moment when it is in the process of changing, the author-function will disappear, and in such a
manner that fiction and its polysemic texts will once again function
according to another mode, but still with a system of constraint—
one which will no longer be the author, but which will have to be
determined or, perhaps, experienced.

All discourses, whatever their status, form, value, and whatever the treatment to which they will be subjected, would then develop in the anonymity of a murmur. We would no longer hear the questions that have been rehashed for so long: "Who really spoke? Is it really he and not someone else? With what authenticity or originality? And what part of his deepest self did he express in his discourse?" Instead, there would be other questions, like these: "What are the modes of existence of this discourse? Where has it been used, how can it circulate, and who can appropriate it for himself? What are the places in it where there is room for possible subjects? Who can assume these various subject-functions?" And behind all these questions, we would hear hardly anything but the stirring of an indifference: "What difference does it make who is speaking?"

QUESTIONS FOR DISCUSSION

What does Jonson think Shakespeare "Hath Left Us"? (253)

1. Why does Jonson think Shakespeare's art only lives while "we have wits to read and praise to give"? (254)

2. Why does Jonson think that Shakespeare is "for all time"? (254)

3. What does Jonson mean when he says that "a good poet's made as well as born"? (255)

4. Does Jonson believe writing is more influenced by art or nature?

Why does Foucault think we should overturn "the traditional problem" of the author? (274)

1. Why does Foucault assert that it is "just as wrong to equate the author with the real writer as to equate him with the fictitious speaker"? (268)

2. Why is the concept of the "author-function" needed if the author has disappeared?

3. Why does Foucault think that our society fears "the proliferation of meaning"? (275)

4. Why does Foucault believe that even after the author-function disappears, fiction will still need some "system of constraint"? (275)

FOR FURTHER REFLECTION

1. What enables some works of literature to transcend time and place?

2. Why do you think we value knowing the author in literary works more than in theoretical or scientific works?

3. Should knowing the context of a work affect the way that you read it?

4. What might an authorless text look like?

DEATH
DEATH

Although grief assumes a range of forms, with individuals responding in innumerable ways to the loss of a loved one, cross-cultural traditions around death and funerals often emphasize community among the bereaved. The sharing of stories and the memorializing of the deceased, in both public and private spheres, bring to the fore aspects of memory and loss that are universally human. In acts of collective remembrance and retelling, a common element in the act of mourning allows the dead to live on in our memories and in new works of art. How the retelling of a life affects the teller is explored in different ways in the selections featured here.

Sara Suleri (1953–) is a Pakistani author now based in the United States. "The Immoderation of Ifat" is a chapter from Suleri's first book, *Meatless Days* (1989), an autobiography which explores the years of her family's migrations to and from England, as well as her own immigration to the United States. The piece is an elegy to her sister Ifat, yet the majority of it focuses on Ifat's life, especially on how momentous events such as Ifat's marriage and the death of their mother alter the sisters' relationship. The memories of unwavering tenderness between siblings take precedence over painful memories of loss.

In his essay "Now We Are Five" (2013), American humorist **David Sedaris** (1956–) writes of the recent suicide of his sister Tiffany. The reminiscence is framed in memories of family beach vacations before and after her death, and highlights how notions of family can change when a key member is absent. While confronting his adult distance from Tiffany, Sedaris paints a portrait of family dynamics in flux over time, where childhood memories contest the painful present of adult reality. The tension in Sedaris's responsibilities toward his sister, when alive and when dead, is one shared by many mourning the loss of a loved one.

The Immoderation of Ifat

Sara Suleri

At first I thought she was the air I breathed, but Ifat was prior, prior. Before my mechanical bellows hit the air to take up their fanning habit, Ifat had preceded me, leaving her haunting aura in all my mother's secret crevices: in the most constructive period of my life she lay around me like an umbilical fluid, yellow and persistent. I was asleep inside her influence when I did not yet know how to sleep. In later years such envelopment would lend a curiosity to my regard, which was uncertain whether an inward musing would not suffice—since there was so much of her inside me—in place of what it meant to look at her. But how could I abstain from looking? For if Shahid was the apple of my eye when I was six, Ifat belonged to a more burnished complexion and was the golden apples of my soul.

Was she twin, or is that merely my imagination? Could it be possible that one egg in its efficient subdivisions became forgetful for a while—my company of cells went wandering off bemused and was not missed—until four years later they remembered to be born, the sleepy side of Ifat? It cannot be, for she was twinned before my time, her face already raising to the power of some other number, which danced about her shoulder like a spirit minuscule. And she needed no lessons from me about how to conduct her always instantaneous sleep! Sleep would come and hold her like a membrane does, until her voice at night was the only one I've heard to tell me quite so clearly, "There are two chords of voice inside my throat." Once it was day again, how I could listen to those humming things, which cajoled each other, danced and ran, in the manner that her face ran, too, weaving in and out of the eddies of her voice. They worked in unison at a display brilliant and precise as water, when water wishes to perform both in and out of light. So of course I was not needed to make Ifat two: before I had even dreamed of number, she had enacted out a multitude. There always were, for instance, several voices in her single throat.

I thought of it, the trick of Ifat's speech and the colloquy that it conducted with her face, when my friend Jonathan was kindly driving me through New Haven's unloveliness. He was driving me home—a kind thing to do—and it set him brooding on all the other ways he could be kind to me. "It's all very well, you know," he murmured, "to be obsessional." We were driving down a one-way street. "But why do it so thoroughly, arrest yourself in a prosopopoeic posture that retards you from your real work?" I looked out the window at people shoveling hateful snow. "Maybe this is my work," I suggested finally. Jonathan's hands left the wheel in a moment of abbreviated exasperation, but then he softened, liberal toward me. "Alright. So now you have to write about your sister's death." "Nonsense!" I replied indignantly, and then the subject changed, as we reached home. But later on I wondered at that conversation, and the scandal in my voice when I cried out, "Nonsense!" What did it mean, I wondered. Then I realized what I must have known all along: of course, Ifat's story has nothing to do with dying; it has to do with the price a mind must pay when it lives in a beautiful body.

Of all her haunting aspects that return to me, I often am most pleased when I recollect her wrist. Ifat imposed an order on her bones that gave her gestures of an unsuspected strength: her wrists were such a vessel. There was no jar, no bottle in the house which could resist that flick of wrist, and in arm wrestling once she dropped Shahid down, to cries of everyone's amazement. We liked to watch her wield her slender tools with such efficient hygiene, so "Let Ifat open the olives," we'd agree, and when of course she did in one clean twist, our admiration exceeded olives. She was the nutty bone our teeth would hit when we wished to take upon our tongue that collusion of taste and texture. Ifat was always two. In moments when her affection felt most fierce to her, she would send out two fingers to bracelet tightly the wrist of whoever was beside her and gave her joy: when that wrist was mine, I had no way of uttering the honor to my radius and ulna. In later years, particularly, Ifat would suddenly and wordlessly grasp my wrist, making my hand, like a dying moth or a creature not knowing what to do with suffocation, flutter out, "Don't let go; don't let go."

"Don't let go, Ifat!" I screamed out in alarm when she veered me back and forth on the world's most perfect swing. There is a chinar tree in Nathia Gali growing upon a silent verge: some large-spirited person has hung a swing from its most massive limb so that the seat swings out to hurtle a body over that chasmic valley, whose terraced rice fields gleam, green and tiny, thousands of feet below. That swing was one of Ifat's passions as a child, and once she had had her manic fill of movement, she would test my mettle by pushing me back and forth over that heart's leap of a fall. I did not know which I liked better: the ecstasy of space such motion gave me or the approval in Ifat's eye when—after I had collapsed trembling on the hill— she'd say, "That was brave of you, Sara, since you are so small!" She was always fair about making concessions to my size: even when I annoyed her, she would glance at me gloomily and say, "I suppose you can't help it, since you are so small." Of course I fought against such diminution, forcing my mind into a trot to keep up with her and the swiftness of her thought. "Shahid is also smaller than you," I reminded her once when she seemed to be slipping beyond my grasp. "That's different, he's a boy." But when I sought to question her on why my girlhood mattered to my size, she had passed away from listening: "Sara," she said firmly, "I can't explain what you're too young to see."

What I could see, however—even then, when she was eight—was the lasting glamour of a face that both did and did not know the nature of its impact. For her beauty's commonplace was not aware of what transpired on her face when feature fell in with spirit. It was my first experience of aesthetic joy to watch her expression spilling over with laughter, or amazement, or whatever else was prompting her to feel alive at a given moment of the day. To such a sight my father responded with a bright delight, looking at her only with open admiration, but I sometimes noticed that my mother would seem saddened to be a witness of that gay excess. It was as though Ifat's grace was frightening to her, as she watched her child and had to contemplate what the world could exact from grace. How I must concentrate, she thought, in order to protect this girl from what could be the portion of such extravagance of face. It made her soul subdued and move in measure when she saw the sudden theater of Ifat's eyes: a theater unable to envisage a curtain or the quick falling of a duskless night. So Mamma gravely curtained Ifat then, adopting a twilight tone that seemed to say, bright daylight of my daughter, look at me and learn. But Ifat was too interested in adoration to consider what else my mother's manner could suggest: "Oh softness of my mother!" she'd exclaim. Thus lesson only gave occasion to what it sought to hide. "What gave you such green eyes, what gave you such softness?" Ifat adored.

Could that be it, an unwitting absorption of my mother's fear, that causes all those sharp angles to accrue around my earliest images of Ifat? I am crying along a roadside in Karachi that is a stony and resistant surface on which to run and cry, but she has left me far behind, so I know that I will never catch up with her and that I no longer want to be the only audience to my tears. Then, shortly after I am three years old, sitting on the deep veranda of a Karachi house, watching in admiration as Ifat twirls her weight upon a heavy rope that holds thick bamboo screens in place, now rolled stiffly up to let in the tepid evening breeze. Ifat dances, twirls and whirls—her white muslin frock is a further admiration round her limbs—until her forehead meets with sickening crack an evil abutment of plaster. How efficiently the fabric of her dress absorbs the abundance of her blood! I hear Ifat screaming "Papa, Papa!" shaking off her entanglement in rope and the sharpness of her fall and the little wounded sounds that Shahid and I keep darting round her. As Papa runs out from his study, Ifat is able to command, almost with impatience, "Now hold me while I die."

She didn't, of course, and her seven-year-old cranium was knitting before the three of us had really satisfied our taste for the glory of her wound. But Ifat still lay in her blue bed and behaved as though nothing could be averted now. It was as though her mastery over us had been extended beyond the weight of years—three over Shahid, four over me—to address us henceforth with the infinite knowledge of the grave. So it did not matter that two days later not even that cumbersome gauze bandage, an ill-tied turban on her head, could keep Ifat in her bed. Even when she was soon up again and playing, she still had that bloodletting over us, making her absolute and awesome to our eyes.

Some two decades later Ifat described her fall to me as though I had not been there, and it was entrancing to witness that event again from, as it were, the opposite angle of the room. She did not pay particular attention to the hurt itself nor to the imperious evocations of death that it unleashed in her. Instead, she told me about what it was like at night to wait for the moistness of that wound to heal and then to run a finger through her hair, feeling the increasingly stiff joy of that dry extraneous growth, with which she could tamper, if she chose. For Ifat, the event clinched her perception of bodily secrecy and the illicit texture of what happens when something is added onto or subtracted from flesh. For me, however, it was and still remains my sharpest consciousness of the publicity of blood.

Keen red blood, coursing down her leopard's skull! The image made me shudder many years afterward when we were merely playing and something in her imperiousness reminded of how she could hurt. For games were Ifat's provenance: she made us play and play until the very intensity of her invention made us feel as though we collaborated with her in the most significant work of our lives. When I woke in the morning, I would slowly think, I wonder what we will play today, and before I was properly awake, Ifat would be upon me, shaking me to action: "You're Belinda and Shahid's Pepito and I'm Diana"; "You're Gray Rabbit and Shahid is Mole and I'm the Crab"; "Today we're going to play at Holmes." Holmes was an elaborate invention through which Ifat made our toys familial to us: each one had its proper station of relationship, and new toys in the fold had to undergo a stringent initiation before they were admitted to that private world. A woollen animal knitted expressly for Shahid (What was Goodboy's sweet face meant to signify? A dog? Perhaps a bear?) was the bad-boy stranger in our games for months until Ifat declared, "He's home—he can be a good boy now." And so we solemnly welcomed him into our midst and named him Goodboy: Goodboy soon became so much a part of us that he even married the Princess of Loveliness—Ifat's favorite doll—after we had determined that he was her long-lost brother, most deserving to have her as his wife. They were intricately brothered and sistered, all our toys, as we made them wed and interwed.

"'Who Killed Cock Robin?'—what a strange song it is, Ifat," I said to her one day. "'I, said the sparrow, with my bow and arrow'—how odd that he should confess it straightaway!" "You know what he's confessing, don't you?" replied Ifat with a meaningful look that always made me feel most ignorant. "It's all about sex!" And then, rising to the horror on my face, she added, "Of course you know that's what nursery rhymes are all about!" Ifat looked pleased at this. "You know, don't you, that all those rhymes are just a way of telling children about the horrid parts of sex?" I at eight did not want to know, feeling squeamish at the relentlessness of her claim. "Don't tell me, Ifat, don't," I begged, until her satisfaction was nearly brimming over. "What!" she exclaimed cheerfully, "'Put on the pan, says greedy Nan, / Let's sup before we go'? 'She cut off their tails with a carving knife / Did you ever see such a sight in your life'?—Come on, Sara, see what you must see!" I crumpled, seeing it, for Ifat's devastating knowledge seemed designed to rob me of the pale of innocence, insisting that innocence was a lie, a most pallid place to be! "Don't you think that there are some things you shouldn't tell me?" I asked her once, gloomily, after she had filled my evening with hair-raising representations of bodily functions. "Don't you think it may be bad for me?" "If you let it fester, that's your fault," Ifat answered in reproof. "Tomorrow I'll tell you why Jack Sprat could eat no fat and his wife could eat no lean!" And then, leaving me to contemplate her dreadful promise, she turned round and went to sleep.

What else could she be coupled with when she had her discourse by her? She presented herself to the world as a pair in the whitest days of her girlhood, so that looking and listening leaked their knowledge into one another in a magic of multiplication. Her talk was like a creature next to her, a golden retriever of Ifat's singular expression or, better still, a lion padding in startling fashion about the house. Years later, when Richard X. swept into my home with his dog Lulu by his side, something of his buoyancy made me tell him cautiously, "You can remind me slightly of my sister." I intended it to be the highest compliment that I could pay, not realizing at the time that to a man so conscious of the peculiarities of manhood such an analogy could only perplex. "Did you like her?" asked Richard in the wistful way he had of always saying in secret, "Please like me." "Like her?—Oh yes," I said quietly, "yes, I did like Ifat." But naming her put the unpronounceability of my life between us in a way that gave him unease: he did not wish to see me framed by family just then but to picture me alone instead and isolate me in his gaze.

"If anyone hurts you, Sara," Ifat said to me on the day I turned nineteen, "make sure you tell me who it is, so that I can kill them, slowly." For a moment she looked mournful with protection but then, at the execution of revenge, quite pleased. "I'll do a Dadi, chop up their livers into little bits and feed them to the crows," she added, echoing my Dadi's favorite curse. We had just driven to Gulberg Market in Lahore, and as she sat waiting for me in the car, she saw two vagabonds drive up to graze me slightly when I crossed the road. I think they only wished to startle me, wanting for some reason to see a woman look afraid, but swiftly came their punishment. Ifat drove fiercely after them, forced their car off the road, and then used her car as a battering ram, causing considerable damage to both vehicles. "Are you mad?" said the vagabonds, aghast. "How dare you touch my sister?" Ifat hissed. By then quite a crowd had gathered, in the habit of Lahore's instant assembly of spectatorship, so Ifat was surrounded with supporters cheering on her bravery. "Don't you have any sisters yourselves, you louts?" they told the astounded vagabonds. "Don't you understand what it is to protect the honor of your sister?" The vagabonds drove off without a word, dented and dumbfounded. "You've lost a headlight," I told Ifat as I got back into the car, noticing her knuckles white with rage. "If anyone hurts a hair of your head, Sara," Ifat told me as we drove home, "I will not let them live." Her voice seemed overburdened with knowledge at that moment: it made me stare down at the birthday cake sitting on my lap and think, "Dear god, don't let her hurt."

I had already watched her accrue the tragedy of adolescence, days she endured only in the deepest mourning. Even then there was an energy to her manner that belied her tone: "Oh, I am Wednesday's child!" she would exclaim. "Wednesday's, full of woe!" In that era she hated her body, which had become beautiful in a way that was too womanly for her tastes, hungry for childhood's swifter grace. So Ifat would hold her face fastidiously, a walking crown above such bodily disdain, as though she would concede to walking beside her body but would not inhabit it, not yet. "Look at the hair on my arms!" she said to me with horror. "It's too horrible—I'd need a forest fire to get rid of all this growth on my limbs!" She was by no means ready to accept the modifications in her own aesthetic that existence was imposing on her and disavowed its strictures, even when they gave her great increments of grace. Thus Ifat left her body sitting by the fire and sauntered off to stare out the window in the opposite direction, for there were always several Ifats with us in a room. Hinged to her like a hotel door, what could I do but keep ushering them in, those successions of her face?

But she had reason to be burdened. Both my parents looked at her with such keen eyes that it must have been a strain on her good humor—she was a most good-humored girl—to sustain the pressure of that gaze. My mother was always cautious, maintaining her exemplary trick of perpetual understatement in order to teach Ifat something of the art of moderation. She developed habits that Ifat passionately admired but could not emulate, for Ifat's habits were my father's. From him she learned her stance of wild inquiry, the arrogant angle at which she held her head. It was her gesture of devotion to him, really, the proud position she maintained when—to the complete devastation of domestic serenity—those two wills clashed. It made me groan aloud to think that Papa could not see that Ifat was simply loving him for what he was when she handed back to him, gesture by gesture, his prickling independence of style. But he could not see deeply enough into the lonely work of this fidelity, noticing only with alarm her flaring spirit, so much like his own. "When Ifat learns to love another man, what will happen to it, her habit of fidelity?" I could read written in my mother's eyes. And so there was an even greater tentativeness to Mamma's touch when she sat down at her piano to play a while and then to softly sing,

> Oh sisters two, how may we do,
> for to preserve this day?
> This poor youngling, for whom we sing,
> Bye bye, lully, lullay.

I felt it sharply, when Ifat learned to love another man. There were always in her great reserves of devotion to dispense: I did not feel deprived but feared that it would be too expensive to her spirit to utter to my father such a complete goodbye. After having lived for years with his endless eloquence of voice, how could she do it, choose to love a silent man? So I warned her against Javed and the ways he could be alien: "He sees your face," I warned, "and not the spirit that constructs your face." Ifat would not listen. It put a gulf between us in those years before she ran away from home and married him, because my disapproval hurt, making her instinctively hide in order to protect her love. "If anything needs that much protection," I told her, "you know it must be wrong." Then I hated myself for being right, when I saw the quick cloud of pain that I had cast about her eyes. So those years in Lahore were difficult with my disapproval, although even I had to laugh on the night when Javed, prowling round the house in amorous pursuit of Ifat, lay down on Dadi's bed. He was waiting for Ifat in the garden and saw what he thought was an empty bed, only to discover that the tiny curlicue of my Dadi was lying next to him, asleep beneath the stars.

What did he signify to her? For a while I was perplexed, until I slowly saw that rather than at a man, I should be looking at the way Javed signified to Ifat a complete immersion into Pakistan. She was living here for good now, she must have thought, so why not do it well? And what greater gift could she give my father than literally to become the land he had helped to make? He, of course, could never see the touching loyalty of this decision, but then our adulthood would often seem to him betrayal's synonym. He could not countenance her love for a polo-playing army man, a spark about the town, not stopping to consider that Ifat was his child and well designed to match adamant with adamant, iron with iron. Javed's elder brother was in prison at that time—for rape, after a trial of great notoriety—but the more prudence that amassed against him, the more resolution to Ifat's loyalty. "Oh, girl," I groaned to myself in exasperation, "why are you so perishably pretty? Who put such pretty notions in your head?" By this time Ifat was in college at Kinnaird, willing a great distance between my father and herself in a determination uncannily like his in tone. And then, with perverse aplomb, she chose to enter into the heart of Pakistan in the most un-Pakistani way possible: she ran away from Kinnaird and called home a few days later to say, bravely, "Papa, I'm married." "Congratulations," he replied, put down the phone, and refused to utter her name again for year. Ifat was then nineteen.

Adrift from each familiar she had known, what energies my sister devoted to Pakistan! First she learned how to speak Punjabi and then graduated to the Jehlum dialect, spoken in the region from which Javed's family came. She taught herself the names and stations of a hundred-odd relations, intuiting how each of them would wish to be addressed. She learned more than I will ever know about the history of the army, and then she turned to polo's ins and outs. The game, she discovered, had originated in the valleys of Kaghan where, in place of a ball, the tribes most commonly played with an enemy's head instead: "Oh," said Ifat, digested it, and moved on to something else. She went with her mother-in-law to the family's ancestral village in the Punjab to perform an annual sacrifice of some poor animal—a goat was killed for god and then doled out to the village's poor. Later she discovered that the rite was a traditional atonement, performed on the spot where Javed's great-grandfather had slain his infant daughter, so aggrieved was he to have a female as a child. "Oh!" said Ifat and listened, white as ice. She listened to her father-in-law, the brigadier, a polo-playing man, tell her that he wanted his four sons to be gentlemen, he did not want them to be cads. She listened to all this, and then she taught herself the most significant task of them all. She learned the names of Pakistan.

For never has there been, in modern times, such a Homeric world, where so much value is pinned onto the utterance of name! Entire conversations, entire lives, are devoted to the act of naming people, and in Pakistan the affluent would be totally devoid of talk if they were unable to take names in vain. Caste and all its subclassifications are recreated every day in the structure of a conversation that knows which names to name: "Do you know Puppoo and Lola?" "You mean Bunty's cousins?" "No, Bunty's cousins are Lali and Cheeno, I'm talking about the Shah Nazir family—you know, Dippoo's closest friends." "Oh, of course, I used to meet them all the time at Daisy Aunty's place!" For everyone has a family name and then a diminutive name, so that to learn an ordinary name is not enough—you must also know that Zahid is Podger, and Seema is Nikki, and Rehana is Chunni, and on and on. To each name attaches a tale, and the tales give shape to the day. "Poor Goga, she's so cut up! I think she really misses Chandni quite a lot." "What is the Chandni story, though?" "Darling, all Karachi knows! When Saeed discovered that she was having an affair with Billo, he just couldn't handle it—he had to have her killed!" We had felt too supercilious, in our youth, to bother with this lingo, so it was somewhat of a surprise to hear such names on Ifat's lips. She was permitted to return only after long negotiations: an energetic lady, Aunty Nuri, undertook to mediate between the brigadier and Pip until—under her auspices—a reconciliation of the clans was tautly staged. "I can't stand it," Shahid told me afterward, "when Ifat talks Punjabi or does this Nikki Pikki stuff!" "Well, it must have been hard work," I mused. In any case, I was distracted. For when we met again, how strange I felt to notice that Ifat's beautiful body, which I had missed so much, was now convex with a child.

I wanted to shield her, but I did not have the means. In the pink house on the hill—the brigadier's invention—Ifat was public, praiseworthy for her beauty, while in ours she was treated with a strict formality. My father would never properly forgive her, and my mother's quaintly decorous way sought to extend privacy to Ifat now that she thought her daughter belonged to a different life. So in the end there was no place left where Ifat could return: in each room she was new. "Will no one ever let that girl be at home," I thought, protection spluttering in me like the sulphur smell of a match that flares beyond the call of duty. Ifat watched my face; "It doesn't matter, Sara," she once told me ruefully. "Men live in homes, and women live in bodies." For she was preoccupied with the creature living inside her: I could watch her make a dwelling of her demeanor, a startling place in which to live. My heart was wrenched to see her lying there later, with her infant boy next to her side, red and wrinkled as an infant is after living so long in water! Ifat's eyes smiled at me from her bed, as she lay with her beauty and her discourse and now a baby, too. Your father called you Taimur, child, as in Tamburlaine, a curious appellation for your sweetest disposition, you little infant boy.

What happened, in the war? Javed had been sent to Bangladesh in the era of the emergency. He came back wounded for a month once, and people said that in his impetuous way he had simply shot himself so he could return to look at Ifat's face. "Don't say such things to me, please!" I said. But then the war began, those bitter days for all. The naming games that went on in the drawing rooms of Pakistan now turned their poison outward: it was no longer enough to say, "Do you know Kittoo?"; it was necessary to add, "He died on the Sargodha front," or "Last night Zafar died." I lived with Ifat in the pink house on the hill, sitting with her as those names came tolling in, cold terror in our eyes. During each air raid, the brigadier would stride into the garden, barking out commands to the soldiers who were operating the antiaircraft guns installed on the top of his house: gradually it became a practice of us all to trail into the garden after him, gazing up at those atrocious noises in the sky. The war was brief, but the waiting of those days was long, and it was followed only by a longer waiting when, after the fall of Dacca, we discovered that Javed was alive in India, a prisoner of war. Ifat was pregnant again, but before the daughter that she bore could see her father, the child would be almost two.

Ifat put on her bridal clothes the day Javed returned. What festivity went quickening through our house in Lahore, making us wince to contemplate the gravity of her joy. Fawzi took a photograph of Ifat on that day: it is an uncanny image, which almost seems to know what it must represent, the twinning impulses of Ifat's soul. She stands white and erect, glancing down at a diagonal to the tugging of her daughter Alia's hand. She seems tall and finely boned, head bowed in the face of its own beauty, quite grave to be what it must be. Her slenderness is such as to suggest a keen fragility, most poignant to me, so that when the photograph first met my eyes I cried aloud, "I must protect this girl!"

Those were peculiar days in Pakistan, but the country made quick provisions to forget the war in Bangladesh; when two years later the prisoners of that war finally returned, they came back to a world that did not really want to hear the kind of stories they had to tell. One day, standing in the dining room, Javed suddenly began to describe what he had felt during his first killing. I stopped still, and my head swam at the thought of what came next, overwhelming me with images of what he must have seen. My terror asked me, how will Ifat do it, make Javed's mind a human home again and take those stories from his head? That was the most arduous labor of Ifat's life, as she began with great reserve to bring her husband home again. She matched her courage with compassion, working hard to counteract those three years brutalized, that waste of life. It made me hold my breath to see such concentration on her face, to see her biting her lip—the mannerism of her childhood—trying brick by brick to break that prison down. The only way in which she can do it, I thought to myself, is by first learning what that prison was: what anecdotes must fill her evenings now, what intensity of detail? "If anyone can do it," I told my mother, "Ifat can." "Yes," said Mamma, "she is generous in that way—if anybody can . . . " And then we looked away from one another, silent with dismay.

After Javed left the army, they moved to Sargodha, an uninteresting part of the Punjab, where he took to cultivating land and opening a stud farm. By the next time we met Ifat, she could tell us with fine verve every detail of how that farm was run and how the world breeds polo ponies. I could not help laughing at this incongruous linkage: the finesse of Ifat's thought and the breeding of a horse! Still, she made her stories funny, almost as if she enjoyed it all, never talking about the effort of her secret work. She would saunter into our house, with three children now, along with her discourse and her face, making abundant company. "Thank goodness you look like yourself, Ifat." I hugged my welcome. "I could not bear it if you looked horsey." "Me?" said Ifat, drawing up her scorn, "Do I have yokel's hands?" For we wished only to joke with one another now, telling minor stories, only dainty tales. I felt that I owed her

the courtesy of silence on her life's score, as though to be unques-
tioning in my attention would be the deftest way to demonstrate
my sympathy. We developed new patterns of conversation, then,
in which phrases floated between us in an unsaid context so limpid
that it could dazzle me. It caused her dazzling face the least distress,
I hoped, to be surrounded by a discretion so complete as to be dazzling. "Always two," I murmured in her direction, "always two." Ifat
smiled a little wearily at that and glanced at me. "They told me I was
everything," she sighed, "They lied; I am not beauty-proof."

She walked as erectly as ever, through the fierce reclamation of
those times. I wondered about the progress of her work, whether or
not her manner of making welcome would suffice: could such a will
for healing, by ill luck, serve to magnify the bruise's sense that it was
just a shoddy bruise? If that were true, more bruising would come—
save her, I begged my limpid context, save her from being bruised.
But I would be angry in Lahore when company eager over Javed's
name brought me tales of wealth and scandal, waiting for my ver-
dict. "You must not say such things about my sister's husband," I said
slowly, "It is impolite." For surely it was discourteous, I felt, for them
to bring such tales to me, as though some third person could ever
understand the nature of Ifat's work. If only you could remain unnoticed, I told her in my mind, then such indignity would not be cast at
the flamboyance of your face. Beauty is a whip they should not use,
but will, your trouble being that even the crudest eye that looks at
you can believe it comprehends. I winced for Ifat, then. "Brave girl,"
I said, "ignore the world: continue with your task."

I think it was an irritant to the world, her continued merriment.
Nor was this pretense: Ifat was good at getting at joy, as the shape
of her eyes would often attest. Some of the most festive moments in
my life occurred when Ifat simply walked into my room: she would
visit on winter afternoons, sitting upstairs in my red room with Tillat and me, the three of us cross-legged upon the bed. And what
exclamation of delight we made when the door quietly opened to my
mother's touch, bringing her into our midst with a little smile and a
pansy in her hand. "I've just been walking in the garden," she murmured absently, "and I found this pansy . . . " It was often her way
of starting conversation, to walk into a room with a flower or pebble,

simply saying, "Look . . . " "Oh, Mamma, what a beautiful pansy!" we exclaimed, ravished by her, and handed it around. "Yes, it is rather, isn't it," she said, turning to leave, until, "Don't go, Mamma, don't go! Stay and talk to us," we begged.

Those were the moments that Ifat and I had to collect and recollect after Mamma died. It changed the tenor of our talk again, for then our context had no option but to rise weightless, entranced by her remaining aura. Ifat told me at exquisite pace the stories of her soul: a few months earlier, some sickness had made her flee her family and come to stay at home. She would lie on the sofa, sleeping fitfully throughout the day, while Mamma would be reading student papers at a table close at hand. "And when I woke, she'd smile at me," marveled Ifat, as though recounting miracle. "When I awoke, she'd smile!" "But I was angry at her, Ifat," I confessed, "I felt that someone was handing me a relic of her, some rag doll, and I refused to kiss those button eyes," Ifat shook her lovely head: "Poor Sara, you should have come home then . . . " We were silent for a while. "I miss her," Ifat sighed.

"Although," she added, "a woman can't come home." Her face had clouded, then, making me watch intently the way that meaning shadowed itself, came and went around her eyes. "Why, Ifat?" I finally asked. "Oh, home is where your mother is, one; it is when you are mother, two; and in between it's almost as though your spirit must retract . . ."—she was concentrating now, in the earnest way she concentrated as a child—"your spirit must become a tiny, concentrated little thing, so that your body feels like a spacious place in which to live—is that right, Sara?" she asked me, suddenly tentative. "Perhaps," I said, "perhaps. But when I look at you, Ifat, I am in home's element!" Ifat's two fingers suddenly grasped my wrist. "You know the profit to me, all these years, from your support?" "But Ifat," I said with sudden tears, "to have you as a sister is a high honor of my life!" Then we rose and turned to other things, conscious of having uttered all that could be said.

Now it is sweet relief to me to know I need not labor to describe what happened in my mind when Ifat died. I was in surprise. The thickness of event made me a rigid thing, whose thoughts came one by one, as if in pain. I found myself inhabiting a flattened day in which nothing could be two: where is the woman of addition? my mind inquired of me. I could not conceive her body, then, nor tolerate the tales of that body's death, the angle of its face, the bruise upon its neck. What would I not have done, I mused, to keep you from that bruise? But then I felt most vain, most vain. "I did not do enough for your strong heart when doing was open to me," I cried out, "How was I to know we had not years and years? Think of me as the cloth they put around you, some indifferent thing, when you most lithe in all your faith became inflexible!" A curious end for such a moving body, one that, like water, moved most generously in light.

Then commenced keen labor. I was imitating all of them, I knew, my mother's laborious production of her five, my sisters' of their seven (at that stage), so it was their sweat that wet my head, their pushing motion that allowed me to extract, in stifled screams, Ifat from her tales. We picked up our idea of her as though it were an infant, slippery in our hands with birthing fluids, a notion most deserving of warm water. Let us wash the word of murder from her limbs, we said, let us transcribe her into some more seemly idiom. And so with painful labor we placed Ifat's body in a different discourse, words as private and precise as water when water wishes to perform both in and out of light. Let it lie hidden in my eye, I thought, her tiny spirit, buoyant in the excessive salt of that dead sea, so that henceforth too she can direct my gaze, a strange happening, phosphorescent!

Around us, in the city, talk of murder rose like a pestilence, making it a painful act ever to leave the house. My face felt nude, and for the first time in my life I wished I were a woman who could wear a veil, an advertisement of anonymity to mirror all the blankness in my mind. At home I had Shahid and Tillat and Nuz, and we talked and laughed as often as we could, but our hearts were strung with silence. Ifat would like it if we laughed, we knew, and so all of us tried: Shahid rediscovered "Uncle Tom Cobbleigh," his favorite song from childhood, and entertained us for hours with his ingenious adaptations: "Oh, what shall we do with Nuzzi Begum? Pill-popping, pill-popping, pill-popping, pill-popping, and Sara and Farni and all, and Sara and Farni and all." Tillat and I totally disgraced ourselves when one of the mourners who came visiting us, a lady with a hear-ing aid, warned us that her battery was down and we would have to speak quite loudly. By the third time I had to bellow, "Yes, it is very sad!" to her persistent "What?" Tillat's strength broke down, and we both burst into some of the most uncontrollable laughter that we have ever laughed. Nuz and I noticed that occasionally our visitors would whisper to each other, "That's the half-sister," so we staged some half-sisterly fights for their benefit: I called her short and dark; she called me cold and proud. Then we would take flowers to the cemetery, a companionable thing to do, and when Shahid spread a sheet of roses on the grave, a look of satisfaction crossed his face that I had last seen when I watched him feed his daughter. It brought to mind the most wrenching question of those days: what could we do for Ifat's children?

As the talk of murder settled into irresolution, the rift between my father's house and the brigadier's became complete. Papa insisted that the children belonged with Javed now, that they could only suf-fer from our influence. "I'm used to thinking more highly of what it means to be loved by me," I answered ruefully. We played with them while we were there, but then they left us for the pink house on the hill, and in our secret minds we all realized that they would, they must, forget. We would not tell one another what we knew, for it seemed the worst disloyalty of all to those children's mother: but what else can happen, our eyes said, once we have all dispersed to various parts of the world? "What can we do, what can we do," the rhythm of my day breathed. So on the morning when they left Lahore, for the pink house on the hill, there was terror in my hands as I held them one by one: "Child's mind, do not forget, I am your mother's sister," my fingers begged. But as they drove away, I turned to see Tillat raise her head in the anguish of such despairing tears that I knew it, then, that they were lost.

Javed has remarried now, and when I visit Pakistan, Ifat's chil-dren look at me shyly, at this strange aunt belonging to an era before their lives capsized: their mother's younger sister, older now than their mother was when she was taken from them. In some police station in Lahore a file of an unsolved murder from 1980 lies for-gotten, or perhaps completely lost. But we have managed to live with ourselves, it seems, making a habit of loss. "The thought most killing to me," I told Tillat, "is—if Ifat could be asked—how firmly she would swear that we would never let the children go." Tillat winced. "We did not have a choice, Sara. What could we do—live with them in Javed's house after what had been said?" We shivered at the contemplation of that old terrain. "I think Ifat would feel most compassionate for us," Tillat murmured, "you know what she was like . . . compassionate . . . " I shook my head. "But to such an extreme that she would probably have imagined that we would be capable of a most radically compassionate act." "Yes, she was extreme," she said. And, suddenly, we smiled at some moment of Ifat's extremity: we did not need to tell them to each other but let those two moments rise between us like a tiny replication of her aura. It was nearly with us, that astonishing radiance, in the way that something you have dreamed the night before can come flashing in and out of your morning, leaving you astonishing, "What was it that I dreamed?"

I like to imagine that there is a space for improvident angels, the ones who wish to get away from too much light. There, a company of Ifat lie, arms across their foreheads, such an intensely familiar thought that it brings tears of delight to the grave eyes of god.

Now We Are Five

David Sedaris

I n late May of this year, a few weeks shy of her fiftieth birthday, my youngest sister, Tiffany, committed suicide. She was living in a room in a beat-up house on the hard side of Somerville, Massachusetts, and had been dead, the coroner guessed, for at least five days before her door was battered down. I was given the news over a white courtesy phone while at the Dallas airport. Then, because my plane to Baton Rouge was boarding and I wasn't sure what else to do, I got on it. The following morning, I boarded another plane, this one to Atlanta, and the day after that I flew to Nashville, thinking all the while about my ever-shrinking family. A person expects his parents to die. But a sibling? I felt I'd lost the identity I'd enjoyed since 1968, when my younger brother was born.

"Six kids!" people would say. "How do your poor folks manage?"

There were a lot of big families in the neighborhood I grew up in. Every other house was a fiefdom, so I never gave it much thought until I became an adult, and my friends started having children. One or two seemed reasonable, but anything beyond that struck me as outrageous. A couple Hugh and I knew in Normandy would occasionally come to dinner with their wrecking crew of three, and when they'd leave, several hours later, every last part of me would feel violated.

Take those kids, double them, and subtract the cable TV: that's what my parents had to deal with. Now, though, there weren't six, only five. "And you can't really say, 'There *used* to be six,'" I told my sister Lisa. "It just makes people uncomfortable."

I recalled a father and son I'd met in California a few years back. "So are there other children?" I asked.

"There are," the man said. "Three who are living and a daughter, Chloe, who died before she was born, eighteen years ago."

That's not fair, I remember thinking. Because, I mean, what's a person supposed to do with *that*?

Compared with most forty-nine-year-olds, or even most forty-nine-*month*-olds, Tiffany didn't have much. She did leave a will, though. In it, she decreed that we, her family, could not have her body or attend her memorial service.

"So put *that* in your pipe and smoke it," our mother would have said.

A few days after getting the news, my sister Amy drove to Somerville with a friend and collected two boxes of things from Tiffany's room: family photographs, many of which had been ripped into pieces, comment cards from a neighborhood grocery store, notebooks, receipts. The bed, a mattress on the floor, had been taken away and a large industrial fan had been set up. Amy snapped some pictures while she was there, and, individually and in groups, those of us left studied them for clues: a paper plate on a dresser that had several drawers missing, a phone number written on a wall, a collection of mop handles, each one a different color, arranged like cattails in a barrel painted green.

Six months before our sister killed herself, I made plans for us all to gather at a beach house on Emerald Isle, off the coast of North Carolina. My family used to vacation there every summer, but after my mother died we stopped going, not because we lost interest but because it was she who always made the arrangements and, more important, paid for it. The place I found with the help of my sister-in-law, Kathy, had six bedrooms and a small swimming pool. Our weeklong rental period began on Saturday, June 8th, and we arrived to find a delivery woman standing in the driveway with seven pounds of seafood, a sympathy gift sent by friends. "They's slaw in there, too," she said, handing over the bags.

In the past, when my family rented a cottage my sisters and I would crowd the door like puppies around a food dish. Our father would unlock it, and we'd tear through the house claiming rooms. I always picked the biggest one facing the ocean, and, just as I'd start to unpack, my parents would enter and tell me that this was *theirs.* "I mean, just who the hell do you think you are?" my father would ask. He and my mother would move in, and I would get booted to what was called "the maid's room." It was always on the ground level, a kind of dank shed next to where the car was parked. There was never an interior stairway leading to the upper floor. Instead, I had to take the outside steps and, more often than not, knock on the locked front door, like a beggar hoping to be invited in.

"What do *you* want?" my sisters would ask.

"I want to come inside."

"That's funny," Lisa, the eldest, would say to the others, who were gathered like disciples around her. "Did you hear something, a little whining sound? What is it that makes a noise like that? A hermit crab? A little sea slug?" Normally, there was a social divide between the three eldest and the three youngest children in my family. Lisa, Gretchen, and I treated the others like servants and did very well for ourselves. At the beach, though, all bets were off, and it was just upstairs against downstairs, meaning everyone against me.

This time, because I was paying, I got to choose the best room. Amy moved in next door, and my brother, Paul, his wife, and their ten-year-old daughter, Maddy, took the spot next to her. That was it for oceanfront. The others arrived later and had to take the left-overs. Lisa's room faced the street, as did my father's. Gretchen's faced the street and was intended for someone who was paralyzed. Hanging from the ceiling were electric pulleys designed to lift a harnessed body into and out of bed.

Unlike the cottages of our youth, this one did not have a maid's room. It was too new and fancy for that, as were the homes that surrounded it. Traditionally, all the island houses were on stilts, but more and more often now the ground floors are filled in. They all have beachy names and are painted beachy colors, but most of those built after Hurricane Fran hit the coast, in 1996, are three stories tall and look almost suburban. This place was vast and airy. The kitchen table sat twelve, and there was not one but *two* dishwashers. All the pictures were ocean-related: seascapes and lighthouses, all with the airborne V's that are shorthand for seagull. A sampler on the living-room wall read, "Old Shellers Never Die, They Simply Conch Out." On the round clock beside it, the numbers lay in an indecipherable heap, as if they'd come unglued. Just above them were printed the words "Who cares?"

This was what we found ourselves saying whenever anyone asked the time.

"Who cares?"

The day before we arrived at the beach, Tiffany's obituary ran in the Raleigh *News & Observer*. It was submitted by Gretchen, who stated that our sister had passed away peacefully at her home. This made it sound as if she were very old, and had a house. But what else could you do? People were leaving responses on the paper's website, and one fellow wrote that Tiffany used to come into the video store where he worked in Somerville. When his glasses broke, she offered him a pair she had found while foraging for art supplies in somebody's trash can. He said that she also gave him a *Playboy* magazine from the 1960s that included a photo spread titled "The Ass Menagerie."

This was fascinating, as we didn't really know our sister very well. Each of us had pulled away from the family at some point in our lives—we'd had to in order to forge our own identities, to go from being *a* Sedaris to being our own specific Sedaris. Tiffany, though, stayed away. She might promise to come home for Christmas, but at the last minute there'd always be some excuse: she missed her plane, she had to work. The same would happen with our summer vaca-tions. "The rest of us managed to make it," I'd say, aware of how old and guilt-trippy I sounded.

All of us would be disappointed, though for different reasons. Even if you weren't getting along with Tiffany at the time, you couldn't deny the show she put on—the dramatic entrances, the nonstop, professional-grade insults, the chaos she'd inevitably leave in her wake. One day she'd throw a dish at you and the next she'd create a stunning mosaic made of the shards. When allegiances with one brother or sister flamed out, she'd take up with someone else. At no time did she get along with everybody, but there was always someone she was in contact with. Toward the end, it was Lisa, but before that we'd all had our turn.

The last time she joined us on Emerald Isle was in 1986. "And, even then, she left after three days," Gretchen reminded us.

As kids, we spent our beach time swimming. Then we became teenagers and devoted ourselves to tanning. There's a certain kind of talk that takes place when you're lying, dazed, in the sun, and I've always been partial to it. On the first afternoon of our most recent trip, we laid out one of the bedspreads we had as children, and arranged ourselves side by side on it, trading stories about Tiffany.

"What about the Halloween she spent on that army base?"

"And the time she showed up at Dad's birthday party with a black eye?"

"I remember this girl she met years ago at a party," I began, when my turn came. "She'd been talking about facial scars, and how terrible it would be to have one, so Tiffany said, 'I have a little scar on my face and I don't think it's so awful.'

" 'Well,' the girl said, 'you would if you were pretty.' "

Amy laughed and rolled over onto her stomach. "Oh, that's a good line!"

I rearranged the towel I was using as a pillow. "Isn't it though?" Coming from someone else, the story might have been upsetting, but not being pretty was never one of Tiffany's problems, especially when she was in her twenties and thirties, and men tumbled helpless before her.

"Funny," I said, "but I don't remember a scar on her face."

I stayed in the sun too long that day and got a burn on my forehead. That was basically it for me and the beach blanket. I made brief appearances for the rest of the week, stopping to dry off after a swim, but mainly I spent my days on a bike, cycling up and down the coast, and thinking about what had happened. While the rest of us seem to get along effortlessly, with Tiffany it always felt like work. She and I usually made up after arguing, but our last fight took it out of me, and at the time of her death we hadn't spoken in eight years. During that period, I regularly found myself near Somerville, and though I'd always toy with the idea of contacting her and spending a few hours together, I never did, despite my father's encouragement. Meanwhile, I'd get reports from him and Lisa: Tiffany had lost her apartment, had gone on disability, had moved into a room found for her by a social-service agency. Perhaps she was more forthcoming with her friends, but her family got things only in bits and pieces. She didn't talk *with* us so much as *at* us, great blocks of speech that were by turns funny, astute, and so contradictory it was hard to connect the sentence you were hearing to the one that preceded it. Before we stopped speaking, I could always tell when she was on the phone. I'd walk into the house and hear Hugh say, "Uh-huh . . . uh-huh . . . uh-huh . . ."

In addition to the two boxes that Amy had filled in Somerville, she also brought down our sister's ninth-grade yearbook, from 1978. Among the messages inscribed by her classmates was the following, written by someone who had drawn a marijuana leaf beside her name:

> Tiffany. You are a one-of-a-kind girl so stay that way you unique ass. I'm only sorry we couldn't have partied more together. This school sux to hell. Stay
> -cool
> -stoned
> -drunk
> -fucked up
> Check your ass later.

Then there's:

> Tiffany
> I'm looking forward to getting high with you this summer.

> Tiffany,
> Call me sometime this summer and we'll go out and get blitzed.

A few weeks after these messages were written, Tiffany ran away, and was subsequently sent to a disciplinary institution in

Maine called Élan. According to what she told us later, it was a horrible place. She returned home in 1980, having spent two years there, and from that point on none of us can recall a conversation in which she did not mention it. She blamed the family for sending her off, but we, her siblings, had nothing to do with it. Paul, for instance, was ten when she left. I was twenty-one. For a year, I sent her monthly letters. Then she wrote and asked me to stop. As for my parents, there were only so many times they could apologize. "We had other kids," they said in their defense. "You think we could let the world stop on account of any one of you?"

We were at the beach for three days before Lisa and our father, who is now ninety, joined us. Being on the island meant missing the spinning classes he takes in Raleigh, so I found a fitness center not far from the rental cottage, and every afternoon he and I would spend some time there. On the way over we'd talk to each other, but as soon as we mounted our stationary bikes we'd each retreat into our own thoughts. It was a small place, not very lively. A mute television oversaw the room, tuned to the Weather Channel and reminding us that there's always a catastrophe somewhere or other, always someone flooded from his home, or running for his life from a funnel-shaped cloud. Toward the end of the week, I came upon my father in Amy's room, sifting through the photographs that Tiffany had destroyed. In his hand was a fragment of my mother's head with a patch of blue sky behind her. Under what circumstances had this been ripped up? I wondered. It seemed such a melodramatic gesture, like throwing a glass against a wall. Something someone in a movie would do.

"Just awful," my father whispered. "A person's life reduced to one lousy box."

I put my hand on his shoulder. "Actually, there are two of them."

He corrected himself. "Two lousy boxes."

One afternoon on the Emerald Isle, we all rode to the Food Lion for groceries. I was in the produce department, looking at red onions, when my brother sneaked up from behind and let loose with a loud "*Achoo*," this while whipping a bouquet of wet parsley through the air. I felt the spray on the back of my neck and froze, thinking that a very sick stranger had just sneezed on me. It's a neat trick, but he also doused the Indian woman who was standing to my left. She was wearing a blood-colored sari, and so she got it on her bare arm as well as her neck and the lower part of her back.

"Sorry, man," Paul said when she turned around, horrified. "I was just playing a joke on my brother."

The woman had many thin bracelets on, and they jangled as she brushed her hand against the back of her head.

"You called her 'man,'" I said to him after she walked off.

"For real?" he asked.

Amy mimicked him perfectly. "For real?"

Over the phone, my brother, like me, is often mistaken for a woman. As we continued shopping, he told us that his van had recently broken down, and that when he called for a tow truck the dispatcher said, "We'll be right out, sweetie." He lowered a watermelon into the cart, and turned to his daughter: "Maddy's got a daddy who talks like a lady, but she don't care, do she?"

Giggling, she punched him in the stomach, and I was struck by how comfortable the two of them are with each other. Our father was a figure of authority, while Paul is more of a playmate.

When we went to the beach as children, on or about the fourth day our father would say, "Wouldn't it be nice to buy a cottage down here?" We'd get our hopes up, and then he would bring practical concerns into it. They weren't petty—buying a house that will eventually get blown away by a hurricane probably isn't the best way to spend your money—but still we wanted one desperately. I told myself when I was young that one day *I* would buy a beach house and that it would be everyone's, as long as they followed my draconian rules and never stopped thanking me for it. Thus it was that on Wednesday morning, midway through our vacation, Hugh and I contacted a real-estate agent named Phyllis, who took us around to look at available properties. On Friday afternoon, we made an offer on an oceanfront cottage not far from the one we were renting, and before sunset our bid was accepted. I made the announcement at the dinner table and got the reaction I had expected.

"Now, wait a minute," my father said. "You need to think clearly here."

"I already have," I told him.

"Okay, then, how old is the roof? How many times has it been replaced in the last ten years?"

"When can we move in?" Gretchen asked.

Lisa wanted to know if she could bring her dogs, and Amy asked what the house was named.

"Right now it's called Fantastic Place," I told her, "but we're going to change it." I used to think the ideal name for a beach house was the Ship Shape. Now, though, I had a better idea. "We're going to call it the Sea Section."

My father put down his hamburger. "Oh, no, you're not."

"But it's perfect," I argued. "The name's supposed to be beachy, and, if it's a pun, all the better."

I brought up a cottage we'd seen earlier in the day called Dune Our Thing, and my father winced. "How about naming it Tiffany?" he said.

Our silence translated to: Let's pretend we didn't hear that.

He picked his hamburger back up. "I think it's a great idea. The perfect way to pay our respects."

"If that's the case, we could name it after Mom," I told him. "Or half after Tiffany and half after Mom. But it's a house, not a tombstone, and it wouldn't fit in with the names of the other houses."

"Aw, baloney," my father said. "Fitting in—that's not who we are. That's not what we're about."

Paul interrupted to nominate the Conch Sucker.

Amy's suggestion had the word "seaman" in it, and Gretchen's was even dirtier.

"What's wrong with the name it already has?" Lisa asked.

"No, no, no," my father said, forgetting, I think, that this wasn't his decision. A few days later, after the buyer's remorse had kicked in, I'd wonder if I hadn't bought the house as a way of saying, See, it's just that easy. No hemming and hawing. No asking to look at the septic tank. Rather, you make your family happy and iron out the details later.

The cottage we bought is two stories tall and was built in 1978. It's on proper stilts and has two rear decks, one above the other, overlooking the ocean. It was rented to vacationers until late September, but Phyllis allowed us to drop by and show it to the family the following morning, after we checked out of the house we'd been staying in. A place always looks different—worse, most often—after you've made the commitment to buy it, so while the others raced up and down the stairs, claiming their future bedrooms, I held my nose to a vent and caught a whiff of mildew. The sale included the furniture, so I also made an inventory of the Barcaloungers and the massive TVs that I would eventually be getting rid of, along with the shell-patterned bedspreads and cushions with anchors on them. "For our beach house, I wanted to have a train theme," I announced. "Trains on the curtains, trains on the towels—we're going to go all out."

"Oh, brother," my father moaned.

We sketched a plan to return for Thanksgiving, and, after saying goodbye to one another, my family splintered into groups and headed off to our respective homes. There had been a breeze at the beach house, but once we left the island the air grew still. As the heat intensified, so did the general feeling of depression. Throughout the sixties and seventies, the road back to Raleigh took us past Smithfield, and a billboard on the outskirts of town that read, "Welcome to Klan Country." This time, we took a different route, one my brother recommended. Hugh drove, and my father sat beside him. I slumped down in the back seat, next to Amy, and every time I raised my head I'd see the same soybean field or low-slung cinder-block building we'd seemingly passed twenty minutes earlier.

We'd been on the road for a little more than an hour when we stopped at a farmers' market. Inside an open-air pavilion, a woman offered complimentary plates of hummus served with a corn-and-black-bean salad, so we each accepted one and took seats on a bench. Twenty years earlier, the most a place like this might have offered was fried okra. Now there was organic coffee, and artisanal goat cheese. Above our heads hung a sign that read, "Whispering Dove Ranch," and just as I thought that we might be anywhere I noticed that the music piped through the speakers was Christian—the new kind, which says that Jesus is awesome.

Hugh brought my father a plastic cup of water. "You okay, Lou?"

"Fine," my father answered.

"Why do you think she did it?" I asked as we stepped back into the sunlight. For that's all any of us were thinking, *had been* thinking since we got the news. Mustn't Tiffany have hoped that whatever pills she'd taken wouldn't be strong enough, and that her failed attempt would lead her back into our fold? How could anyone purposefully leave us, *us*, of all people? This is how I thought of it, for though I've often lost faith in myself, I've never lost it in my family, in my certainty that we are fundamentally better than everyone else. It's an archaic belief, one that I haven't seriously reconsidered since my late teens, but still I hold it. Ours is the only club I'd ever wanted to be a member of, so I couldn't imagine quitting. Backing off for a year or two was understandable, but to want out so badly that you'd take your own life?

"I don't know that it had anything to do with us," my father said. But how could it have not? Doesn't the blood of every suicide splash back on our faces?

At the far end of the parking lot was a stand selling reptiles. In giant tanks were two pythons, each as big around as a fire hose. The heat seemed to suit them, and I watched as they raised their heads, testing the screened ceilings. Beside the snakes was a low pen corralling an alligator with its mouth banded shut. It wasn't full grown, but perhaps an adolescent, around three feet long, and grumpy-looking. A girl had stuck her arm through the wire and was stroking the thing's back, while it glared, seething. "I'd like to buy everything here just so I could kill it," I said.

My father mopped his forehead with Kleenex. "I'm with you, brother."

When we were young and set off for the beach, I'd look out the window at all the landmarks we drove by—the Purina silo on the south side of Raleigh, the Klan billboard—knowing that when we passed them a week later I'd be miserable. Our vacation over, now there'd be nothing to live for until Christmas. My life is much fuller than it was back then, yet this return felt no different. "What time is it?" I asked Amy.

And instead of saying, "Who cares?," she said, "You tell me. You're the one with a watch on."

At the airport a few hours later, I picked sand from my pockets, and thought of our final moments at the beach house I'd bought. I was on the front porch with Phyllis, who had just locked the door, and we turned to see the others in the driveway below us. "So is that one of your sisters?" she asked, pointing to Gretchen.

"It is," I said. "And so are the two women standing on either side of her."

"Then you've got your brother," she observed. "That makes five—wow! Now, *that's* a big family."

I looked at the sunbaked cars we would soon be climbing into, furnaces every one of them, and said, "Yes. It certainly is."

QUESTIONS FOR DISCUSSION

Why does remembering that Ifat was "extreme" enable Suleri to feel a continuing closeness to her sister? (300)

1. Why does Suleri say Ifat's story is about "the price a mind must pay when it lives in a beautiful body"? (284)

2. Growing up, why does Suleri feel that "Ifat was always two"? (284)

3. Why is Ifat's merriment "an irritant to the world"? (296)

4. After Ifat's death, why does Suleri describe laboring to place "Ifat's body in a different discourse"? (298)

When Sedaris's father expresses doubt that Tiffany's suicide had anything to do with the family, why does Sedaris think, "But how could it have not?" (311)

1. How does Sedaris feel about the "show" he describes Tiffany putting on? (304)

2. Why does Sedaris buy the beach house?

3. How serious is Sedaris when he asks, "How could anyone purposefully leave us, *us*, of all people?" (311)

4. After the beach house trip, why does Sedaris simply agree with the real-estate agent when she says that five siblings make "a big family"? (312)

FOR FURTHER REFLECTION

1. Is writing about the circumstances of someone's death an invasion of that person's privacy?

2. After someone dies, why are there often competing stories about the death and its meaning?

3. How can memories of a relative who has died continue to affect family dynamics?

4. Would you want a family member to memorialize you in writing?

Acknowledgments

All possible care has been taken to trace ownership and secure permission for each selection in this anthology. The Great Books Foundation wishes to thank the following authors, publishers, and representatives for permission to reprint copyrighted material:

The Pangs of Love, from THE STORIES, by Jane Gardam. Copyright © 2014 by Jane Gardam. Reproduced by permission of Europa Editions and David Higham Associates.

The Golden West, by Daniel Fuchs, from STORIES FROM THE NEW YORKER 1950–1960. Copyright © 1960 by the New Yorker Magazine, Inc. Reproduced by permission of Condé Nast.

Equality, Value, and Merit, from THE CONSTITUTION OF LIBERTY, by Friedrich A. Hayek. Copyright © 1960 by the University of Chicago. Reproduced by permission of the University of Chicago Press and Taylor and Francis Books UK.

Selection from Liberalism, by Ronald Dworkin, from PUBLIC AND PRIVATE MORALITY, edited by Stuart Hampshire. Copyright © 1978 by Cambridge University Press. Reproduced by permission of Cambridge University Press.

An Arundel Tomb, from THE COMPLETE POEMS, by Philip Larkin, edited by Archie Burnett. Copyright © 2012 by the Estate of Philip Larkin. Reproduced by permission of Farrar, Straus and Giroux, and Faber and Faber Ltd.

Love Is Not a Pie, from COME TO ME: STORIES, by Amy Bloom. Copyright © 1993 by Amy Bloom. Reproduced by permission of HarperCollins Publishers and the Gersh Agency. Published in the United States by HarperCollins Publishers. Originally appeared in Room of One's Own (1990), Image (Ireland, 1991), and The Best American Short Stories, 1991.

Vivisection, from AN INTRODUCTION TO THE STUDY OF EXPERIMENTAL MEDICINE, by Claude Bernard, translated by Henry Copley Greene. Reproduced by permission of Dover Publications, Inc.

Selection from THE FEMININE MYSTIQUE, by Betty Friedan. Copyright © 1983, 1974, 1973, 1963 by Betty Friedan. Reproduced by permission of W. W. Norton and Company, Inc., Curtis Brown, Ltd., and the Orion Publishing Group, London.

ACKNOWLEDGMENTS

Ode 3.2, from THE ODES: BOOK III, by Horace. Translated by A. S. Kline. Copyright © 2003 by A. S. Kline. Reproduced by permission of A. S. Kline.

Dulce et Decorum Est, from THE POEMS OF WILFRED OWEN, by Wilfred Owen, edited by Jon Stallworthy. Copyright © 1983, 1963 by the Executors of Harold Owen's Estate. Reproduced by permission of the Wilfred Owen Royalties Trust.

What Is an Author?, by Michel Foucault, from MODERN CRITICISM AND THEORY: A READER, edited by David Lodge. Copyright © 1988 by Addison Wesley Longman Limited. Reproduced by permission of Taylor and Francis Books UK.

The Immoderation of Ifat, from MEATLESS DAYS, by Sara Suleri. Copyright © 1989 by the University of Chicago. Reproduced by permission of the University of Chicago Press.

Now We Are Five, by David Sedaris. First published by the *New Yorker*. Copyright © 2013 by David Sedaris. Reproduced by permission of Don Congdon Associates, Inc.